D0850836

The Tudor Discovery of Ireland

THE TUDOR DISCOVERY
OF IRELAND

Christopher Maginn and Steven G. Ellis

FOUR COURTS PRESS

Set in 10.5 pt on 13 pt Bembo for
FOUR COURTS PRESS
7 Malpas Street, Dublin 8, Ireland
www.fourcourtspress.ie
and in North America for
FOUR COURTS PRESS
c/o ISBS, 920 N.E. 58th Avenue, Suite 300, Portland, OR 97213.

A catalogue record for this title
is available from the British Library.

ISBN 978–1–84682–573–6

This publication was grant-aided by the Publications Fund of
National University of Ireland, Galway.

Printed in England
by Antony Rowe Ltd, Chippenham, Wilts.

Contents

List of illustrations   6

List of abbreviations   7

Preface   9

Introduction   13

PART I DISCUSSION OF THE TEXT   25

1.1   Patrick Finglas' Breviate   27
1.2   A description of the power of Irishmen   35
1.3   Havens of Ireland   42
1.4   William Darcy's articles   45
1.5   Articles for the reformation of Ireland   49
1.6   Revenues of Ireland   50
1.7   Pedigrees of the Burkes   53
1.8   Ordinances and provisions for Ireland   56
1.9   The Hatfield Compendium   63

TEXT OF THE HATFIELD COMPENDIUM   67

PART II DISCOVERY AND REFORM   111

2.1   Discovery and the origins of Tudor reform   113
2.2   'To attayne to the knowledge off the state and maner of this londe'   135
2.3   The reformation of the country taken in hand   157

Conclusion   187

Bibliography   191

Index   199

Illustrations

1 Map of the lordship of Ireland, c.1520   8
2 Image of Galloglass and kerne   36
3 Image of first page of Hatfield Compendium   68
4 Portrait of Henry VII   115
5 Portrait of Henry VIII   136

Abbreviations

AFM	*Annála ríoghachta Éireann: annals of the kingdom of Ireland by the Four Masters from the earliest period to the year 1616,* ed. John O'Donovan, 7 vols (Dublin, 1851)
AU	*Annála Uladh, Annals of Ulster,* ed. W.M. Hennessy and B. MacCarthy, 4 vols (Dublin, 1887–1901)
BL	British Library
CP	Cecil Papers, Hatfield House Library, Hertfordshire
CSPI	*Calendar of state papers relating to Ireland, 1509–1670,* 24 vols (London, 1860–1912)
EHR	*English Historical Review*
HMC	Historical Manuscripts Commission
IHS	*Irish Historical Studies*
JRSAI	*Journal of the Royal Society of Antiquaries of Ireland*
LPL	Lambeth Palace Library, London
L. & P. Hen. VIII	*Letters and papers, foreign and domestic, Henry VIII,* 21 vols (London, 1862–1932)
NAI	National Archives of Ireland
NLI	National Library of Ireland
ODNB	*Oxford dictionary of national biography,* ed. H.C.G. Matthew and Brian Harrison (Oxford, 2004)
PRIA	*Proceedings of the Royal Irish Academy*
SP	State Papers
SP Hen. VIII	*State papers, Henry VIII,* 11 vols (London, 1830–52)
TNA	The National Archives, London (Kew)

-N-

O'Cahan

MacDonnell

O'Donnell

O'Neill
(Clandeboye)

Carrickfergus

O'Neill
(Tyrone)

Lough Neagh

Lough Erne

Magennis

Maguire

MacMahon

O'Hanlon

Lower
MacWilliam
Burke

O'Rourke

O'Reilly

LOUTH

MacDermot

O'Malley

Drogheda

O'Connor

Lough Ree

MEATH

Lough Corrib

Upper
MacWilliam
Burke

Dublin

O'Flaherty

DUBLIN

Galway

KILDARE

O'Dempsey

Earl of
Kildare

MacNamara

O'Connor

O'Toole

O'Brien

Lough Derg

O'More

O'Byrne

O'Mulryan

CARLOW

Limerick

MacMurrough

KILKENNY

LIMERICK

TIPPERARY

Earl of
Ormond

WEXFORD

KERRY

Waterford

Earl of Desmond

Wexford

CORK

WATERFORD

Powers

MacCarthy More

Cork

O'Sullivan Beare

MacCarthy Reagh

0   50 miles

—————— Boundary of Royal Authority

-------- County Boundaries

1 Map of the lordship of Ireland, c.1520 (adapted from Christopher Maginn,
William Cecil, Ireland, and the Tudor state (Oxford, 2012)).

Preface

This book was as unconventional in its evolution as it is in its present structure. My desire to reproduce faithfully (and so in its entirety) a lengthy and previously unexamined sixteenth-century manuscript, along with a dissection of its contents as a means of exploring the phenomenon of knowledge acquisition and its relationship to the determination of Tudor policy for Ireland, ensured that this unusual structure would be the case. Much of its peculiar development stems from the fact that the book, as it is now, was not at all apparent to me when I began work on it in late 2009. I was at that time engaged in writing a book about William Cecil and Ireland, and so had cause to scrutinize a great many of that famous Tudor statesman's papers preserved at Hatfield House Library in Hertfordshire. It was there that I came upon the manuscript – what I have called here the Hatfield Compendium – that serves as the centrepiece of this book. Vicki Perry, then the assistant archivist of the Historic Collections Library and Archives at Hatfield House, kindly made me a copy of the manuscript so that I might consult it more closely and at my leisure. Because the manuscript was evidently written in the days of Henry VIII, and so predated the main period of William Cecil's service to the Tudors, it was of little immediate interest to me beyond the fact that it came to reside among Lord Burghley's papers; and, in any case, a host of other professional commitments made it so that I could not devote sustained attention to the manuscript or its diverse contents. So my appreciation of what I had in this document was slow in coming. I eventually transcribed it over a productive summer spent at the National University of Ireland, Galway, in 2010; only then did I begin to see some of its historical value. Still, the significance of several of the manuscript's sections continued to elude me. It was only through my frequent discussion of the manuscript and its contents with Professor Steven Ellis in Galway that I came to see the importance of publishing an edition of the Hatfield Compendium.

It was then that I began to envisage writing a short book, which presented an annotated transcription of the manuscript with a technical discussion and extrapolation of its contents, rather than submitting the work as a long contribution to an academic journal. Steven and I had, some years earlier, collaborated on a large book of historical synthesis; this project offered an opportunity for us to reprise that partnership, only this time working with a more narrowly focused primary source which was at once puzzling, challenging and of genuine and immediate use to the two of us in our respective research agendas. Steven was by then head of the School of Humanities at NUIG and holder of the established Chair of History in Galway, and so was burdened with a great many administrative and teaching responsibilities. And he, too, had other things to be writing and thinking about, notably his own comparative study of Counties Meath and Northumberland in the early Tudor period. But after some gentle cajoling from me, Steven agreed to write several of the technical expositions of the text, and made a number of comments and suggestions for changes in the sections that I had already written. Yet, as the book's technical sections began to come together, and as I started to gather my thoughts to compose some sort of an introduction to all of this, I found myself thinking more fundamentally about the nature and the basic function of a piece of evidence such as the Hatfield Compendium. My work on William Cecil had already shown me the difficulties experienced by the Tudors, and the men who served them, in their efforts to rule a territory which they never visited and generally knew very little about. The Hatfield Compendium, as a body of information, a kind of dossier intended at its most basic level to impart knowledge to those who read it, forced me to think about how Englishmen in positions of political power and influence came to learn about what was becoming an important part of the composite Tudor state. I soon realized that the exploration of this abstract means of considering the Anglo-Irish relationship would require not only a more robust introduction, but also space beyond the book's technical sections to reappraise aspects of Tudor Ireland in light of what I was now understanding as a process of knowledge acquisition: what I termed here in the present study 'the Tudor discovery of Ireland'. And central to understanding and demonstrating the translation of discovery into political practice required an exploration of an elusive concept which ran through so much of the political discourse in Tudor times and which has featured prominently (though uncritically) in the historiography of sixteenth-century Ireland: 'reformation', or, as it is now more commonly known to Irish historians, 'reform'.

A discussion of these twin processes – discovery and reform – required more primary research and secondary reading and thus also a substantially longer, and a more intellectually demanding, book. I think that my decision to include a long interpretive section, what became Part II of this book, to accommodate the discussion of these concepts was (I suspect) far more than Steven had bargained for when he originally agreed to help me piece together this documentary puzzle. But his initial (and quite understandable) hesitation gave way to encouragement when I began to write up and share with him some of my initial ideas for this final part of the book. He generously allowed me, on my frequent returns home to Galway, to tap his unrivalled knowledge of early Tudor source material relating to Ireland, most especially with regard to the political and economic developments in the reigns of Henry VII and Henry VIII. Steven also agreed to write the pages of the book that deal with that most crucial episode of the reign of the first Tudor sovereign: the administration of Sir Edward Poynings (1494–5). Once the structure and intellectual thrust of the book was (finally) finalized in my mind, it was just a matter of finding the time to write it.

In 2013 I was awarded a Fordham University Faculty Fellowship, which allowed me the sustained break from teaching and administrative responsibilities necessary to complete this book. I was also the recipient of the Irish American Cultural Institute Fellowship in Irish Studies, which allowed me to take up residence at the Centre for Irish Studies at NUIG for the better part of 2014. The IACI/NUIG Fellowship, together with a Visiting Fellowship at the Moore Institute at NUIG, which I was awarded for summer 2014, afforded me the opportunity both to write and conduct additional research in a stimulating scholarly environment and to present some of my ideas to the academic community in Galway. Steven again read and commented on all that I wrote and supplied me with additional pieces of information to consider. As it happened, NUIG's James Hardiman Library was the first university library in the world to obtain digital access to the Cecil Papers at Hatfield House Library. This technological innovation enabled me, from my office or from home, to 'blow up' portions of the Hatfield Compendium in Hertfordshire and to subject the manuscript to a close and repeated visual examination in a way that previous generations of scholars could not (and no doubt could scarcely have imagined).

In the writing of this book I accrued many debts. Dr Louis de Paor, Dr Nessa Cronin, Dr Méabh Ní Fhuartháin, Dr Leo Keohane and the staff at the Centre for Irish Studies were excellent hosts during the period of my fellowship. I would also like to thank Professor Dan Carey, the director of the Moore Institute in Galway, which welcomed me as a research fellow in summer 2014, and to acknowledge the benefit I derived from my conversations about aspects of the book with the staff of the history department at NUIG. Four Courts Press readily agreed to publish our work and the staff there, notably Martin Fanning and Anthony Tierney, have been a pleasure to work with. The Hatfield Compendium and the images of it are reproduced from the Cecil Papers with the kind permission of the Marquess of Salisbury. Mr Kieran Hoare, the archivist at the James Hardiman Library in Galway, Dr Gerald Power, Dr Brendan Scott and Dr Tomás Finn each read most of our book manuscript at various stages in its gestation and made many helpful comments and criticisms. However, for the mistakes that have eluded the vigilance of our friends and colleagues we alone are responsible.

Christopher Maginn
Lackagh, Co. Galway
July 2014

NOTES ON CONVENTIONS

The rendering of Irish personal and familial names in English poses no small difficulty. Here we have chosen to employ, in an effort to maintain consistency, well-established English forms of Irish surnames – MacGillapatrick rather than Mac Giolla Phádraig, O'Neill rather than Ó Néill – and Anglicized forms of Irish Christian names and epithets: Hugh rather Aodh, Teige rather than Tadhg; Oge rather than Óg, and Boy as opposed to Buí. The year has been taken to begin on 1 January rather than on 25 March, as was the custom in the Tudor territories. To distinguish between the two coinages which circulated in Ireland after 1460 we have distinguished between pounds Irish (IR£) and pounds sterling (£). An Irish pound was worth roughly two-thirds, or 13s. 4d. sterling.

Introduction

Before the Tudor conquest of Ireland there was the Tudor discovery of Ireland. It was not a discovery of the Columbian variety – the Anglo-Irish relationship already stretched back centuries by the time Henry VII became the first Tudor king of England in 1485; and there were, by then, tangible manifestations of the antiquity of that relationship in place, most notably the presence in Ireland of English subjects and institutions of English government and society which directly linked the lordship of Ireland to the nation and crown of England. Nevertheless, the rapid acquisition of knowledge about Ireland, which began under the early Tudors and which was to continue right the way through the reign of Elizabeth I, constituted a discovery of no small importance for the development of the English state. The means by which the Tudors, and the most influential members of the political establishment who served them, came to be acquainted with Ireland – with its history, with its politics and economy, with its peoples and with its geography – and how that acquired knowledge was put into practice is the subject of this book.

That a discovery did, in fact, take place becomes apparent when we consider just how little the Tudors knew about Ireland. Unlike their Yorkist predecessors, the Tudors had no natural ties to Ireland. Henry VII's initial ignorance of his English kingdom has been well documented – he had probably only visited England on one occasion prior to his famous victory at Bosworth Field and subsequent accession to the throne. The preference of subsequent Tudor kings and queens, even in an age of peripatetic monarchy, to confine most of their movements, and thus the movements of their courts, to the south-east of England is also well known.[1] Ireland, however, was entirely alien to the Tudors and the

---

1 S.B. Chrimes, *Lancastrians, Yorkists and Henry VII* (London, 1966), pp 176–7; S.G. Ellis, 'The limits of power: the English crown and the British Isles' in Patrick Collinson (ed.), *The short Oxford history of the British Isles: the sixteenth century, 1485–1603* (Oxford, 2002), pp 47–9. Henry VIII was the last Tudor to progress as far to the north as York (in 1541). By the end of her long reign Elizabeth I, Henry VII's granddaughter, had travelled no further north than Staffordshire and no further west than Bristol; and in her last years the queen confined her movements exclusively to the Thames Valley: Tim Thorton, 'Henry VIII's progress through Yorkshire in 1541 and its implications for northern identities', *Northern History*, 46 (2009), 231–44; Zillah Dovey, *An Elizabethan progress: the queen's journey to East Anglia, 1578* (Frome, 1996), p. 1. It is worth noting in this context that Henry VIII was the last of the Tudor sovereigns ever to leave the kingdom of England.

depth of their ignorance of that place is a point that has been too little regarded by historians. It was an ignorance that Henry VII and his Tudor successors failed to remedy through the most effective means available to an early modern monarch seeking to build and reinforce ties of loyalty: the royal progress (though it could be said that a Tudor king or queen at the head of a conquering army might have been more appropriate in an Irish context and would have achieved the same result by different means). Yet while Henry VII, and perhaps Henry VIII, contemplated leading a grand military expedition to their lordship of Ireland, such a course of action does not appear to have even entered into the thinking of the later Tudors, even as England's relationship with Ireland steadily deepened, and steadily worsened, over the course of their reigns. In the end, no Tudor sovereign was to set foot in Ireland during the nearly six score years which that royal dynasty occupied the throne.

The same can be said of the vast majority of those men who advised, counselled and assisted the Tudor sovereigns in the ruling of their territories. Their ignorance is an equally important aspect of the Anglo-Irish relationship. In Tudor times, greater value was typically placed on knowledge acquired directly through personal experience than on knowledge gleaned, indirectly, through either oral accounts or from written sources.[2] Ireland was not Muscovy, of course; still less was this neighbouring island across the narrow sea from Wales the distant 'new founde land' lately discovered across the broad Atlantic.[3] Indeed, at the courts of the Tudor sovereigns, there was regularly a prominent councillor, sometimes several of them, who possessed personal knowledge or experience of Ireland, either on account of their Irish birth or through their service to the crown there. Henry VII, for example, could turn to members of his council for counsel on his lordship, such as the Irish-born nobleman Thomas Butler, seventh earl of Ormond, or the soldier/administrators Sir Richard Edgecombe and, later, Sir Edward Poynings, both of whom saw service in Ireland. Thomas Howard, third duke of Norfolk, was an influential member of Henry VIII's privy council whose knowledge of Ireland stemmed from his stint as chief governor there in the early 1520s. In the reigns of Edward VI and Mary I there were scarcely any high-ranking politicians at the English court with experience of Ireland, but Queen Elizabeth might turn to her Irish-born cousin, Thomas Butler, tenth earl of Ormond, and to royal councillors like Thomas

2   J.H. Elliott, *The Old World and the New, 1492–1650* (Cambridge, 1970), p. 40. This point is made with regard to Ireland in Christopher Maginn, *William Cecil, Ireland, and the Tudor state* (Oxford, 2012), p. 82.

3   Inna Lubimenko, 'England's part in the discovery of Russia', *Slavonic Review*, 4 (1927), 104–18; Stéphane Mund, 'The discovery of Muscovite Russia in Tudor England', *Revue belge de philology et d'histoire*, 86 (2008), 351–73; Evan T. Jones, 'Alwyn Ruddock: "John Cabot and the discovery of America"', *Historical Research*, 81 (2012), 224–54.

Radcliffe, third earl of Sussex, and Sir James Croft, both of whom were former governors of Ireland. Such men, however, were always few in numbers relative to other royal councillors and were typically of secondary importance in Tudor government. The principal engineers of Tudor policy, such as Archbishop Morton and Bishop Foxe under the first Tudor; Wolsey and Cromwell in the reign of Henry VIII; Somerset, Northumberland and Pole under the mid-Tudors; and William Cecil, Leicester, Walsingham and the younger Cecil at Elizabeth's court, could lay claim to no first-hand knowledge of Ireland.

In the absence of the Tudors' and their advisors' first-hand experience of Ireland, written accounts of that country and conditions there took on added significance, which is as much as to say that the Tudor discovery of Ireland most often occurred on the page. This knowledge was not acquired for knowledge's sake. It was put to a very tangible purpose: it formed the basis of what historians would call the 'Tudor', or sometimes the 'Elizabethan', conquest of Ireland. But, until the last years of the sixteenth century, the Tudor sovereigns and most of the men who served them did not see themselves engaged in a grand conquest of Ireland. For them – with the notable exception of the influential Elizabethan governor of Ireland Sir Henry Sidney, who located the completion of the English conquest of Ireland in Elizabeth's reign precisely during his deputyship – the only conquest which had taken place was that undertaken in the twelfth century by Henry II.[4] In a speech given in Star Chamber in 1599 at the very end of the Tudor century, Robert Cecil, Elizabeth's principal secretary, is recorded as having said: 'w[th]in this five yeres, Her Ma[tie] helde Irelande in as good tearmes as … anye her p[re]dicessors ever held yt'. His remarks came at the height of the earl of Tyrone's rebellion, the so-called Nine Years War (1594–1603), when the Elizabethan regime was struggling to maintain control of Ireland and the queen's councillors were responding to criticisms of the crown's handling of the government of Ireland. Secretary Cecil exonerated his queen from any blame, and in a defiant rhetorical turn asked: 'What would you have the queene doe? Shoulde shee make a conquest of all Ireland agayne? … And doe you thincke yt hadd beene easye for the Queen of Englande to sett the kinge of Ffraunce in his kingdome, to p[ro]tectt all the Lowe Countreys, to encounter the kinge of Spayne and all his forces, & to have spent her men & tresure in conquering Irelande?'[5] A few years later, in his famous exposition of why it had taken the English crown so long to 'subdue' Ireland, Sir John Davies, King James I's attorney-general, indicated that it was not until 'the nine and thirtieth year of Queen Elizabeth [that is, 1596], when the royal army was sent over to suppress the earl

---

4   *The statutes at large passed in the Irish parliaments held in Ireland, 1310–1800*, 20 vols (Dublin, 1786–1801), i, p. 330.

5   A report of Secretary Cecil's speech in Star Chamber, Nov. 1599, TNA, SP 12/273/37, fo. 79.

of Tyrone's rebellion' that the kingdom was 'brought under the obedience of the crown of England'. For it was that army, he continued, 'which made in the end an universal and absolute conquest of all the Irishry'.[6]

Prior to this, the crown saw itself as committed to making Ireland into an English dominion, ultimately a second Tudor kingdom, modelled in political, legal, socio-economic, cultural and eventually religious terms on England. Such modelling was frequently violent and its various manifestations – colonization, war, deliberate cultural destruction and massacres – taken together, looks very much like what we would nowadays call a conquest; however the fact that the Tudors and Tudor officials did not see themselves as undertaking the conquest of Ireland until the last years of Elizabeth's reign is significant.[7] Rather, contemporaries employed the language of 'reformation' when writing and thinking about Ireland, by which they generally meant the fundamental overhaul of government, law and society, so as to restore – as they understood it – the state of English rule there. By Tudor times Englishmen were certain of the transformative powers of English culture, laws and governing institutions; in Ireland, where it was believed that Englishness once flourished, it was just a matter of reactivating and renewing a pre-existing cultural and political framework. The Tudors never committed, in any formal or official sense, to Ireland's reform; reform was an elastic concept with no agreed-upon political meaning – it meant different things to different people at different times in the fifteenth and sixteenth centuries. But it can be said that the English crown began on this path in the reign of Henry VIII when, according to an Elizabethan recollection, the old king 'tooke in hande the generall reformacon of the country'.[8] Thus the ideological force that drove the Anglo-Irish relationship in the Tudor period was not conquest, but English efforts to 'reform' Ireland. A key to understanding 'reform' is to acknowledge the Tudor discovery of Ireland which first took place in the late fifteenth and early sixteenth centuries; and the keys to this discovery are the documents from which the Tudors and the men who served them came to learn about the neighbouring island.

One of these documents, hitherto overlooked by historians, captures the twin processes of knowledge acquisition and the implementation of acquired knowledge in a way that other such documents do not. It resides among the

---

6   John Davies, *A discovery of the true causes why Ireland was never entirely subdued ... until the beginning of his majesty's happy reign* (London, 1612), pp 5–6.

7   David Edwards, 'Beyond reform: martial law and the Tudor reconquest of Ireland', *History Ireland*, 5 (1997), 16–21; idem, 'The escalation of violence in sixteenth-century Ireland' in David Edwards, Pádraig Lenihan and Clodagh Tait (eds), *Age of atrocity: violence and political conflict in early modern Ireland* (Dublin, 2010), pp 34–78, esp. p. 78.

8   'Towching the reveues both auncient and present', BL, Cotton MSS, Titus B XII, fo. 324v. See also LPL, Carew MS 635, fo. 62v (*Cal. Carew MSS*, iv, no. 398).

Cecil Papers preserved in Hatfield House Archives in Hertfordshire, England.[9] The anonymous and undated manuscript was placed among the undated papers belonging to the reign of Henry VIII (1509–47) in the first volume of the *Calendar of the Salisbury (Cecil) manuscripts*, published in 1883, where it was laconically described as 'Ireland. Brief of the getting and of the decay of Ireland, and ordinances and provision for the same. –Undated'.[10] During King Henry's pivotal reign there were a number of political treatises written about the state of government and society in Ireland; many (though not all) of the treatises were composed by leading members of Ireland's English population (or the Anglo-Irish as they are commonly known). These writings, known to historians as reform literature, sought both to demonstrate the allegedly woeful position of the king's subjects in Ireland and to suggest how best to bring about Ireland's 'reformation'.[11] There were, the reader of these works learned, two related though separate problems undermining the lordship that demanded the crown's attention: those emanating from Irishmen whose independence, coupled with their supposed bellicosity, savagery and memories of military defeat and dispossession, threatened the king's subjects; and those emanating from Englishmen who had, over time, notably through their alliance with Irishmen and adoption of Irish culture, come to deviate from English political, legal and cultural norms and so risked contaminating the wider English community in Ireland.

The existence of this kind of literature, together with the description contained in the *Calendar of the Salisbury (Cecil) manuscripts*, suggested that the anonymous document in question was nothing more than a copy of a Henrician treatise which treated of the history of Ireland before advancing suggestions for its reform. The most likely candidate was the 'Breviate of the gettyng of Irelande and the decaye of the same'. Historians of Ireland are very familiar with this piece. Written by Sir Patrick Finglas, a leading light of the gentry of the English

---

9 Hatfield House Archives, Hertfordshire, Cecil Papers MS 144, fos 1–15v.

10 *Calendar of the manuscripts of the … marquess of Salisbury …, preserved at Hatfield House*, 23 vols (London, 1883–1973), i, p. 52. A decade earlier the royal commission on historical manuscripts had similarly described the MS as 'Brief of the getting and of the decay of Ireland': *Fourth report of the royal commission on historical manuscripts* (London, 1874), p. 202. For an archival history of the Cecil Papers themselves – where it is explained that the designation MS 144 indicates that the document described here was bound into a guard book and catalogued between 1831 and 1856 when it and other documents were 'rescued from a mass of old domestic Accounts & family Deeds accidentally discovered in a decaying state' – see R.H. Williams, 'The Cecil Papers: four centuries of custodial history', www.cecilpapers.chadwyck.co.uk/info/essay.do, accessed 17 Feb. 2014.

11 The most influential exploration of this literature is Brendan Bradshaw, *The Irish constitutional revolution of the sixteenth century* (Cambridge, 1979), pp 32–57, 164–85; but see also the discussion of this material in D.G. White, 'Tudor plantations in Ireland to 1571' (PhD, University of Dublin, 1968), ch. 1. See also below, note 16; also note 12.

Pale, the Breviate offers a history of the establishment and decay of the English colony in Ireland in the later medieval period followed by a detailed strategy for the lordship's 'reformation'.[12] To judge by the many later sixteenth-century copies that survive, Finglas' treatise enjoyed a healthy circulation in government circles in the decades after its composition. So it was not at all surprising that a copy should end up in England among the disparate papers of Sir William Cecil, afterwards Lord Burghley. Cecil was the most powerful figure in Elizabethan England after the queen and maintained a keen interest in Ireland, and the records associated with it, throughout his many decades of service to the Tudor dynasty.[13] The only clue that the Hatfield House document was anything more, or something else, was its length: the calendar noted that it was thirty pages long, longer than most examples of the early Tudor reform genre and substantially longer than any of the known copies of Finglas' Breviate.

An examination of the original document revealed it to be a compendium of assorted manuscripts containing information on Ireland. Some of the material is informative, offering historical, geographical and contemporary political, socio-economic and military knowledge, and some of it is prescriptive, setting out both theoretical proposals and more specific legal advice to bring about the lordship's reform. Upon closer inspection the various pieces of information were drawn up at different points in the late fifteenth and early sixteenth centuries. But this mate-rial was deliberately gathered together and placed in a single document written in an unbroken secretary hand sometime late in the reign of Henry VIII. The com-pendium, which will be referred to here as the Hatfield Compendium, seems to have been prepared as an elaborate dossier on Ireland for a government official, or officials, who wished (or who were offered the opportunity) to achieve a work-ing knowledge of the country from one source. In its entirety, the Hatfield Compendium amounts to some 14,000 words and stretches across fifteen manu-script folios. It contains both material otherwise unknown to historians and ear-lier, and more complete, versions of manuscripts which historians have typically employed in their researches on Tudor Ireland. The document does indeed begin with a copy of Finglas' Breviate; but there is much more to follow: an invaluable tract known as the 'A description of the power of Irishmen', which presents a detailed reckoning of the military strength, or 'power', of dozens of lords from across the island; a listing of many of Ireland's harbours, or 'havens'; and another

---

12 See below, p. 21.

13 For Cecil's sustained and multi-faceted interest in Ireland see, Maginn, *William Cecil, Ireland, and the Tudor state*. Brendan Bradshaw transcribed and edited an anonymous reform treatise which he found among the Cecil Papers at Hatfield House: 'A treatise for the reformation of Ireland', *Irish Jurist*, 16:2 (1981), 299–315 (CP, MS 201, fos 116–23v). This treatise was com-posed in Queen Mary's reign and, apart from its presence among the Cecil Papers, is unrelated to the manuscript presently under discussion.

Henrician reform treatise concerned principally with the decay of English law in Ireland written by the Co. Meath gentleman Sir William Darcy of Platten. Then there is a puzzling (for it is fragmentary) set of 'Articles for the reformation of Ireland', which give way to a commentary on the royal revenues deriving from lands in Ireland. This is followed by pedigrees of the various branches of the Burkes, one of Ireland's oldest and most prominent English lineages whose inheritance passed to the crown of England in the later fifteenth century, and a lengthy and richly detailed set of 'Ordinances and provisions for Ireland', which inter alia codifies ordinances for the military and social organization of the English Pale. The 'Ordinances' conclude with the identification of passes to be cut through the forests and the wastes that often separated English areas of Ireland from the Irish lordships beyond in the early Tudor period. Were the Hatfield Compendium to have been given a page outlining its various contents it would have looked something like this:

1   Sir Patrick Finglas' Breviate (fos 1–5)
2   A description of the power of Irishmen (fos 5v–8v)
3   The havens of Ireland (fo. 8v)
4   Sir William Darcy's articles (fos 9–9v)
5   Articles for the reformation of Ireland (fo. 9v)
6   Revenues of Ireland (fos 10–10v)
7   Pedigrees of the Burkes (fo. 10v)
8   Ordinances and provisions for Ireland (fos 11–15v)

The compendium preserved at Hatfield House offers a unique view on a crucial phase in the Anglo-Irish relationship, when the Tudors were beginning their discovery of that part of their inheritance about which they knew least, but which would come to trouble them, and the state forming around them, most. The documents, which together comprise this Compendium, were intended to serve, at their various points of composition, as sources of information – a textual means through which the Tudor sovereigns and members of the political establishment in England were to learn about Ireland. But they were also a medium by which the English of Ireland and Englishmen serving the crown in Ireland, the wellsprings of information on the country, could, by exploiting the intended audience's ignorance of the place, control and construct an image of the country and its inhabitants so as to engage and interest their king and his servants in the well-being of his subjects in Ireland. An exploration of the Hatfield Compendium and its contents can thus also tell us a great deal about the political and economic state and aspirations of the English of early Tudor Ireland. Yet the prescriptive element in these writings reminds us of the fact that the ultimate aim of the men who penned these documents was to convince the English crown to embark upon the reform of Ireland: discovery was to be almost immediately superseded by political, economic and social change which, contemporaries believed, would bring Ireland back to a previous perfect condition. Beginning in the reign of Henry VIII, the Tudor regime did engage more directly and more regularly in Ireland – the advent of what we understand as the Tudor conquest of Ireland. But this engagement and interaction began as discovery, a process which went hand-in-hand with suggestions for reform. And as these twin processes became translated into political policy and action, the undertaking assumed qualities and a direction which, at one level, alienated the very community whose theorists had so stridently argued for it in the first place and, at another, saddled the Tudor state with one of the most ambitious endeavours ever to be attempted in the early modern world.

The present book is divided into two parts. The first offers a technical discussion and dissection of the Compendium's eight component parts, concluding with a similar analysis of the Compendium itself. Where possible, composition dates, the identification of authors and the intended audience will be established for each component part. And because the Hatfield Compendium contains so much original and unpublished material it is reproduced here, at the end of part one, fully transcribed and, where it is thought necessary, annotated. In this way, the modern reader will be confronted with the same material that was assembled for a reader in Tudor times. The second part of this book is interpretative and more discursive in nature. In three chapters, which will proceed in a broadly chronological fashion from the accession to the throne of Henry VII through the end of the reign of Henry VIII, part two will chart the development of the twin processes that are central to understanding the Anglo-Irish relationship in this period and which are so evident in the Hatfield Compendium: the acquisition by Englishmen of knowledge about Ireland – discovery – and the crown's efforts to effect change in Ireland based on this knowledge – reform.

Discovery is a process that has gone almost entirely unnoticed by historians in their accounts of the history of Tudor Ireland. This oversight may, as we have seen, be attributed to the fact that England's association with Ireland was already long established by the Tudor period. The process of knowledge acquisition, it may be argued, is also so deeply embedded in the historical record that it has not attracted the same notice as, for example, the formulation of policy, bureaucratic innovations, the outbreak of violence or the framing of laws. Yet understanding by what means and when the Tudor regime obtained knowledge about this territory over which the English crown claimed to rule is essential. In his magisterial study of Philip II and the Spanish king's exercise of power in the second half of the sixteenth century, Geoffrey Parker, quoting Michel Foucault, observed: 'It is not possible for power to be exercised without knowledge, it is impossible for knowledge not to engender power'.[14] Indeed historians of Spain have stressed the importance

14 Geoffrey Parker, *The grand strategy of Philip II* (New Haven and London, 2000), p. 65.

of Philip II's desire for detailed information about his New World possessions, an eagerness which has been said to be symptomatic of that king's 'Renaissance thirst for knowledge'.[15] It may well be that Philip II was extraordinary in this regard: his willingness to work through the paperwork pertaining to his many possessions is the stuff of legend; his attention to detail notorious. By contrast, the Tudor kings and queens, with the possible exception of Henry VII, expressed little personal, bureaucratic or intellectual interest in Ireland, and were generally prepared to leave the task of gathering and distilling information about the neighbouring island to the men who served them. Yet the fact remains that the exercise of Tudor power in Ireland was based on knowledge, and that the Tudors and their leading advisors in the absence of first-hand experience discovered Ireland in much the same way as Habsburg kings acquired knowledge about the Indies.

Reform is a concept that is more familiar to historians of Tudor Ireland. It is now generally accepted that the corpus of reform literature which appeared in Henry VIII's reign marks the most tangible manifestation of this concept and represents the ideological starting point for understanding Tudor thinking about Ireland. But little consensus has emerged as to the intellectual ownership of the concept – whether it sprang from an 'Anglo-Irish reforming milieu' as Brendan Bradshaw memorably described it – or over its origins; whether reform was a concept inherited from the medieval period or an outgrowth of sixteenth-century Renaissance humanism. Or over how, and to what extent, the ideas contained in the reform literature passed out of the purely theoretical realm and entered political thinking, which was ultimately translated into deeds.[16] Indeed, reform is a concept that, though it is frequently evoked, has not been thoroughly defined or subjected to systematic investigation, with the result that historians' treatment of reform varies: narrowly, as an act meant to renew the institutions and the functioning of English government in Ireland; more broadly, as a social, political and religious policy specific to Ireland which sought to make the kingdom and its inhabitants like England and the English; as a style of government that the Tudors might employ in other territories, like Wales, where they also exercised incomplete political and cultural authority; and, most recently, as an historical canard which has distracted historians from the increasingly violent

15 Geoffrey Parker, *Empire, war and faith in early modern Europe* (London, 2002), ch. 4; John Elliott, *Empires of the Atlantic world: Britain and Spain in America, 1492–1830* (New Haven and London, 2006), p. 34 (quotation).

16 Bradshaw, *The Irish constitutional revolution*, pp 32–57, 164–85; Ciaran Brady, *The chief governors: the rise and fall of reform government* (Cambridge, 1994); Fiona Fitzsimons, 'Cardinal Wolsey, the native affinities and the failure of reform in Henrician Ireland' in David Edwards (ed.), *Regions and rulers in Ireland, 1100–1650: essays for Kenneth Nicholls* (Dublin, 2004), pp 78–121; Ciaran Brady, 'From policy to power: the evolution of Tudor reform strategies in sixteenth-century Ireland' in Brian Mac Cuarta (ed.), *Reshaping Ireland, 1550–1700: colonization and its consequences* (Dublin, 2011), pp 21–42.

nature of the Anglo-Irish relationship in Tudor times.[17] Another potential problem is that because the reform material generally increases in quantity over the course of the sixteenth century, and because so much of it has survived to be read and explored by the modern researcher, it can be assumed that contemporaries also had a comprehensive knowledge of these manuscripts and also benefitted (as the modern historian surely does) from a linear progression of knowledge. However the English government's record keeping was notoriously poor in Tudor times and it was at its worst in Ireland; information pertaining to the reform of Ireland committed to paper could be lost, forgotten or simply ignored more easily than it could be acquired, interpreted and then applied.

Meanwhile, the concept of reform and early Tudor reform literature which it produced has been very much overshadowed by the more elaborate reform tracts that were penned toward the end of the sixteenth century during Elizabeth's reign. These works, principally those of English-born colonists, such as Richard Beacon, William Herbert, Barnaby Rich and, most importantly, Edmund Spenser, have been seized upon by historians and literary specialists alike as evidence of the genesis of modern ideas, such as colonization, racial superiority and ethnic cleansing, which were supposedly coursing through the minds of the men who were at once remaking England's relationship with Ireland and forging the ideas which would soon underpin the expansion of English power and culture throughout the world. That these tracts were often longer and written in a finely crafted literary style – often in exquisite Elizabethan prose (rather than in an unadorned and more purely political format which characterized the earlier Henrician material) – has made the later genre all the more attractive.[18] Ciaran Brady has recently pointed to the importance of the early Tudor reform writings in the evolution of the ideas expressed in the later Elizabethan material, but as yet historians have done little to reorientate scholarly focus on the ideas expressed in the earlier works.[19]

---

17 S.G. Ellis, *Reform and revival: English government in Ireland, 1470–1534* (London, 1986); David Edwards, 'Collaboration without Anglicisation: the MacGiollapadraig lordship and Tudor reform' in P.J. Duffy, David Edwards and Elizabeth FitzPatrick (eds), *Gaelic Ireland, 1250–1650: land, lordship and settlement* (Dublin, 2001), pp 77–97; Christopher Maginn, 'The limitations of Tudor reform: the policy of "surrender and regrant" and the O'Rourkes', *Breifne*, 43 (2007), 429–60; Ciaran Brady, 'Comparable histories?: Tudor reform in Wales and Ireland' in S.G. Ellis and Sarah Barber (eds), *Conquest and union: fashioning a British state, 1485–1725* (London, 1995), pp 64–86; Edwards, 'The escalation of violence in sixteenth-century Ireland', pp 34–78.

18 See, for example, Willy Maley (ed.), 'A supplication of the blood of the English most lamentably murdered in Ireland, cryeng out of the yearth for revenge (1598)', *Analecta Hibernica*, 36 (1994), 1–90, which also provides a list (at p. 4) of all of the sixteenth-century reform treatises which had been published to 1994. See also Nicholas Canny, *Making Ireland British, 1580–1641* (Oxford, 2001).

19 Brady, 'Tudor reform strategies' in Mac Cuarta (ed.), *Reshaping Ireland, 1550–1700*, p. 26.

Part two of this book will reunite the process of discovery with reform by looking at the interplay between knowledge acquisition and the origins of reform as a concept and their appearance in the historical record of the early Tudor period. Knowledge acquisition, as an analysis of the Hatfield Compendium will show, was inseparable from the proposals for the reform of Ireland which emerged as one of the defining features of the Anglo-Irish relationship in Tudor times. And though the Hatfield Compendium itself belongs firmly to the age of Henry VIII, this book will demonstrate that the documents and therefore also the information and ideas for reform contained in it were rooted in late medieval English thinking about Ireland and that this line of thought continued to serve, into the late sixteenth century and beyond, as a touchstone for Englishmen seeking to make Ireland into an English kingdom. In this way, by recovering the importance of the Hatfield Compendium and by placing its component parts and, ultimately the Compendium itself, within a chronologically broader sweep of Anglo-Irish interaction, the present book will reconstruct the Tudor discovery of Ireland and seek to show how discovery evolved in the early Tudor period into the crown's commitment to Ireland's reform, and how this commitment ultimately assumed a coercive form with such disastrous consequences for the relationship between England and Ireland in the early modern period.

PART I

Discussion of the text

I.1

Patrick Finglas' Breviate

The Hatfield Compendium opens with a copy of 'A breviate of the gettyng of Ireland and of the decaye of the same'. It was the work of Patrick Finglas, an up-and-coming lawyer and a member of a prominent gentry family whose name derived from the Co. Dublin village where they had settled.[1] The Breviate, however, was one of at least three recensions – evident in four known versions – of a treatise that Finglas had composed some years earlier entitled 'A briefe note of the gettinge and decaye of Ireland'. For the sake of clarity, the several versions of Finglas' work discussed here will be labelled in bold and numbered: [**Versions 1, 2, 3 and 4**]. The original 'brief note' appears to have been lost – all that has survived is a later Elizabethan, or possibly an early Stuart, copy preserved at the archiepiscopal archives at Lambeth Palace in London among the papers collected by the administrator and antiquarian George Carew (1555–1629) [**Version 1**].[2] Finglas, recently begun on a career in the royal service – he was appointed the king's serjeant-at-law in 1508 – was said to have preferred his treatise to Henry VIII around the year 1515.[3] It furnished the young king with a detailed history of the English conquest – 'the getting' – of Ireland in the late twelfth century and then set out the history of the 'decay' of the English colony there which, according to Finglas, set in 150 years or so thereafter. More than a decade later, Finglas, by then chief baron of the exchequer and a member of the privy council in Ireland, penned the first recension of his treatise [**Version 2**]. The copy which has survived, also among the Carew papers at Lambeth, was endorsed: '1529 An abbreviatt of the gettinge of Irland and the decay of the same wch was written as may be conceved, about the 20: of K. H. 8. raygne'.[4] Here, Finglas rehearsed the information contained in his 'brief note', though he included some additional historical detail, and then appended, in a single paragraph, his suggestions for Ireland's reform. Then, seemingly in the year before his death in summer 1537, Finglas returned to his treatise, this time adding much more detailed and elaborate suggestions for Ireland's reform after rehearsing his history of its 'getting' and its subsequent 'decay'.[5] This

---

1   CP, MS 144, fos 1–5.   2   LPL, Carew MS 635, fos 185–7.

3   S.G. Ellis, *Reform and revival: English government in Ireland, 1470–1534* (London, 1986), p. 224. The 'briefe note' is headed: 'preferred unto Kinge Henry the Eight about the viith yere of his raigne [Apr. 1515 to Apr. 1516]'.

4   LPL, Carew MS 600, fos 204–7.

5   Finglas died sometime between 18 July and 12 Aug. 1537: BL, Additional MS 19865, fo. 2; BL, Cotton MSS, Titus B XI, fo. 359.

final bout of work on his treatise produced two recensions which appeared, undated, under the titles 'the decay of Ireland written by Patrick Finglas, one of the Barons of the exchequer in Ireland', and 'A brevyate of the conqueste of Irland and of the decay of the same' [**Versions 3 & 4**]. The former survives as a later copy – again preserved among the Carew papers; the latter is a contemporary document which is to be found among the Henrician State Papers where, as we shall see, it was incorrectly placed in the *Calendar of state papers relating to Ireland* under the year 1533.[6] The Breviate (which in sixteenth-century English meant a short account rather than an abridgement of a longer tract) is entirely in the hand of Finglas' son, Thomas, protonotary of the common bench.[7] It is a near-identical copy of this last recension of the Breviate [**Version 4**] that appears in the Hatfield Compendium, only here the Breviate is organized into a series of 'items' numbered from one to fifty-six in Arabic numerals.

Finglas' reform treatise is well known to historians primarily because it was transcribed and printed *in extenso* by the eighteenth-century historian Walter Harris. Harris included the Breviate [**Version 4**] in a book that offered full transcriptions of written specimens from the history of Ireland.[8] His object was faithfully to reproduce for the reader these documents, rather than to interpret them or to subject them to critical analysis, so as to highlight some of the richness and antiquity of Ireland's history. Harris' transcription of the Breviate was based on a seventeenth-century copy preserved in the archives of Trinity College in Dublin. Though Harris entitled the piece 'A Breviat of the Getting of Irland, and of the Decaie of the same' and duly attributed it to Patrick Finglas 'Chief Baron of the Exchequer in K. Henry the VIIIth's time', the manuscript from which Harris worked was, as a matter of fact, also a part of a compendium of documents, not altogether unlike the Hatfield Compendium. In the Trinity manuscript the Breviate flows straight into what are called in the Hatfield Compendium the 'Ordinances and Provisions for Ireland' before continuing on to a separate document, what we know to be 'Darcy's articles' (discussed below in section 1.4). Harris, however, mistakenly believed the three documents to be

---

6 LPL, Carew MS 621, fo. 92; 'A treatise by Patrick Finglas', TNA, SP 60/2/7, fos 17–24 (*Calendar of state papers relating to Ireland of the reigns of Henry VIII, Edward VI, Mary and Elizabeth, 1509–73*, ed. H.C. Hamilton (London, 1860), p. 9). This document was not included in the otherwise comprehensive *Letters and papers, foreign and domestic, Henry VIII*, 21 vols (London, 1862–1932).

7 Bradshaw, *The Irish constitutional revolution*, p. 95. For a specimen of Thomas Finglas' hand, see Thomas Finglas to Cromwell, 21 July 1534, TNA, SP 60/2/18, fo. 50.

8 TCD MS 842, fos 25–36; Walter Harris (ed.), *Hibernica, or, some ancient pieces relating to the history of Ireland*, 2 vols (Dublin, 1747, 1750), i, pp 39–52. For Harris' original transcription, see NLI, MS 16, fos 25–42. For other copies of Finglas' Breviate in Trinity College, Dublin, see TCD MSS 581, 786.

the singular work of Finglas entitled the Breviate. This has caused no small amount of confusion: accepting that Finglas was also the author of the 'Ordinances and Provisions for Ireland', historians have linked him to Thomas Cromwell's similarly worded *Ordinances for the government of Ireland* which were printed in 1534 and, on the strength of this, have ascribed to the Breviate a date contemporaneous to the printed *Ordinances*.[9] Apart from treating what were three separate documents as one, the seventeenth-century copy of the Breviate from which Harris worked is, in most respects, identical to the later recension of the Breviate [**Version 4**] that opens the Hatfield Compendium. (The 'Ordinances and Provisions for Ireland' are another matter and will be discussed at length below, in section 1.8.) There are, however, many errors in Harris' transcription, which makes the printed version of the Breviate unreliable.

Historians are also familiar with Finglas' treatise because it was summarized over the first six pages of the more widely accessible *Calendar of the Carew manuscripts* published in the nineteenth century.[10] But the document that opens the calendar, and which was placed under the year 1515, is in fact the 'decay of Ireland', written more than two decades later in 1536–7 [**Version 3**]. The editors of the calendar were well aware that several versions of Finglas' work, all of them later copies, existed among the Carew papers at Lambeth. Indeed they went so far as to include the additional information contained in the Breviate [**Version 2**] in the footnotes running below their transcription of 'the decay of Ireland', noting that Finglas' reference to having reported the inherent military weakness of the Irish to 'the duke of Northfolke' meant that the Breviate was written after 1524 – Thomas Howard, who had served as lord lieutenant of Ireland 1520–2 and who had, in 1520, secured for Finglas appointment as chief baron of the exchequer, did not succeed his father as the third duke of Norfolk until May 1524.[11] In dating 'the decay of Ireland' [**Version 3**] to 1515, however, the editors failed to consider that Finglas did not become chief baron until 1520, and so could not have been described as occupying this post before then. 'The decay', moreover, contains suggestions for the 'reformation' of Ireland, which urge the king to confiscate abbeys and castles on the borders of the English Pale and then redistribute them to 'younge lordes knyghtes and gent[lemen] out of Englande, which shall dwelle upon the same'. The later recension of the

9 Bradshaw, *The Irish constitutional revolution*, p. 100; Alan J. Fletcher, *Drama and the performing arts in pre-Cromwellian Ireland: sources and documents from the earliest times until c.1642* (Cambridge, 2001), pp 508–9; Marian Lyons, *s.v.* 'Patrick Finglas', *ODNB* (eds), H.G.C. Matthew and Brian Harrison (Oxford, 2004); Valerie McGowan-Doyle, *The Book of Howth: the Elizabethan re-conquest of Ireland and the Old English* (Cork, 2011), p. 6.

10 *Calendar of the Carew manuscripts, preserved in the archiepiscopal library at Lambeth*, ed. J.S. Brewer and William Bullen, 6 vols (London, 1867), i, no. 1.

11 Ellis, *Reform and revival*, p. 34.

Breviate [**Version 4**] contains nearly identical suggestions for confiscation and redistribution. Thus 'the decay of Ireland', and indeed the (later) Breviate [**Versions 3 & 4**], must have been written following both the enactment by the Irish parliament in May 1536 of the Act of Absentees, which authorized the seizure of church lands by endowing the crown with the possessions held by English foundations in Ireland, and the attainder of Gerald Fitzgerald, ninth earl of Kildare, and those men who had followed his son 'Silken' Thomas into ill-fated rebellion in 1534. The former act also resumed to the crown the lands in Ireland belonging to the duke of Norfolk, the 'heirs general' of the earl of Ormond – Thomas Boleyn, the ninth earl of Ormond, was by then in political eclipse and without an heir following the execution for treason in May 1536 of his son George, Viscount Rochford – and, also, the Talbot earl of Shrewsbury. The province of Leinster, where the preponderance of the church lands, the attainted lands and the absentee lands lay, emerged in Finglas' final recensions as the key to the reform of the entire lordship. This accounts for the suggestions that castles and manors, such as Athy and Rathangan, which had belonged to Kildare, the castle of Carlow, part of Norfolk's inheritance, Arklow, which belonged to Ormond, and the lordship of Wexford, part of Shrewsbury's inheritance by right of the earldom of Waterford, should be confiscated. So, Finglas' treatise, which he first wrote in 1515 [**Version 1**], underwent additions and alterations in 1529 [**Version 2**] and again in 1536–7 [**Versions 3 & 4**].

But what moved Finglas, first to compose, and then to revise his work at these dates? The year 1515 has long been regarded as a seminal year in the history of Tudor Ireland for two reasons. First, it saw the beginning of a criticism from within the English Pale of the ninth earl of Kildare, which over the next two decades would rise to a fever pitch; and, looking back from the spectacular fall of the house of Kildare in a blaze of armed rebellion in 1534–5, Gerald Fitzgerald, the ninth earl of Kildare's visit to court in May 1515 very much looks like the beginning of the end for him and his family.[12] This year also marked the first appearance in the published State Papers of the reform literature that would become such an important feature of the reigns of Henry VIII and his children; that both the printed versions of the Henrician State Papers and the Carew manuscripts open in 1515 with separate tracts crying out from the page for the reform of Ireland has served to magnify the year's importance still further. Indeed 1515 saw an anonymous author write the weighty (and undated) tract the 'State of Ireland and Plan for its Reformation'; the ninth earl of Kildare make his first visit to court as lord deputy of Ireland; and Sir William Darcy's articles outlining the

---

12 S.G. Ellis, *Ireland in the age of the Tudors: English expansion and the end of Gaelic rule, 1447–1603* (London, 1998), p. 114; Colm Lennon, *Sixteenth-century Ireland: the incomplete conquest* (Dublin, 1994), pp 79, 82.

recent history and decay of Ireland presented to the king's council in London.[13] It was also the year that Finglas preferred his treatise on the history of the English colony in Ireland to King Henry.

But why should Finglas have chosen to do so in 1515? If Kildare's enemies were looking for an opportunity to strike at the earl then surely the death in 1513 of his father, the 'Great Earl' (Gearóid Mór), would have presented a more favourable circumstance. Certainly, to judge by Kildare's confirmation as deputy in 1515, and the royal grants he received on foot of his visit to court, Henry VIII saw no deficiency in the earl or in his style of government. The written evidence from 1515, moreover, generally makes only indirect criticism of Kildare rule, though – as will be discussed in greater detail below – Darcy's tract was more pointed in places. The version of Finglas' tract presented to Henry VIII in 1515 [**Version 1**] limited itself to a discussion of the 'getting' and 'decay' of the English colony in Ireland: it was purely historical and contains none of the prescriptions for reform or the explicit criticisms of Kildare evident in the later recensions. In terms of the Hatfield Compendium, the information in this version concludes at 'Item' thirty-seven; by the time of Finglas' final recension more than twenty years later the tract had grown to fifty-six items. Still, Henry VIII had already been king for nearly six years in 1515 – this would seem an arbitrary time to seek to educate him about Ireland and what was supposedly wrong there.

A possible explanation for the flurry of activity in and around 1515 may be found in a letter of John Kite, the English-born archbishop of Armagh. Writing in May 1514 to his patron Thomas Wolsey, the bishop of Lincoln and one of the young king's most prominent councillors, Kite related how he had assured the English of Ireland that King Henry's coming was imminent, though he sought assurance himself from Wolsey 'off the kings co[m]myng indede'. Kite had nevertheless concluded that 'the kyng is as moche bound to reforme this land as to mayntayn the goode ordre & justice off England'.[14] Newly arrived from England, this former royal chaplain's comments may have inspired the more verbal among Ireland's English population to begin writing in an effort to provide the king and his council with the historical, social and political background necessary for men planning not only the first visit to the lordship of an English king in well over a century but also the reform of the lordship.[15] The English of Ireland were not alone in their belief that a significant change in Tudor policy toward Ireland was at hand. It was around this same time, c.1513–14, that the anonymous morality play called *Hickscorner* was written in England. The play may be read for its many thinly veiled criticisms of the policies pursued

13   State of Ireland and plan for its reformation, c.1515, TNA, SP 60/1/9, fos 13–28v (*State papers, Henry VIII*, 11 vols (London, 1830–52), ii, pp 1–31).

14   John Kite to Wolsey, 14 May 1514, TNA, SP 60/1/3, fo. 4.

15   *SP Hen. VIII*, ii, p. 27 (quotation). See also below, p. 137.

by the government of the young Henry VIII. It satirizes, for instance, the possibility, suggested in the 'State of Ireland', that an Englishman from every parish in England, Cornwall and Wales should be resettled in Ireland as a means of achieving the lordship's reform.[16] The eponymous Hickscorner enters the play as a man just put ashore at home in England having sailed the world over. He relates to two characters, 'Free Will' and 'Imagination', that he had in his travels lately witnessed the sinking of a 'grete naue full of people that wolde into Irlonde and they came out of this countre. They wyll neuer more come [again] to Englonde'. Yet Hickscorner explains that his bad tidings should be greeted with good cheer because had these good Englishmen successfully traversed the Irish Sea: 'I se them all drowned in the rase of Irlonde'.[17] The significance of the year 1515 as a historical marker thus may lie more in the belief in Ireland, and indeed in England, that the bullish young king, reconciled with France since August 1514, had committed to Ireland's reform, than in the year in which a coherent political movement against Kildare found expression.

Finglas revisited his treatise in 1529 in very different circumstances. The material that he added that year was a response to the belief, expressed by 'some men' according to Finglas, that the increased sophistication of the Irish in martial affairs meant that it was more difficult to reform Ireland in the reign of Henry VIII than it was at the time of the original conquest. The sentiment was understandable. The previous three years were a time of especially weak government, marked as they were by the absence in England of the earls of Kildare and Ormond, renewed Irish raids on the English Pale and, most spectacularly, the kidnapping of the vice-deputy, the baron of Delvin, by O'Connor Faly. Thomas Howard, the former governor and by then the duke of Norfolk, was implored by members of the Irish privy council to inform the king that Irishmen '(being never so strong as nowe) have spied their tyme, and our debilitie nevermore then at this houre'.[18] Finglas countered, noting that Englishmen's knowledge of warfare was superior to that of Irishmen and that the ability of the crown to avail of the hundreds of 'castelles and pyles' built in Ireland in the centuries since the Conquest would ease the task of reform. This emphasis on the lordship's existing military infrastructure was a familiar refrain – it had been communicated in similar terms to Edward IV by the parliament of Ireland some fifty-five years earlier:

> in aduertysyng the Kynges highness to the lyghly recouere of the sayd
> land it is so the furst conquest therof was obtened w^t a full smale nombre

16 Ian Lancashire (ed.), *Two Tudor interludes: Youth and Hick Scorner* (Manchester, 1980), pp 63, 244; *SP Hen. VIII*, ii, pp 25–6.
17 *Hickscorner, c.1497–1512*, ed. John Farmer (London, 1908), lines 326–9, 362.
18 *SP Hen. VIII*, ii, p. 130.

of Englyssh men at which tyme all the land was under Iryssh obeysaunce, and at thes dayes all the cities castelx and walled townes of the same land inviron ben under the kynges obeyssaunce.[19]

Finglas claimed to have reported this information to Norfolk, 'and others that have bene there'. This reference to 'there' probably indicates that Finglas wrote this section while in England and that a visit to court occasioned the addition – the copy in the Hatfield Compendium, by contrast, refers to Norfolk 'and other greate capitaynes that have ben *here*' [that is, Ireland].

The evidence available for dating the final recensions of Finglas' treatise is even more plentiful. As we have noticed above, the monastic lands and castles of Leinster became central to the treatise at this stage in its evolution, and these last recensions must have been written after the enactment in May 1536 of the Act of Absentees and before Finglas' death in summer 1537. By then, the lord deputy, Leonard Grey, together with the Irish privy council, of which Patrick Finglas continued to be an active member, had also adopted the 'reformyng of Leynster' as the necessary prelude to a more general reform of Ireland.[20] But they had to convince a king still smarting from the expenditures involved in the suppression of Kildare's rebellion to authorize such a potentially expensive undertaking. The result was the drawing up by the lord deputy and council of Ireland of 'A memoriall or a note for the wynnyng of Leynster'.[21] The 'memoriall', sent over to the king and his council in February 1537, has much in common with Finglas' treatise. It too looked to the historical example of the first conquest and had as its central thrust the confiscation and redistribution of abbeys and castles on the borders of the English Pale. The 'memorial', however, shares passages that are strikingly similar to those included in the final recension of Finglas' treatise. The 'memorial', for example, extols the virtues of 'the nobilitie of those Inglishemen, wich came at the conqwest', for 'thei sought neither for delicate fare, neither desired thei to lye in walled townes, uppon soft beddes'.[22] The Breviate, meanwhile, warns that the lands in Leinster should not be given to men who 'coveyte easye beddes ne goode fare'; rather these men should follow in the example of the 'noble lordes knygthes and gentlemen that conquered this

19 TNA, C 47/10/29 (printed in Donough Bryan, *The great earl of Kildare, Gerald FitzGerald, 1456–1513* (Dublin, 1933), pp 20–1).

20 Lord Deputy and Council to Henry VIII, 29 Oct. 1536, TNA, SP 60/3/79, fos 165–6; Lord Deputy and Council to Henry VIII, 23 Nov. 1536, TNA, SP 60/3/83, fos 175–7v (quotation); Christopher Maginn, *'Civilizing' Gaelic Leinster: the extension of Tudor rule in the O'Byrne and O'Toole lordships* (Dublin, 2005), pp 46–9.

21 Memorial for the winning of Leinster, Feb. 1537, TNA, SP 60/4/7, fos 19–25; Grey to Cromwell, 10 Feb. 1537, TNA, SP 60/4/8, fo. 26.

22 Memorial for the winning of Leinster, Feb. 1537, TNA, SP 60/4/7, fo. 24; Brady, *Chief governors*, p. 249.

lande under kynge Henrye Fitz Emprese [Henry II] the whiche regarded not easye lyghyng delycate fare ne pompeous apparaille'.[23] Patrick Finglas was the common denominator running through both documents, and it is likely that his treatise was revised for a final time, with the help of his son, Thomas, in conjunction with the drawing up of the 'memoriall' in early 1537.

By the time of his death in August 1537, Patrick Finglas had produced an important statement of the history of English Ireland, and his several additions to the work, made over two decades, ensured that his Breviate received pride of place in the Hatfield Compendium. His fellow Palesman, and successor in the office of king's serjeant-at-law, Patrick Barnewall, noted Finglas' passing in a letter to Cromwell and added that he feared 'the kinges highnes … shall lack his s[er]vice', for he was 'that man that effectually favored the kinges causes and the co[m]en wele of that his graces land'.[24] The usefulness of Finglas' writings as a history is evident from the many (mostly antiquarian) copies of his work that were later made in Elizabeth's reign.[25] A copy of the Breviate appears, for example, among the notes of Elizabeth's secretary, Sir Francis Walsingham, embellished with annotations and elaborate genealogies of some of the principal figures named in the history.[26] Later, the Breviate achieved the status of an historical authority in its own right when Sir John Davies described it as an 'ancient discourse of the Decay of Ireland' and drew from it liberally in his influential tract *A discovery of the true causes why Ireland was never entirely subdued* (1612).[27] For the modern historian, Patrick Finglas' work represents a unique living document of the Henrician period.

23 CP, MS 144, fo. 4v.
24 Barnewall to Cromwell, 17 Aug. 1537, LPL, MS 602, fo. 116.
25 BL, Additional MS 4792, fos 70–83; Book on the state of Ireland, c.1575, TNA, SP 63/54/29, fo. 96; TNA, SP 63/214, fos 13v–14v; 50–3; 63–7; 71–4v; 75–9 (where an excerpt from Gerald of Wales' *The Conquest of Ireland* is indiscriminately interspersed within a copy of Finglas' Breviate); BL, Additional MS 48015, Yelverton MS 16, fos 243–8; BL, Cotton MSS, Titus B XII, fo. 594 (a fragment).
26 Walsingham's notes, 1579, BL, Cotton MSS, Titus B XII, fos 486–90v. For the importance which Walsingham attached to procuring the written history of England, see Barry Shaw, 'Thomas Norton's "Devices" for a Godly realm: an Elizabethan vision of the future', *Sixteenth Century Journal: Journal for Early Modern Studies*, 22:3 (1991), 501.
27 John Davies, *Historical tracts: by Sir John Davies* (London, 1786), pp 23 (quotation), 122, 153, 154, 158, 189. The seventeenth-century antiquarian, James Ware, later identified Patrick Finglas, imprecisely, as 'the Author of the book of the Causes of Ireland's Calamities and the Remedies therof': *The antiquities and history of Ireland* (Dublin, 1705), p. 90.

I.2

A description of the power of Irishmen

If Finglas' treatise was concerned primarily with the history, the present and future state of English Ireland, then the second document in the Hatfield Compendium was concerned with that which was thought to threaten it most: Irishmen.[1] The anonymous author of the document, titled 'A discruption [sic] of the power of Irishemen', takes the reader on a journey from Leinster clockwise through Ireland's 'fyve portions called kvyeghes [cúigí = provinces]', though six 'portions' are in fact identified. It lists the location and military strength, or 'power', of the dozens of individual lords – eighty-six in toto – who together comprised the Irish polity, or the 'king's Irish enemies' as they were frequently called in official English discourse. Generally, military strength is given in terms of the horsemen, battalions of gallo-glass (numbering between sixty to eighty heavily-armed footmen whose ancestors had come to Ireland from the outer isles of Scotland) and kerne (lightly-armed Irish infantry) that a lord could call upon in time of war.[2] The list includes militarily weak and politically marginal sub-lords, who could muster no more than four horsemen and two dozen kerne, middling lords, who could muster twice as many men and support a battalion of galloglass, all the way up to provincial overlords, some of whom are described as 'prynce and lorde', and who were reckoned to have at their disposal 200 horses, three galloglass battalions and 300 kerne.

No effort was made to tot up the overall 'power' of Irishmen, though the total number of horse, galloglass and kerne available to Irishmen were tallied individually for the six regions identified. Desmond, with 6,282, had the high-est number of Irish soldiers followed by Connacht with 5,396; they were fol-lowed by Ulster with 4,021 fighting men, Thomond with 3,374, Leinster with 2,354, and Meath with 610. This makes the overall 'power' of Irishmen an impressive 22,663 men.[3] But the document goes on to state that one 'knave' served every galloglass and looked after the fighter's equipment. Similarly, a 'lad' served every two kerne; and every horseman, we are told, had two or three horses, and each of his horses was looked after by a 'knave'.[4] When these ancil-

---

1   CP, MS 144, fos 5v–8v.

2   There are three exceptions: O'Driscoll in Munster and O'Malley in Connacht are described as using 'longe galleys'; and Desmond is said to have had a 'battayle of crossbowmen and gun-ners': CP, MS 144, fos 6, 6v.

3   In arriving at this sum, we have taken each 'battayle' of galloglass, which was reckoned to have numbered between sixty and eighty men, to be comprised of seventy galloglass.

4   The anonymous author of 'The state of Ireland and plan for its reformation' bemoaned what

2 Albrecht Dürer, 1521, 'Thus go the soldiers: Ireland behind England. Thus go the peasants in Ireland' (image courtesy of Staatliche Museum Preussicher Kulturbesitz, Kupferstichkabinett, Berlin © bpk).

lary military men (and boys) are added to the numbers of actual fighting men the overall number of Irishmen engaged in military activity rises to 40,031.[5] But those lords of English descent bordering Irish areas were also quite capable of deploying Irish 'power', as measured by a lord's, or a family's, potential to muster horse, galloglass and kerne. Following the summary of Irish 'power' in Leinster, Desmond and Connacht, the author gives some account of the state and military strength of lords in the exposed areas of the Englishry, though it is much less comprehensive: for instance, the ability of Ireland's most powerful marcher lord, the eighth earl of Kildare, to avail of Irish 'power' is unrecorded, even though he is known to have assembled by c.1500 a standing force of 240 Irish troops.[6] Nevertheless, in the document English lords were listed as possessing 7,022 Irish fighters (we can estimate that they were supported by 5,730 men and boys). Thus the total number of Irishmen engaged in military activity listed here is approximately 52,069. If we consider that the *entire* population of Ireland

he described as the 'infynyt nombre of [Irish] horsseladdes' which regularly accompanied the king's deputy in Ireland: *SP Hen. VIII*, ii, p. 13.

5 These numbers are based on the assumption that each horseman had at least two horses, and so enjoyed the services of two 'knaves'.

6 S.G. Ellis, *Tudor frontiers and noble power: the making of the British state* (Oxford, 1995), p. 128.

in the early Tudor period, including English areas and indeed women, is esti-
mated to have been only 500,000, then this document would suggest that well
above one in ten people in Ireland were engaged in military activity.[7] If we place
the male Irish population at, say, 200,000–250,000 (in other words, if we assume
that Ireland's English population and women comprised half the population and
then subtract them from the overall population) then it is possible that above
twenty per cent of Irishmen were engaged in military activity as their chief
occupation at the dawn of the Tudor age.

It is difficult to say how accurate are the numbers given here in the 'description'. Some of the figures listed for Munster and Connacht seem inflated – some
of the former wildly so: the MacCarthys were said to have had 4,000 kerne
between them – while the numbers given for Ulster, the home of such powerful lords as O'Neill and O'Donnell, seem too low. O'Neill, for example, is listed
here as being able to muster approximately 200 horse, but in 1447 he pledged to
assist Richard, duke of York, with more than twice that number.[8] This has led
to the plausible suggestion that the author of this document, or at least the
source for this information, had a good knowledge of Leinster, the midlands and
east Munster but was less familiar with the rest of Ireland.[9] Still, this assiduous
reckoning of the military strength of Irishmen is unrivalled in the Tudor period
not only for the information it provides on the military strength of the Irish
polity but also for what it suggests about the demographic situation in Ireland
and, as will be discussed below, national identity in the late fifteenth century.

The document concludes with a series of remarks describing society in
Ireland, given as 'items' numbered one through eleven (a twelfth remark went
unnumbered). These were intended to explain to the reader the political and
cultural reasons for the warlike nature of parts of the lordship. The picture that
emerges is one of a politically fragmented society but one that was regarded by
the author as being part of a single Irish political and cultural order. What was
happening in Ireland, the author makes clear, was above all else a struggle
between two nations: the king's subjects, the English of Ireland, and the Irish,
who were the king's enemies. 'All the forsaide Irishmen', he says, 'hateth the

7   K.W. Nicholls, 'Gaelic society and economy' in Art Cosgrove (ed.), *A new history of Ireland*; ii,
    medieval Ireland, 1169–1534 (Oxford, 1987), p. 409.
8   Edmund Curtis, 'Richard duke of York as viceroy of Ireland, 1447–60', *JRSAI*, 62 (1932),
    171.
9   The earl of Desmond, whose sprawling lordship stretched across the province of Munster, is
    the only named lord whose lordship is described in terms of its length: 120 miles. He is listed
    as having at his disposal 400 horsemen, eight battalions of galloglass, a battalion of crossbow-
    men and gunners and a whopping 3,000 kerne: CP, MS 144, fo. 6v; Edwards, 'The escalation
    of violence in sixteenth-century Ireland', p. 53. The earl of Desmond's claim, in 1529, that he
    could muster 16,500 foot and 1,500 horse was meant to impress Charles V and was pure exag-
    geration: McCormack, *Earldom of Desmond*, pp 50–1.

kynges lawes and s[u]biectes mortally ... when thei see their advauntage thei then do the beste they can on the kynges subiectes to their destruction'. But as grim as things were in Ireland for the king's subjects they had providence on their side: 'God do p[ro]vide for the kynges subiectes here that he sendeth dailye dissencions amonge the saide Irishemen ... so as thei cannot loke on us the kynges subiectes ne p[er]ceyve our debylite ne strenghte'.[10] In these sections the reader learns that some Englishmen in Ireland might also hate the king's laws, and that English lineages, such as the MacWilliam Burkes in Connacht, were of 'no better condicyons then Irishmen and weareth their habytes and ben so frended and allyed with them that thei take their parte agaynst the kynges subiectes and hateth the kynges lawes and geveth no ayde ne assistance to his deputie'.[11] Yet, throughout, the author adheres to a strict racial division between Irish and English.[12] Savage, whose lordship was located in Ulster's Ards peninsula, is a possible exception. Though his ancestors had in the late medieval period carved out a piece of east Ulster from the Irish, the author includes his military strength with that of the Irish of Ulster. But even here the two-nation framework is evident: Savage is referred to as 'an Englishman ... so envirouned with Irishmen that he is nerehande expulsed out of his landes'.[13]

All of this is familiar enough to historians of Tudor Ireland. In the early 1930s, Liam Price transcribed 'A description of the power of Irishmen' from a copy in the British Library and published it in a well-known Irish antiquarian journal.[14] This copy from which Price worked was made in Elizabeth's reign by the antiquary and cartographer Laurence Nowell, who in 1560 travelled to Ireland to gather information for William Cecil, then the principal secretary.[15]

---

10 CP, MS 144, fo. 8v.   11 CP, MS 144, fo. 7v.

12 Whether historians should interpret this period using a 'two nation' framework has been the subject of debate and is symptomatic of more general disagreement in the historical community over identity in late medieval and early modern Ireland: S.G. Ellis, 'More Irish than the Irish themselves? The "Anglo-Irish" in Tudor Ireland', *History Ireland*, 7:1 (1999), 22–6; K.W. Nicholls, 'Worlds apart? The Ellis two-nation theory of late medieval Ireland', *History Ireland*, 7:2 (1999), 22–6. See also Christopher Maginn, 'Gaelic Ireland's English frontiers in the late middle ages', *PRIA*, sect. c, 110 (2010), 173–90.

13 CP, MS 144, fo. 8v.

14 BL, Cotton MSS, Domitian A. XVIII, fos 100–4. Liam Price, 'Armed forces of the Irish chiefs in the early 16th century', *JRSAI*, 62 (1932), 201–7. There was a notice (in *The Academy* (1881), 158) that the scholar Edmund Hogan, SJ, planned to publish the copy of 'The description of the power of Irishmen', which was then housed in the British Museum. But Hogan does not appear to have done so. Other Elizabethan copies of the manuscript may be found in the State Papers (Hanmer Collection) in TNA, SP 63/214/3, fos 10v–11v, 48–50, 58–62, 87–90, and in the NLI, MS 669 and BL, Additional MS, 48015, Yelverton MS 16, fos 213–16. Later, in the mid-sixteenth century, there was an attempt to juxtapose the information contained in 'The description' with present conditions in Ireland: BL, Lansdowne MS 159, fos 20–3.

15 R.M. Warnicke, 'The Laurence Nowell manuscripts in the British Library', *British Library Journal*, 5 (1979), 201–2.

But this version of the document from which Price worked, and which historians have used most extensively, is inferior in several respects to the version that appears in the Hatfield Compendium.[16] The numbers given are more or less the same in both, thus they share the same possible inaccuracies, but the version in the Compendium is older – the oldest copy of this document yet discovered – and its explanatory sections which follow the military quantifications are frequently more fulsome. For example, the British Library copy, as transcribed by Price, lists:

> The Butlers in Kilkenny 8oh[orse]. 2b[attayles]. 200k[erne]
> The Geraldines of Mounster environed w[th] Irisshe scarsly can keepe themselves.

The same listing in the Hatfield Compendium reads:

> It[e]m ther is in Leynester beforesaide the countie of Kylkenye wherin parte of the Buttlers dwelleth and they wylbe lxxx horsmen ii battaylles and ii[c] kiearne and they be so envyrou[n]ed with Irishemen, and yerelye debate betuxte them and the ['Geraldynes', *is crossed through*] awarre of the Geraldynes of Mownster that scantly thei can kepe themselfes, so as lytle they can helpe the kynges deputie

Price's transcription of the manuscript in the British Library concludes thus:

> They provide for the benefices from Rome though they can scarcely reade, the profites wherof the [*sic*] spend against us. But God provides setting continuall dissension emongst them & mortall warre.

The Hatfield Compendium concludes as follows:

> It[e]m God do p[ro]vide for the kynges subiectes here that he sendeth dailye dissencions amonge the saide Irishemen, so as more then three of the saide capitaynes loveth not other and make mortall warre dailye on thother so as thei cannot loke on us the kynges subiectes ne p[er]ceyve our debylite ne strenghte. It[e]m also they have meanes to be stronge, all the benefyces of their cou[n]treis shalbe geven to the saide lordes sonnes and p[ro]vided from Rome, thoughe one of them scau[n]te can his pater

16 See, for example, S.G. Ellis, 'The collapse of the Gaelic world, 1450–1650', *IHS*, 31 (1999), 458–9; David Edwards, *The Ormond lordship in county Kilkenny, 1515–1642: the rise and fall of Butler feudal power* (Dublin, 2003), p. 154.

noster, and they spende the p[ro]fyites of the same on their kynnesmen to make them well apparoulled to the warre agaynste us Englishemen.[17]

Price thought the British Library manuscript to have been 'compiled somewhere about the year 1540'. But Kenneth Nicholls, pointing to the appearance in the document of Redmund MacShane, whom he convincingly showed to be lord of a sept of O'Byrnes based in the Leinster Mountains in the years 1483–91, established a substantially earlier date (c.1490) for the information contained in the document.[18] Indeed close scrutiny of the Irish annals reveals that other chiefs named in the 'description' were also in action in the years prior to 1490. In 1488, for example, Donough, son of the Art MacDonough, a minor Leinster lord included in the 'description', was reported to have killed the son of O'Murrough, another minor Leinster lord.[19] The Donough Oge MacCarthy, listed in the manuscript as lord of Duhallow in Desmond, was named as the killer of Barry More in 1486.[20] And the Ulster lord Conn MacHugh Boy O'Neill, identified in the manuscript as lord of Clandeboy, was reported to have died in 1482.[21] Moreover, in its section devoted to Leinster, the document in the Compendium refers to 'a parte of the coun[n]tie Catherlaghe, w[ch] therle of Kyldare dyde conquere on Irishemen and but latelye inhabyted'. As Steven Ellis has shown, Gerald Fitzgerald, eighth earl of Kildare, built up a large rental in Co. Carlow through the exploitation of a 1483 statute that vested in him all waste lands between Calverstown and Leighlinbridge.[22] So it seems more likely than not that the document was originally drawn up, as Nicholls suggested, in the early 1490s and was based on information that was current in the preceding decade.

To say definitely what occasioned the assembly of this information, and at this time, is impossible; however a suggestion or two may be offered. In 1494 Henry VII informed Charles VIII, the king of France, that he had decided to put Ireland 'in order', and drew specific attention to those whom he called the 'Irlandois sauvaiges'.[23] Later that year Henry dispatched Sir Edward Poynings to Ireland at the head of a sizeable English expeditionary force. It is thus possible that the information was compiled to give the king (and thus Poynings) an idea

17 CP, MS 144, fo. 7.

18 K.W. Nicholls, 'Crioch Branach: the O'Byrnes and their country' in Conor O'Brien (ed.), *Feagh McHugh O'Byrne, the Wicklow firebrand* (Rathdrum, 1998), pp 8, 108.

19 *Annála Uladh, Annals of Ulster … a chronicle of Irish affairs … 431 to 1541*, ed. W.M. Hennessy and Bartholomew MacCarthy, 4 vols (Dublin, 1887–1901), s.a. 1488.

20 *Annála ríoghachta Éireann: annals of the kingdom of Ireland by the Four Masters from the earliest period to the year 1616*, ed. John O'Donovan, 7 vols (Dublin, 1851), s.a. 1486.

21 *AU*, s.a. 1482.

22 Ellis, *Tudor frontiers*, pp 119–20.

23 Instructions to Richmond, King of Arms, 10 Aug. 1494, BL, Cotton MSS, Caligula D VI, fo. 19.

of what he was up against in Ireland. In copying this document for the Hatfield Compendium the scribe accidentally wrote 'yor' deputy in the section explaining how the Burkes of Connacht, being 'so envyroned with Irishmen and dyssevered themselfes', were not in a position to lend military assistance to the deputy.[24] 'Yo^r' was struck out and 'the' was inserted in its place. The mistake almost certainly indicates that the document was originally written for the king; and, as will be argued below, that the Hatfield Compendium was not. We know that Henry VII gave serious consideration to leading a military expedition to his lordship in person in 1506 and may, in the years prior to this, have sought out detailed information about Ireland and the Irish. In April 1498 John Wise, in a letter to Thomas, earl of Ormond, made reference to the fact that he had 'written to the kings grace of thorde and maner of this lande in euery thing accord[ing] to his formour comaundements'.[25] Wise was formerly chief baron of the exchequer in Ireland and was a trusted royal servant. But he was also a Waterford man whose regular exposure to, and interaction with, Irishmen in Munster, and the O'Briens in particular, meant that he was possessed of both the local knowledge necessary to write such a wide-ranging and painstakingly detailed document and the connections at court that would allow his work to reach the king.[26]

25 John Wise to earl of Ormond, 30 Apr. 1498, TNA, SC 1/52/64 (*Calendar of Ormond deeds, 1172–1603*, ed. Edmund Curtis, 6 vols (Dublin, 1932–43), iv, p. 336).

26 *Statute rolls of the Irish parliament, Richard III–Henry VIII*, ed. Philomena Connolly (Dublin, 2002), pp 95, 115; Maginn, *William Cecil, Ireland, and the Tudor state*, pp 20–3, 25. See also below, pp 130–2.

I.3
Havens of Ireland

In this section of the Hatfield Compendium the reader is presented with another circuit of Ireland. Entitled 'Havens of this lande of Irelande', this section is purely geographical, offering a bare listing, arranged in three columns, from top to bottom, of the island's harbours for ships. It begins in Loughfoyle and the Bann, the northernmost havens given, and then traces Ireland's extensive coast-line clockwise until it concludes at the haven of Sligo in the north-west. In all, seventy-two havens are identified, but no sense is given as to where they were situated geographically, or how they differed from one to another. The listing, it would seem, was intended chiefly to impress upon the reader the ample quantity of sheltered places for shipping in Ireland. It may also be that it served a more purely bureaucratic function. In October 1515 articles for a parliament scheduled to be held in Ireland the following year were drawn up in England. One of the articles read: 'That no person lade or discharge goods at any creek, except in the main ports, without special leave of the customs'.[1] It is thus possible that the listing in the Hatfield Compendium represents an attempt to identify all havens in the country with a view to making clear where one could and could not legally discharge goods. It is impossible to date this section of the Compendium with any specificity or to speculate about the identity of its compiler; but the reference to 'this lande of Irelande' in the title is strong evidence that it pre-dated the erection of Ireland into a kingdom in 1541. (The tendency thereafter was to refer to Ireland as a 'realm' rather than as a 'land'.)

The list's comprehensiveness is impressive, considering that it was likely drawn up in the early Tudor period, a time when knowledge in England of Ireland's geography, most especially of the west and north-west, was limited. In the commonplace book of Christopher Cusack, sheriff of Meath – a copy of which survives from the early sixteenth century but which contains disparate material which is probably much older – there is a geographic description of the island of Ireland in which its most southerly and northerly points are aligned against St Michael's Mount in Cornwall and Dumfries in Scotland, respectively. Here, it was inaccurately stated that Ireland was larger than England: 'Irland should be mo[r] then Ingland by iiii[xx] miles' its author concluded.[2] Later, in 1543 Sir Anthony St Leger, lord deputy of Ireland, offered Henry VIII a detailed

1   *L. & P. Hen. VIII*, ii, no. 996.
2   TCD MS 594, fo. 36. The description in Cusack's commonplace book is nearly identical to the undated and anonymous 'Geographical account of Ireland', which was placed in the year 1514 in the State Papers of Henry VIII: TNA, SP 60/1/5, fo. 7 (see also below, p. 138).

description of Ireland's havens – 'The more parte of the notable havons of Ireland'; but he named only thirty-seven, and was quick to point out those havens which lay within (or near) the Irishry and which were, in effect, beyond royal control.[3] It was only in Elizabeth's reign, as Tudor rule extended throughout the island, that a greater awareness of such geographical detail was achieved in governing circles, and mainly through the increasing use of maps.[4] This is evident, for example, in the well-known, and richly detailed, maps of Ireland drawn in the 1560s by Laurence Nowell and John Goghe.[5] When these are compared with the crude 'Cotton' map of Ireland drawn in the 1520s – this drawing represents the earliest known attempt under the Tudors to map the island – and a later Italian map of Ireland from 1565 – in which Dublin and its hinterland are plotted too far south, and Sligo is depicted as lying north-east of Donegal – the new-found superiority of English knowledge of Ireland's geography and topography becomes immediately apparent.[6] Of course the act of listing havens, and ultimately plotting them on maps, did not conjure these locations into being. For centuries Englishmen and Irishmen had relied on local knowledge to move about the country, by land and by sea, without a reliance on lists of places or maps. Lists of places, such as that included in the Hatfield Compendium and on maps, were not intended to replace local knowledge. Rather they represent an effort to impart some of this local knowledge to those unfamiliar with Ireland, so allowing them to measure and to visualize that which they could not see first-hand.

There are many similar lists of Ireland's havens scattered among sources contemporary to the Tudor period. Nowell, for instance, included a list of 'Havens in Ireland' in a book of information, which he compiled about the country in the early 1560s. A copy of his list, which identified seventy-one havens, may be found in the British Library. (It would seem that Nowell's was the basis for at least one other copy in the British Library.)[7] Other lists of havens appear among

3 Havens of Ireland, 6 Apr. 1543, TNA, SP 60/11/2(i), fo. 15. St Leger provided a brief description of each haven: 'Dublyn, a badde haven. Wicklowe, but a crecke'.

4 William Smyth, *Map-making, landscapes and memory: a geography of colonial and early modern Ireland, c.1530–1750* (Cork, 2006), ch. 1.

5 'General description of England and Ireland', c.1564, BL, Additional MS 62540, fos 3v–4r; 'Hibernia: insula non procul ab Anglia vulgare Hirlandia vocata', 1567, TNA, MPF 1/68.

6 The well-known 'Cotton' map is reproduced in Smyth, *Map-making, landscapes and memory*, pp 40–1. Bolognino Zaltieri's 1565 map of Ireland, published in Venice, is a copy of Sebastiano de Ré's 1558 map of Ireland. The former is reproduced in S.G. Ellis, 'The Tudor borderlands, 1485–1603' in John Morrill (ed.), *The Oxford illustrated history of Tudor and Stuart Britain* (Oxford, 1996), pp 66–7. See also the Elizabethan effort to set out the depths of some of the harbours in Munster: the depths, anchorages etc., of the harbours of Ireland, 21 Apr. 1567, BL, Cotton MSS, Titus B XII, fo. 482.

7 BL, Additional MS 48015, Yelverton MS 16, fo. 217; BL, Additional MS 48017, Yelverton MS 17, fo. 75v.

the papers on Irish customs and antiquities gathered together by the Elizabethan antiquarian Meredith Hanmer. These are also nearly identical to the Hatfield list, differing only in the omission of one or several havens.[8] In another Elizabethan list, which identifies eighty-three havens, there was an uncompleted effort made to describe each of the 'havens in Ireland'.[9] The Hatfield Compendium thus boasts the oldest known list of Ireland's havens. Whether it or another master list of havens served as the copy upon which these later listings were based is now impossible to ascertain.

8   TNA, SP 63/214, fos 8, 36 (the former list identifies 67 havens; the latter 70).
9   TNA, SP 63/214, fos 38–43. Still more lists of havens may be found in: ibid., fos 44–6, 55.

1.4
William Darcy's articles

Following the stark listing of Ireland's havens, the Hatfield Compendium acquires much greater specificity. Sir William Darcy's articles put in to the king's council meeting at Greenwich on 23 or 24 June 1515 record an otherwise unknown meeting of the king's council of England.[1] The document was previously known only from later Elizabethan copies preserved among the Carew manuscripts at Lambeth Palace and among the manuscripts from which Harris worked at Trinity College, Dublin.[2] The present copy, which is around fifty years earlier than these versions, is also a fuller, and probably more accurate, record of the articles which may have been copied from the original council register and records now lost. It gives the date of the meeting as 23 June, instead of 24 June as in the Carew copy; the orthography is more in line with early Tudor practice; and there are some minor differences in the wording of particular sections. For instance, of the five shires of the earldom of Ulster, Carew names the fifth as Belacke, whereas the Hatfield Compendium and Harris give Lecale. Of the introduction of Irish exactions within the English Pale, the Carew copy says they were 'renved w[th]in theis 30 yeres, coyne & lyverie and cartinge cariadges Jorneys & other impositions, farr hostinges & Journyes and wyllfull warr begane synce that tyme', whereas Hatfield reads 'renued within this xxx[ti] yeres bene cuddies carttyng carriages io[r]neyes and other imposicions farre hostynges and io[r]neyes and wylfull warre began synce that tyme'.

The main difference, however, relates to the second part of the document. The 'articles' themselves comprise six brief points about Irish exactions and military impositions; but there then follows a second, much longer section outlining the 'causes of the sore decay' of the king's subjects; and tacked onto the end of this new copy are four additional 'causes' not found in the Carew copy, so making eight in all. These include a description of the decline of English weaponry, dress and language within the English Pale; and they also make three

---

1   Letters were written in the king's name to the marquis of Mantua and the Doge of Venice from Greenwich 24 June 1515: *L. & P. Hen. VIII*, ii, no. 611; *Calendar of state papers and manuscripts relating to English affairs, existing in the archives and collections of Venice and in other libraries of northern Italy*, ed. Rawdon Brown, 6 vols (London, 1864–86), ii, no. 631.
2   LPL, Carew MS 635, fos 188–8v (*Cal. Carew MSS*, i, no. 2); Harris (ed.), *Hibernica*, pp 51–2. In fact, Harris omitted Darcy's actual Articles altogether, and simply tacked on at the end of his printed copy the first three Causes of the Sore Decay, without the heading. So, in Harris' copy, the final section listing the Passes leads straight into the first three Causes.

assertions: that 2,000 marks 'wyll not repayre the kynges castelles and maners ther'; that the king's revenues are now better 'thes xxiiii yeres' than in the previous sixty, 'notwythstandyng all the forsaide ungracious ordre and preside[n]ce ben dailye used'; and that the statute making it treason to impose coign and livery on the king's subjects is not now enforced.[3]

The circumstances surrounding the articles' composition are partly known. They were submitted to the king's council during the course of a visit to court by the lord deputy of Ireland, Gerald Fitzgerald, ninth earl of Kildare, and, at least in part, were intended as a criticism of his government.[4] Darcy was in a strong position to offer this. After service in local government as sheriff and subsidy collector, Darcy had, in effect, taken over the responsibilities of the treasurer of Ireland from the late 1490s, serving first as receiver general, and then from 1504, when the office of lord treasurer had been revived for the Lord Gerald, the future ninth earl of Kildare, on his return to Ireland, as his deputy.[5] His comments about the disrepair of the king's castles and manors and the buoyancy of the revenues were thus clearly based on his expert knowledge as treasurer; and we know that his experience commanded respect at court because in 1519–20, when the decision was taken to appoint the earl of Surrey as lord lieutenant of Ireland, Darcy advised the king that the profits of the revenues amounted to 2,000 marks yearly, as Cardinal Wolsey later reported to Sir John Stile, then undertreasurer. Stile's response was that Darcy's own accounts for 1502–3 and 1504–5 showed that the total revenues did not then exceed IR£1,587 13s. 3¼d. per annum.[6] Darcy's comments about the sharp decline in the wearing of English gowns and the use of longbows in many Pale parishes probably also reflected personal experience: he was one of the few gentry in western Meath still to wear gown and doublet.[7]

In other respects, however, Darcy was probably less well informed. His comment about the execution of Thomas Fitzgerald, seventh earl of Desmond, for imposing coign and livery on the English Pale was factually based, but despite Darcy's claim that James Fitzgerald, sixth earl of Desmond (d.1463), was the first to impose coign and livery on the king's subjects, its incidence in the English parts certainly had a much longer history than Darcy surmised. According to Darcy, English rule had once extended throughout sixteen counties, but within

3 CP, MS 144, fo. 9v. The statute concerning coign and livery in the last clause is almost certainly the Act of Marches and Maghery (1488).

4 D.B. Quinn, 'Henry VIII and Ireland, 1509–34', *IHS*, 22 (1961), 320–1.

5 S.G. Ellis, 'An English gentleman and his community: Sir William Darcy of Platten' in Vincent Carey and Ute Lotz-Heumann (eds), *Taking Sides? Colonial and confessional mentalités in early modern Ireland: essays in honour of Karl S. Bottigheimer* (Dublin, 2003), p. 31; idem, *Reform and revival*, pp 32–3, 100.

6 *SP Hen. VIII*, ii, 77–8.   7 *Ormond deeds,* iv, app. no. 76.

the last fifty years the earls of Ormond and Desmond had both introduced coign and livery and other Irish practices throughout their territories. Thus, where 'goode Englishe ordre and rule' had once been kept, now 'the kynges lawes be not obeyed and all the kynges subiectes ben in no bett[er] case then the wylde Irishe'.[8] The earldom of Ulster had had five shires, 'besydes dyvers lordeshippes and man[n]ers, as the wryter hereof can shewe and declare', but for lack of a resident lord, the Irish had 'near hande conquered' the five shires. Darcy was able to name the five shires; and while his assertion that the earl of Ulster 'mought dispend a year in the lande above xxx^m markes' was probably based on the exchequer estimate of the king's revenues in 1485 stating that the earl's lands in Ulster and Connacht had once yielded 32,000 marks, this was pure fiction.[9] Finally, within the last thirty years, he alleged, coign and livery and other Irish exactions had been reintroduced by the deputy into the Pale. Thus, so Darcy sweepingly asserted, all the king's subjects 'be nerehand Irishe', speaking Irish and wearing Irish dress, 'so as they are cleane goone and decayed', and not eight of the lords and gentry 'but ben in debte and their landes be made waste and without briefe remedye be had thei must sell their landes other leave them and [departe] unto some other landes'.[10]

We need not take too seriously the more sweeping claims in Darcy's articles: such hyperbole was normal in Tudor petitions. Yet, Darcy had a particular axe to grind, in that he had recently been replaced as treasurer by Kildare's client, Christopher Fleming, Lord Slane.[11] In fact, given his unrivalled knowledge of the king's revenues and aspects of early Tudor government in Ireland, Darcy could hardly have failed to provide a more convincing analysis than these crude and sketchy articles had root-and-branch reform been the main aim. In fact, it is far from clear that Lord Deputy Kildare's government was being seriously criticized in 1515 beyond his remark of 'wylfull warre made by the Kiynges deputie without thassent of the lords and Kynges counsell'. Darcy's articles were also

---

8   CP, MS 144, fo. 8v. Later, in the 1570s, Lord Chancellor Gerrard used the same exchequer records to trace the origins of these Irish exactions to the fourteenth century: see Charles McNeill (ed.), 'Lord Chancellor Gerrard's notes of his report on Ireland, 1577–8', *Analecta Hibernica*, 2 (1931), 93–291.

9   CP, MS 144, fos 8v, 9; TNA, E 101/248, no. 17 (printed in *Analecta Hibernica*, 10 (1941), 17–27). Speaking in Star Chamber decades later Robert Cecil remarked that 'some men will speake & tell of great revenewes that the crowne of England hath hadd out of Ireland and howe Ulster hathe yealded of ytself 30000li yerelie. But theis are fables of olde Malmesbry and suche other flitter for legenda aurea then to be wryten in any story'. A report of Secretary Cecil's speech in Star Chamber, Nov. 1599, SP 12/273/37, fo. 79.

10 Ibid., fo. 9.

11 Memoranda roll, 4–5 Henry VIII m. 12 (NAI, Ferguson coll., iv, fo. 19; BL, Additional MS 4791, fo. 196); Ellis, 'An English gentleman and his community', pp 33–4; Gerald Power, *A European frontier elite: the nobility of the English Pale in Tudor Ireland, 1496–1566* (Hannover, 2012), pp 59–61.

critical of the Butlers for introducing Irish customs, and the purpose of Kildare's visit to court was more probably to reinforce the normal contacts between king and ruling magnate, and perhaps also to allow the young King Henry to acquaint himself more closely with conditions in this outlying province of the Tudor territories at a time when the English of Ireland believed a royal expedition to Ireland to be a real possibility. In that sense, Darcy's articles may have been useful in stimulating a rare debate in the king's council about Tudor policy for Ireland. Kildare returned to Ireland in September 1515 with a new commission as governor and a sheaf of royal grants.[12]

12 *L. & P. Hen. VIII*, ii, nos. 996–1001; Kildare to Henry VIII, 1 Dec. 1515, TNA, SP 60/1/7, fo. 9.

1.5
Articles for the reformation of Ireland

This section is comprised of what is apparently the beginning of a tract, hitherto unknown to historians, entitled 'Artycles for the reformation of Irelande'. Only one (the first) of the 'Artycles' is preserved here. It appears at the (faded and badly damaged) bottom of folio 9v and is distinguished from Darcy's articles by a line drawn across the page; that it represents the beginning of what were a series of articles is evident from the word 'Item' written, and only just legible, at the lowermost right-hand side of the folio in anticipation of an article to follow on the next folio. But whatever was to come was either deliberately omitted or, more likely, damaged or, perhaps, became separated from the rest of the Compendium when it became mixed in with an unrelated pile of 'old domestic Accounts & family Deeds'.[1] Unlike so much of the rest of the material in the Compendium the surviving article is not meant to be informative. Rather it is prescriptive, telling the reader what sort of men should occupy the key offices in the government of Ireland: the lord deputy, the lord chancellor, the treasurer, the three chief judges and the master of the rolls. The basis for the appointment was to depend on social rank and, importantly, on whether the occupant was born in England or Ireland. The portion of the manuscript that contains the suggestion that the 'deputie of the lande of Irelande alway be an erle or some noble man of [.....] lande' is damaged at a crucial point. It is possible that the line read: 'some noble man of [this or that] lande', that is, Ireland; but men born in England were to fill the rest of the positions mentioned here, and most other Henrician tracts which offer a prescription for Ireland's reform recommended that the king's deputy be English-born. In the fifteenth century, moreover, the English of Ireland typically requested that an Englishman from England, preferably a member of the king's family, be sent over to govern them and lead the reform of Ireland.[2] The chief office under the crown in Ireland would thus also appear to have been reserved for an Englishmen under this scheme. Beyond that, it is impossible to say, or even to speculate, with any certainty when this was written or who lay behind this small portion of an otherwise unknown tract setting out how Ireland might be reformed.

1   See above, p. 17, note 10. The unbroken page numbering at the upper right-hand corner of the Compendium would suggest that whatever came after fo. 9v was lost prior to the cataloguing of the manuscript in the mid-nineteenth century. It is possible that these missing folios are still mixed in among other manuscripts at Hatfield House.
2   See, for example, *SP Hen. VIII*, ii, pp 182, 481, 507; *L. & P. Hen. VIII*, iv (ii), no. 2405 and *Statute rolls of the parliament of Ireland, reign of King Henry VI*, ed. H.F. Berry (Dublin, 1910), p. 50.

1.6

Revenues of Ireland

These anonymous and undated articles relating to the king's revenues in Ireland constitute a series of proposals for raising additional revenue. Unheaded in the Hatfield Compendium, they are a much fuller version of a document that appears frequently in Elizabethan antiquarian works where it is called 'Revenues of Ireland'.[1] The centrepiece is an ingenious but entirely unrealistic proposal for a transformation of the Irish parliamentary subsidy into a tax of a penny per acre of arable land throughout Ireland. This proposal apparently draws on a description known from a document which now survives as a copy in Christopher Cusack's commonplace book,[2] but which here is described as having been 'made long before the Incarnation of Christ', in order to calculate the number of cantreds and betagh towns throughout Ireland's five provinces. It notes that in the intervening years woods had been felled and 'tilling land thereof made the which is not comprehended in the said description'. A betagh town, derived from the Irish *baile biatach*, that is a 'food, or victualler's, town', supposedly contained 960 acres of arable land, and there were thirty betagh towns in a cantred, and so it is calculated that the sum total of betagh towns in Ireland was 5,920 [*recte* 5,820].

The opening part of the document is evidently missing from the Hatfield Compendium. The basis of the first surviving section with its calculations about Ireland's division into portions, cantreds and betagh towns was probably a version of the more detailed comments in the Cusack document: this likewise records that Ireland was divided into five portions, with each portion credited with the same number of cantreds as here, amounting to 184 in total, and with each cantred containing thirty towns, making according to the Cusack document 5,530 towns in all. The first part of the Cusack document is in Latin: it outlines points which, following some apparently unrelated (though quite detailed) comments in English on Ireland's geographical location in relation to England and Scotland, are then developed (in some detail and again in English) later in the text. The Cusack document then ends with the following piece of speculation: 'yf Ireland were reconcilit and English as England is to the King is obeaunce and enabitid and occupied w^t Englis men the king might haue euery yere of common subsidy of the landes vj^s viij^d of euery plowe land sm^a tot. in the

---

1   TNA, SP 63/214, fos 8v–9, 37, 56; BL, Additional MS 48015, Yelverton MS 16, fo. 218; 48017, Yelverton MS 17, fo. 75v.

2   TCD MS 594, fos 35v–6v. This copy is noted as having been made on 1 Nov. 1511.

yere xxij^{li} m^l li & xl marke [£22,026 13s. 4d.] besid. customis also of his land. and portes and ffishynis w^c was of old time C m^l marke [100,000 marks] by ye yere[3] besid. rentes of hold inhabitants of vllyster conna3th mi3th leynyster and mowynst^r w^c was in the old erle of march is days xxij^{li} m^l [£22,000] besid. all other things as of abundaunce of chirches and wardes of mariadges &c.'

It is possible to imagine how speculation along these lines could later in the Hatfield Compendium be translated into more detailed proposals for raising additional revenue. In the Hatfield document, the new subsidy of a penny per acre of arable land was supposedly to raise £23,900. In addition, all the clergy were to pay the king a subsidy of a shilling in the pound ('xiid out of every libre') for the next ten years on their spiritualities. How much this would realize was unknown, but a note follows that the clergy of 'the four obedient shires' had hitherto contributed twelve pence 'out of every mark taxed' (a shilling in the mark, or 13s. 4d.). In order to raise this new clerical subsidy, the archbishops were to bind their suffragans to appoint collectors in their dioceses to answer to the king's officers each year; and if necessary the lord lieutenant and the army were to assist them. Again there is a note outlining, by way of explanation, practice in regard to the established parliamentary subsidy: it recalls that 'in Edwarde the iii^{des} dayes' the subsidy was levied at 6s. 8d. per ploughland [=120 medieval acres of arable land], the same rate as in the Cusack document, 'which is above a penny an acre' [actually, only ⅔d. an acre], whereas now each acre in 'the four shires' paid above 1½d. an acre. In addition, the king still received the annual rents ('chief rents') reserved on grants of lands to tenants-in-chief following the conquest.

The remaining articles are much more conventional, but also offer more clues as to the date of their composition. There is a proposal for a resumption of the feefarms and customs of all the cities and towns, to be received as those of Dublin and Drogheda are, followed by a note that all the foregoing should be enacted in the first parliament held [hereafter? – the document is torn here]. The document then notes the rents and profits of the king's manors per annum, and his 'estate' and casualties. To these articles, two of a more personal character were apparently added somewhat later, perhaps in 1525–6. The first recalls that the author ('I') delivered a 'book of the king's manors and lands to his commissioners at their being here', with advice to keep it safely. The second relates that the 'forsaid book' was sent to the king with the chief justice of king's bench, 18 September 'x[vj?]' Henry VIII (16 Henry VIII would be 1524).

As regards their authorship and the date of their composition, the articles probably need to be seen in conjunction with the final document in this compendium, the Ordinances and Provisions for Ireland, discussed in section 1.8

3   100,000 marks a year was likewise the estimate of the revenues from the rivers, havens and fishing included in the 1474 address of the Irish parliament to King Edward IV: TNA, C 47/10/29 (printed, Bryan, *The great earl of Kildare*, p. 21).

below. There, the suggestion is made that the Ordinances were chiefly the work of Sir William Darcy and compiled later in 1519 in the very early stages of the preparations for the appointment as governor of Thomas Howard, earl of Surrey. This is a much shorter document, but the author may well have been the same: note in particular the references to 'the four obedient shires', the older fifteenth-century term for the English Pale which Darcy is known to have pre-ferred, and the rather antiquarian character of some of the articles. If so, the doc-ument was written a little later than the Ordinances. The reference to 'the lord lieutenant' fixes the date to Surrey's governorship, and Surrey's parliament in 1521–2 considered a bill for the resumption of customs and feefarms (see also below, section 1.8).[4] We know also that Darcy was closely involved, during the preparations for Surrey's expedition, in advising the king and Cardinal Wolsey about the state of the revenues (see above, section 1.4, and below, section 1.8).[5] He was, for instance, successively receiver-general of the king's revenues in the English Pale, undertreasurer, deputy-treasurer and surveyor of the king's castles from c.1501 to 1514.[6] And after Surrey's recall, he is again found serving as undertreasurer in 1523, and so was well placed to furnish the king's commis-sioners, who visited Ireland between June and August 1524, with the book of the king's manors and lands. By then, he was also well over sixty years old, which might explain the author's comment that the book should be surely kept, 'for if I were gone the same would not lightly be gotten again'.[7] This was not a mere conceit of an old man; Darcy in fact was speaking to a problem which plagued Tudor rule in Ireland: an ignorance of crown revenues there (and, as we shall see, much else beside). Writing in the late sixteenth century, an Elizabethan official in England investigating royal revenues in Ireland remarked that 'in the greate breaking owte of the Irisherie' in the later Middle Ages 'the countrie being then, as it wer, exposed to the spoille, all Englishe memories and antiqui-ties were consumed and burntt especially of wrytinges, as cowrt rolles and evi-dences, amongst them all moste all those wch sholde give lighte to the matter some fewe onely war saved nowe remayning in the threasurie there, by wch one maye rather coniecture for that they ar imperfecte'.[8]

4   D.B. Quinn (ed.), 'The bills and statutes of the Irish parliaments of Henry VII and Henry VIII', *Analecta Hibernica*, 10 (1941), 121–2.
5   See also *SP Hen. VIII*, ii, p. 77.
6   NAI, Ferguson collection, ii, fo. 57v; iii, fo. 336, NAI, Ferguson repertory, iv, fos 60, 98; Ellis, *Reform and revival*, pp 32–3, 100; idem, 'An English gentleman and his community', pp 31–2.
7   Quinn, 'Henry VIII and Ireland', p. 332; Ellis, *Reform and revival*, pp 32–3, 100; idem, 'An English gentleman and his community', pp 36–7.
8   BL, Cotton MSS, Titus B XII, fo. 323.

I.7
Pedigrees of the Burkes

In this section of the Compendium short genealogies of the principal branches of the Burke (originally the de Burgh) lineage – called 'pedigrees' in the MS – are presented in three paragraphs; a fourth paragraph rehearses the breadth of the lands under the lordship of Richard Burke, second earl of Ulster – the so-called 'red earl' – the most prominent of the lineage named in the first pedigree. Taken together, they tell something of the history of a venerable English family's involvement in Ireland through the lineal identification of its patriarchs and the lands which they possessed.

The first paragraph presents a pedigree that traces the descendants of William FitzAdelm Burke, who at the time of the English conquest of Ireland received a grant of Connacht from King Henry II. He was grandfather of Walter Burke the progenitor of the line of Burkes who held the titles earl of Ulster and lord of Meath and Connacht. The next two paragraphs show (sometimes imperfectly) the descendants of William 'Liath' [grey] Burke, the grandnephew of Walter Burke and progenitor of the two great collateral branches of the Burkes which survived in Connacht into the early modern period: the Lower (northern) MacWilliam Burkes of Mayo and the Upper (southern) MacWilliam Burkes who were concentrated round Galway.[1]

There were many such lineages in Ireland, but the Burkes were exceptional. In the fourteenth century the family's senior line became intertwined through marriage with the blood of the Plantagenet kings of England. Following the extinction of the senior male Burke line in 1333, upon the death of William, third earl of Ulster – the so-called 'brown earl' – the lineage's possessions passed in and out of the hands of princes of the blood before ultimately devolving to King Edward IV in 1461, making the Yorkists, and thus the Tudors after them, through the marriage of Henry VII to Elizabeth of York, the heirs to the largest inheritance in Ireland.[2] There can be little doubt that the inclusion of these pedigrees in the Compendium was to show the direct link which existed between the English

1   Martin Burke, 'Notes on the persons named in the obituary book of the Franciscan Abbey at Galway', *Journal of the Galway Archaeological and Historical Society*, 7 (1911), 1–28. See the footnotes below, pp 97–8.
2   In Sept. 1494 the patent granting lands in Co. Meath to James Ormond noted that they were 'parcel of the lands and tenements of the earldom of March, now in the king's hands in right of Elizabeth the Queen Consort': *Calendar of the patent rolls, Henry VII, 1494–1509* (London, 1916), p. 8.

crown and parts of Ireland, notably Connacht where the collateral branches of the Burkes were concentrated, which had been all but lost to royal authority.

Dating this section poses some difficulty. These same genealogies appear (in Latin) in an Elizabethan collection of material relating to Ireland, but the version in the Hatfield Compendium is older.[3] The second pedigree, that of the Lower MacWilliam Burkes, lists the four grandsons of Sir Edmund 'Albunaghe' [the Scot], the last of whom, Richard, died in 1473. The reference, in paragraph three, to 'Oyllycke father to the vii sonnes that now ben' is a potential key to dating the section, yet it is hard to know to which Ulick of the Upper MacWilliam Burkes the sons were born: Ulick 'an fhíona' [of the wine] (*d*.1423), Ulick 'ruadh' [the red] (*d*.1485), or Ulick 'fionn' [the fair] (*d*.1509). Reference in paragraph four to the 'iiii shires', rather than to the English Pale, would suggest a dating prior to 1494 when Sir Edward Poynings introduced the latter term into the political vernacular of the lordship of Ireland. So it seems reasonable to suggest that the information assembled in this section was gathered, like some of the other material in the Hatfield Compendium, for Henry VII in the last decade of the fifteenth century.

The fourth and final paragraph in this section stands out on two counts. In the first place, it is not a pedigree. Rather it presents a geographical description of the lands under the lordship of Richard Burke, second earl of Ulster. Second, the paragraph is a fragment of a fuller English account of the earl's landed possessions. The entry was included by the seventeenth-century Irish antiquary Dualtagh Mac Firbisigh in his *Book of Genealogies*:

> The red earl was lord in demayne and sarvice for the most part from Bealagh-Lughyd in Tuamona to Balliehony, which is an hundred miles, and from the Norbagh by the seaside to Bailie Mac Skanlon by Dundalke, and also from Limbricke to Waterford, besides all his lands in four shires, and in the county of Kilkenny and Tipperary.[4]

A nearly identical version of the (supposed) reach of the 'red' earl's lands and influence appears, in Irish, in the *Historia et genealogia familiae de Burgo*, also known as *Senchas Búrcach*, completed in north Connacht in the late sixteenth century.[5] But its appearance here in the Hatfield Compendium, and in later Elizabethan collections of historical materials relating to Ireland, would suggest that English language accounts of the second earl of Ulster's landed possessions

3 See, for example, TNA, SP 63/214, fos 15, 68–9.

4 *Leabhar mór na ngenealach: the great book of genealogies. Compiled (1645–66) by Dubhaltach Mac Fhirbhisigh*, ed. Nollaig Ó Muraíle, 5 vols (Dublin, 2004), iii, pp 110–11.

5 Roderic O'Flaherty, *A chorographical description of west or h-Iar Connaught*, ed. James Hardiman (Dublin, 1846), p. 189; TNA, SP 63/214, fo. 15.

were also in circulation. Thus the purpose of this brief and peculiar looking section of the Compendium was to show Tudor officials that all those lands which had once belonged to the Burkes – one of the most important families in the history of the medieval lordship of Ireland – had been the rightful possession of the crown of England since the reign of Edward IV.

1.8

Ordinances and provisions for Ireland

The Hatfield Compendium concludes with the anonymous and undated 'Ordynaunces and provisions for this lande of Irelande'. This section accounts for more than a quarter of the material in the compendium. It is comprised of 110 numbered articles (again given in arabic numerals). This copy of the Ordinances – which, unlike most of the other component parts of the Compendium, does not appear in the antiquarian works undertaken in Elizabeth's reign – is much fuller than the copy in Trinity College Dublin (where the articles are unnumbered), from which Harris' printed edition is derived and which commences abruptly halfway through article 12, omitting the first 11 articles and also articles 26, 76, 77, 87, and part of article 57. The Trinity manuscript also conflates articles 32 and 33, omitting the first part of article 33, and it offers a number of variant (and generally inferior) readings of particular words and phrases. Yet, as its title and early articles suggest, the Ordinances are an entirely separate document from the several versions of Finglas' Breviate.

The main thrust of the Ordinances is on military matters – relations with the Irish, arrangements for hostings against them for defence, and for livery of the deputy's retinue – but they begin with articles for the enforcement of the law and existing statutes, and conclude with some more varied articles, including very detailed articles relating to coinage, trade, the revenues, weights and measures. Take article 80 for example:

> It[e]m that no m[er]chau[n]tes wyfe use any taverne or sellyng of ale upon payne of xxs totiens quotiens as often as any of them do the contrarye but let the[m] be occupied in makyng of wollen clothe and lynnen clothe

Such glimpses into the social and economic aspects of society in early modern Ireland are very rare, but are relatively plentiful here. The Ordinances end with one for the deputy to spend eight days every summer 'cuttyng paases of the woddes nexte adioynyng the kynges subiectes whiche shalbe thoughte moste nedefull'. A list of thirty-three wooded areas earmarked for cutting is then given. Most of these passes to be cut appear to have been in Leinster running along the extremities of the English Pale.[1]

---

1   Nearly identical lists of passes to be cut were copied in Elizabeth's reign – most often placed after a copy of 'A description of the power of Irishmen' – but upon close inspection these are inferior to the list in the Hatfield Compendium: TNA, SP 63/214, fos 13, 50, 62; BL, Additional MS,

In regard to the dating of the document, there are a number of clues. Article 43 offers an addition to the Act of Marches and Maghery (1488), while articles 59 through 61 recapitulate particular points concerning the duties of justices and wardens of the peace which are familiar from orders attached to a commission of the peace and of array issued for the barony of Slane in 1499.[2] Other articles suggest a slightly later date. Article 93 appears to refer to a statute of 1508 against exporting hobbies;[3] and articles 74 through 76 envisage a withdrawal of the Irish coinage which had been struck until quite late in Henry VII's reign, together with a revised tariff for English coins circulating in Ireland. The governor at the time, however, was probably the earl of Kildare: the ordering of the captain and spears for Co. Kildare is left to the deputy (article 29) whereas in the case of the other three shires the gentry of each shire were to elect a captain of the spears for each hosting; and in regard to the cessing of kerne on marchlands, a total of 120 kerne was specified for Cos. Kildare and Carlow combined (article 31).[4] There were also a number of articles regulating the deputy's conduct: they generally adopt a neutral tone, but article 108 is more pointedly phrased, alleging that 'if the deputie ... may lyverye at his pleasure lordes and gentlemen landes, let never the saide lordes ne gentlemen call that lande theirs at leynghte, but call it the deputie landes, and take ensamble therof at Mounestere'.

Nonetheless, the opening articles seem more concerned with preparations for a change of deputy. Accordingly, one possible date is the lead up to the appointment of Sir William Skeffington in 1534. It has been suggested that 'some of the proposals in Sir Patrick Finglas' Breviate appear more or less verbatim in the Ordinances', namely the printed Ordinances for the government of Ireland of 1534.[5] The fact that, as is now clear, the Ordinances were not part of Finglas' Breviate does not, of course, preclude the possibility that Finglas had also drafted these, although the phrasing of individual articles might suggest otherwise.[6] There are,

48015, Yelverton MS 16, fo. 217v. Thirty of these passes are listed (and rendered in a more recognizably modern form) in C.L. Falkiner, *Illustrations of Irish history, topography, mainly in the seventeenth century* (London, 1904), p. 147, where it is observed: 'it is not now possible to identify all the counties in which these passages were situate'. For an earlier attempt to identify some of these same defiles, see H.F. Hore, 'Woods and fastnesses in ancient Ireland', *Ulster Journal of Archaeology*, 6 (1858), 160. On the woodlands of Ireland more generally in this period, see K.W. Nicholls, 'Woodland cover in pre-modern Ireland' in Duffy et al. (eds), *Gaelic Ireland*, pp 181–206.

2   NAI, Lodge MSS, 'Articles', fo. 221.

3   Quinn (ed.), 'The bills and statutes', 107.

4   For a fuller discussion of the defensive arrangements of the English Pale based on some of the evidence contained in these Ordinances, see S.G. Ellis, *Defending English ground: war and peace in Meath and Northumberland, 1460–1542* (Oxford, 2015), ch. 5.

5   Bradshaw, *The Irish constitutional revolution*, p. 100, referring to TNA, SP 60/2/26, fos 64–71v (*SP Hen. VIII*, ii, p. 207–16).

6   For instance, Finglas, in article twenty-five of his Breviate (printed below), refers to 'the lytle

however, some striking resemblances between the Ordinances and the printed *Ordinances*, most notably the following articles:

> 59 It[e]m that the justyces of peace shalbe made in everie shyre and they to make wardeynes of the peace in everie baronye and constables in everie paraiche, and that they kepe ['mynisters' *is crossed through*] mustres ones everie quarter of the yere
>
> 60 It[e]m everie man havyng foure libr[e] of free goodes and so upwarde unto x libr[e] is wourthy to have his bowe some arrowes or a byll and fro x libr[e] is wo^{r}thy to have his iacke sallet bowe arrowes and a byll upon payne of vis viiid as often as he be founde wythout the same
>
> 61 It[e]m that shootyng be used in everie parishe within thEnglishe Pale everie holydaye so that the weather be fayre on payne of iiis iiiid
>
> 62 It[e]m that everie housbondman havyng a ploughe wythin thEnglishe Pale shall sett by the yere xii asshes in the dytches and closses of his ferme upon payne of iis
>
> 63 It[e]m whersoever any crye be rered in any place that all these that are adioynyng nexte unto the same place where such cryes be made shall aunswere to the same crye in their most defensible araye upon payne of iiis iiiid that make defaulte totie[n]s q[u]otiens

In the printed *Ordinances*, the articles appear as follows:

> Item, that justices of peace shall be made in everye shire, and they to make wardinges of the peace in every barony, and constables in every paryshe; and that they kepe musters ones every quarter of the yere.
>
> Item, that shotyng be used in every parish within the Englishe pale, every holyday, so that the wether be fayre, upon payne of 3^s 4^d of forfayture to the Deputie.
>
> Item, that every husbande having a ploughe within thInglishe pale, shall sette, by the yere, 12 ashes in the diches and closes of his ferme, upon peyne of 2^s to be forfayte to the Deputie.
>
> Item, where so ever any crye be reared, in any place, that al those, that be adjoynyng next unto the same place where such cries be made, shal answere to the same crie in theyr most defencible array, upon peyn of forfayture to the Deputye 3^s 4^d, that make defaulte, totiens quotiens.[7]

As may be seen, the articles are more or less verbatim, except for the addition of the phrase 'to the Deputy' in the version of articles 61 through 63 in the printed

Englishe Pale withyn the counties of Dublyne Mydthe and Uryell', whereas the Ordinances generally prefer 'the four shires', including Co. Kildare.

7   *SP Hen. VIII*, ii, p. 214.

Ordinances, and the omission there of article 60. The reason for the omission is that this particular article had already appeared in a slightly different form towards the beginning of the printed *Ordinances*.[8] As already noted, however, these articles concerning the duties of justices and wardens of the peace are known from earlier sources, although not article 62 about planting ash trees. There are also other articles in the Ordinances which have apparently been slightly reworked for the printed *Ordinances*. One of the most revealing reworkings is the following article concerning appropriate weapons for a hosting:

> 22 It[e]m that no Englishman[n] dwellyng wythin maughre grou[n]de do take no spere wth hym to the felde excepte he hath a bowe or pavyce upon payne of furfeite of vis viiid and losyng of his spere totiens quotiens

> Item, that no Englysshe man, dwellynge within the harte of the Inglyshe pale, do take any speare with hym to the felde, excepte he take a bowe and arrows, upon peyne of forfayture 6^s 8^d, and losing of his spere, totiens quociens.[9]

Now the phrase 'maghery ground' in article 22 has a technical meaning relating to the Act of Marches and Maghery (1488) in which the boundaries of march and maghery were specified and on which were based the numbers of troops to be provided and the particular weapons brought to each hosting by gentry dwelling either in the maghery or in the marches respectively, and this point is clarified by other articles in this section. In the printed *Ordinances*, however, 'maghery ground' is glossed more vaguely as 'the heart of the English Pale' and the particular point of the article is obscured by the intrusion of other unrelated articles. The most striking duplication of particular articles, however, is one urging that 'the statute of Spanish wines be put in execution' – a statute not otherwise known – although, again, the wording is somewhat different:

> 82 It[e]m that the statutes of the Spanyshe wynes be put in execution: that is that no hydes be geven for any man[er] wares excepte it be for wheate salte yron or smale wynes upon payne of forfeture of the same or the valo^r and all men sendyng any hydes out of this lande shall fynde suerties to the customers that the returne of the saide hydes shall come in such wares as is afforsaide

> Item, the statute of Spanyshe wynes be putte in execution; that is, that no hydes be yoven for any maner wares, except it be for wheate, salt, yron, or Gascoyne and Rochel wines, upon pein of forfeiture of the same, or the valu.[10]

8   Ibid., ii, pp 208–9.   9   Ibid., ii, p. 213.   10   Ibid., ii, p. 216.

In general, the implication of all this is that, when drafting, the authors of the printed *Ordinances* (principally the king's secretary, Thomas Cromwell, as we know) had a copy of the Ordinances to hand, and occasionally derived articles from them, but not systematically. This does not necessarily mean, however, that the Ordinances were first compiled in 1533–4. Even where articles in the printed *Ordinances* were clearly adapted from the Ordinances, significant changes were sometimes made, as in regard to the numbers of kerne to be cessed on the marches at each hosting:

> 30 It[e]m that all gentyles of the marches of Mydthe shall cesse on their m[ar]che landes vi^xx kierne of their own[n] kyerne to be indyfferentlye cessed to everie hoostyng and a capytayne to be elected for them, and that capytayne to have a lytle bann[er] and all the kierne to followe the same of that shyre and to be alwayes redye togetthres
>
> 31 It[e]m the shiere of Uriel to cesse xl kierne the countie of Dublyne xl kyerne the counties of Kyldare and Catherlaghe vi^xx kyerne and their cap-itaynes to be elected and everie capytayne their lytle gytton

This is reworked in the printed *Ordinances* as follows:

> Item, that the gentyls of the marches of Myth shall cesse on their marche landes 120 kerne, to be indifferently cessed to every ostyng; and the shyre of Uriell to cesse 80 kerne; the marches of the countie of Dublin 24 kerne; the kerne of the countyes of Kyldare and Cartlagh, as the Erle of Kyldare used to cesse there: and all the sayde kerne to be attendaunt uppon the Deputie.[11]

This might suggest that the inclusion in the printed *Ordinances* of material from the Ordinances represents a reworking of articles that had been compiled rather earlier.

One particular context which would fit well with the internal evidence of the Ordinances is the lead up to Surrey's expedition (1520–2). It may be that they were drafted later in 1519 (and clearly also in Ireland) by someone closely connected with the Dublin administration, and at an early stage in the prepara-tions leading to the appointment as governor of the earl of Surrey but before the particular character of this new initiative was known in the lordship. In the event, Surrey was given the more honourable title of lord lieutenant, but in the initial planning, as here, he is described as the king's deputy.[12] Thus, in the early

---

11 Ibid., ii, p. 213.
12 A device how Ireland may be well kept in obedience, TNA, SP 60/1/28, fos 70–2 (misdated

part of the Ordinances (articles 6 through 9), it is envisaged that the deputy's retinue, paid for from the Irish revenues 'in avoydyng thabomynable extorcyon of
cou[n]ye and lyverye', shall comprise 100 yeomen and 20 gunners, costing £820
a year; 120 galloglass, costing £400 per annum; 200 kerne, costing £200; and 40
horsemen. Article 10 notes, however, that 'the foresaid charges cannot be borne
until the revenues be increased'. These articles also seem to relate to three sets
of memoranda which were certainly associated with the preparations for Surrey's
expedition. The first begins with 'The army for Irland besid[e]s the deputies
awne charche', listing 400 of the king's guard, 24 of the king's gunners, and 100
Irish horsemen, an army of numerically similar size to that envisaged in the
Ordinances, but with local troops replaced by the king's guard: Surrey later
complained bitterly about the value of the latter in the circumstances of Irish
warfare, and they were soon replaced.[13] The second offered 'consideracions why
coyne and lyverey may not bee clerely and subdaynly leid downe', as suggested
in article 6, noting also that the deputy would need kerne and galloglass to
pursue the Irish into woods and marshes.[14] And almost as an afterthought, article 106 suggests that the deputy should receive half the feefarm and customs of
Waterford, Cork, Youghal, Limerick and Galway, the other half to go for
repairs to their walls and for their defence. This proposal reappears in a more
prominent position in a set of 'Remembrances for Ireland' compiled in early
1520, where it has been recast to propose a statutory resumption of all the feefarms and customs of these same towns and cities, plus Kinsale, on the grounds
that their walls are now well built and repaired.[15] And by around February, a
more general resumption of feefarms and customs of the towns is envisaged,[16]
realized by the sending over of a (failed) bill for Surrey's parliament for a general
resumption of customs, cocket, and feefarms alienated since 1327.[17]

As to the document's authorship, article 104 recommends that the lords and
the king's council 'shall add correct and amend all that is containeth in this book
after their discretions'. This may suggest that the present version of the
Ordinances had been partially revised and extended after an initial draft by its
main author: the content of the last six articles (articles 105–10) is very varied

2 Dec. 1521: see *L. & P. Hen. VIII*, iii, no. 670) where he is described as the king's deputy and
may arrive by Easter next (= 8 Apr.), and SP 1/19, fo. 222 (*L. & P. Hen. VIII*, iii, no. 669),
ordering the king's guard to appear before the council on 24 Mar. to accompany 'our lieutenant' to Ireland at Easter.

13 TNA, SP 60/1/28, fo. 70 (*L. & P. Hen. VIII*, iii, no. 670); *SP Hen. VIII*, ii, pp 31–2, 48, 54–
5.

14 TNA, SP 60/1/28, fo. 71 (*L. & P. Hen. VIII*, iii, no. 670(ii)).

15 TNA, SP 1/30, fo. 90 (*L. & P. Hen. VIII*, iv, no. 80 where this document was tentatively
placed under the year 1524).

16 *L. & P. Hen. VIII*, iii, no. 670.

17 Quinn (ed.), 'Bills and statutes', 121–2.

and they may have been added later. It is, however, clear from the general content of the Ordinances that the principal author was almost certainly a Palesman and a royal official who was intimately familiar with arrangements for the defence and administration of the English Pale. The prominence given to Meath in the arrangements for hostings (articles 23 and 30) may also suggest he was a Meath landowner. As to who that author was, the most likely candidate is Sir William Darcy. Darcy's known Articles of 1515 consistently refer to the English Pale as 'the four shires', its traditional fifteenth-century name. The first sixty articles of the Ordinances likewise refer to the Pale by its older name of 'the four shires' (usually spelled 'the iiii^{or} shyres'), but beginning with the articles recapitulating the duties of JPs a few specific references to 'the English Pale' appear from article 61 onwards. Darcy is known to have been involved in advising on the preparations for Surrey's expedition. He had long service as undertreasurer, knew the state of the Irish revenues better than anyone else, and had undoubtedly advised the king on this: two of the articles (articles 10, 105) refer specifically to the state of the revenues.[18] More generally, the Ordinances exhibit the same preoccupation with English military order and weaponry, which were, as we know, one of Darcy's trademarks.[19] Thus, while the suggestions advanced here concerning the authorship of the Ordinances, their dating, and the context in which they had been drafted lack unambiguous corroboration from the Ordinances themselves, they fit the known circumstances fairly well.

18 See above, p. 52.
19 Ellis, 'An English gentleman and his community', pp 31–5.

1.9

The Hatfield Compendium

So when was the Hatfield Compendium drawn up? For whom was this document, the only known specimen of its kind, compiled and for what purpose? The Compendium includes 'A description of the power of Irishmen', which was originally drawn up sometime in the early 1490s, but the Compendium could not have been compiled prior to early 1537 when the last recension of Finglas' 'Breviate' was completed. The inclusion of this version of the Breviate, its priority of placement, coupled with the fact that the entire Compendium was carefully written in a single Henrician hand, suggests that it was penned, likely by a professional clerk, at some point from 1537, but probably before 1541 when England's medieval relationship with Ireland was transformed by the latter's erection into a kingdom. Because the Compendium is written in a clerkly hand it lacks the definite orthological markers that would allow the ready identification of the scribe. However, there are some superficial resemblances to an anonymous document endorsed 'a reputacon for misorder in Irelond to be reformed' drawn up in England sometime in late 1533.[1] The author of this paper was most probably Walter Cowley, formerly the king's attorney in Ireland and a client of Thomas Cromwell; it was on one of his frequent visits to England that Cowley addressed the paper to Cromwell so that his patron might in turn present it to his master the king.[2] It may be that one of Cromwell's administrative staff wrote up the copy of Cowley's paper which survives.[3] There are a few

1 Report to Cromwell, 1533, TNA, SP 60/2/3, fos 4v–10. The 'report', whose preface is addressed to the king, refers to Ireland as '*there* w'in *that* yo[r] said lande', as opposed to '*this* yo[r] gracis realme of Englande': fo. 4v (emphasis added).

2 Terry Clavin, 'Walter Cowley' in *Dictionary of Irish biography* (eds), James McGuire and James Quinn (Cambridge, 2010); Ellis, *Reform and revival*, p. 224. Walter Cowley, whom we know to have been born in Ireland, probably in Dublin, was the son of Robert Cowley, who was born in England. The author of the 'report', in an effort to set forth his own credentials to add gravity to his comment on Ireland, wrote: 'And forasmuche also I was bo[r]ne there w'in that yo[r] said lande lernyd by summe lytle experience there it p[ro]voketh me to that enterprise, coveyting the weale of my native cuntrey and besides that I accompt me more bounden to the same then many others my father being an Englishman bo[r]ne w'in this yo[r] gracis realme of Englande': Report to Cromwell, 1533, TNA, SP 60/2/3, fo. 4v.

3 G.R. Elton, 'Thomas Cromwell: aspects of his administrative work' (PhD, University of London, 1948), p. 348. Most of the handwriting in Cowley's paper is (so far as can be determined) a direct match with the handwriting found in Thomas Cromwell's letter to Thomas Alen, 9 July 1534, TNA, SP 60/2/17, fo. 49. For a specimen of Walter Cowley's own handwriting, see his letter to Cromwell: 21 Dec. 1531, TNA, SP 60/1/74, fo. 152.

orthological peculiarities in the Hatfield Compendium which are not found in Cowley's piece,[4] but it is conceivable that the same clerk in Cromwell's service penned both documents.

As we have seen, some of the component parts of the Compendium were originally intended for the eyes of the king, but the Compendium itself would seem to have been compiled for a royal servant who was to benefit from the crash course on the several aspects of Ireland which this body of information offered. Some indication of this may be seen in those two instances in the Compendium where the clerk copied 'yo[r]', as in 'your deputy' of Ireland, before striking out 'your' from the text to insert 'the deputy' of Ireland into the text.[5] The Compendium's Irish subject matter, and its broadly political concerns, give the work coherence, and distinguish it from the medieval miscellany genre, which is defined as much by the wildly disparate contents of its manuscripts as by modern efforts to explain how this genre was understood and utilized by contemporaries.[6] Given this, and the dating suggested above, it may well be that the Compendium was prepared for the four royal commissioners, led by Sir Anthony St Leger, the future lord deputy, who arrived in the lordship in September 1537 with wide-ranging powers to enquire into the state of government and society. None of these Englishmen, so far as we know, had had any knowledge or experience of Ireland prior to this service, and so would have benefited from a lengthy dossier which placed so much information about the lordship's history, politics, geography and inhabitants at their fingertips.

The commissioners' ignorance and inexperience of Ireland was well known to judge by the number of 'books' on the state of Ireland with suggestions for its reform which were directed to them by men with experience of Ireland. Each of these books, however, is self-consciously prescriptive and bore the definitive political stamp of its author.[7] In a letter to the commissioners, John Alen, the

4   For example, in the Hatfield Compendium the clerk tends to render gentlemen, 'gent', and write manor, 'mano[ir]'.
5   CP, MS 144, fos 7, 10.
6   Derek Pearsall, 'The whole book: late medieval English miscellanies and their modern interpreters' in Stephen Kelly and J.J. Thompson (eds), *Imagining the book: medieval texts and cultures of Northern Europe* (Turnhout, 2005), pp 17–29.
7   John Alen's articles, July 1537, TNA, SP 60/4/31, fo. 88; Robert Cowley to Cromwell, July 1537, TNA, SP 60/4/32, fos 89–94 (where Cowley writes of the necessity of putting an army in readiness for the 'generall reformacion' of Ireland: 'hertofore I delyvered your Lordship severall bokes concernyng that matier'); Lord Deputy Grey to Commissioners, Sept. 1537, TNA, SP 60/5/14, fos 25–6v; John Alen to Commissioners, Sept. 1537, TNA, SP 60/5/15–16, fos 27–40; Thomas Luttrell to Commissioners, Sept. 1537, TNA, SP 60/5/17, fos 41–5v; Book addressed to the Commissioners, Feb. 1538, TNA, SP 60/6/15, fos 31–8v (this is a copy of Alen's book of Sept. 1537, TNA, SP 60/5/16). There is a copy of this latter 'book' in BL, Additional MS 48015, Yelverton MS 16, fos 249–58v.

master of the rolls, made reference to their being 'contentyd that I shulde with others joyne to geders for the conseyveing of a booke, whyche hytherto by those joined with not being perfecteyd'; instead, he wrote out his own ideas 'whiche mought be a sure grounde for you to folowe'.[8] The multi-authored Hatfield Compendium, by contrast, is, by its very make-up, a more neutral document. We know that the commissioners were instructed to take with them an assortment of records, most of them relating to the crown's revenues and the parliament of Ireland, which was then prorogued and awaiting direction from the crown. Three of the commissioners acknowledged prior to their departure the receipt of twelve books containing acts for parliament and also books of account.[9] But in addition to acts to be passed in parliament and extents of the king's revenues there were 'other thinges writinges and munimentes' which had been prepared 'for their dispeche'.[10] It is possible that the Hatfield Compendium was one of these other writings, specially compiled, perhaps by one of Cromwell's clerks in later 1537, for a group of royal commissioners bound for Ireland, but who could lay claim to no knowledge of the place.

Precisely how and when this Henrician manuscript came to reside among the papers of William Cecil, and nowhere else, is (and will probably remain) a mystery. It is also unclear whether the Hatfield Compendium was ever brought over to Ireland, or whether the document which we now have before us remained permanently in England as a work of reference or a master-copy. Cecil was an avid collector of manuscripts and his interest in Ireland in the second half of the sixteenth century has already been observed. Though the document bears none of the marginalia and endorsements that so often mark his handling of a paper, such an information-rich source would have had many practical uses for someone like Cecil who devoted his considerable energies to overseeing the government of Ireland for decades, but who, like the monarchs he served, never set foot there. The Hatfield Compendium probably served as the original document from which the Elizabethan antiquary Laurence Nowell later worked to compile information on Ireland.[11] In the 1560s Nowell lived in Cecil House in the Strand – the London home of William Cecil – where he served as tutor to the principal secretary's ward, Edward de Vere, the seventeenth earl of Oxford. Here, under Cecil's patronage, Nowell and other scholars exchanged information about, and most importantly manuscripts from, England's past. Their study of the past, along with the geography of England, was part of a wider effort to understand English identity and England's place in history, what has been called 'the discovery of England'.[12] The

8   *SP Hen. VIII*, ii, p. 487.
9   Commissioners' receipt, 31 July 1537, TNA, SP 60/4/39, fo. 149.
10 Henry VIII to Commissioners, 31 July 1537, TNA, SP 60/4/37, fo. 124.
11 See above, p. 38.
12 Robin Flower, 'Laurence Nowell and the discovery of England in Tudor times' in *Proceedings*

history of Ireland, we can be certain, was included in that discussion, and it is possible that the Hatfield Compendium featured prominently.

But for the royal commissioners in 1537 a document like the Compendium would have had more immediate uses. They were entering a land whose inhabitants interpreted the crown's destruction of the Fitzgeralds in 1535 as the beginning of a phase in the Anglo-Irish relationship in which the English crown would be more actively involved in the affairs of Ireland. For officials in the Irish government, the time to march against the Irish was at hand: they argued that the boundaries of the English Pale in Leinster should be extended, as a prelude, they hoped, to the rapid extension of Tudor rule throughout Ireland – a 'general reformation' as they put it. For the Irish, if we accept the accounts of government officials who spoke for them, the conquest of Ireland seemed an all-too-real possibility following the arrival of an English army that had displayed military prowess superior to most anything the Irish polity could muster. In England, Cromwell had assumed an active role in the preparation and progress of the royal commissioners' mission and the king was in an expectant mood, though his expectations were more measured in comparison to his English subjects in Ireland. Henry VIII ordered his commissioners to establish order and the rule of law in his lordship of Ireland, to root out corruption in the administration, to make the crown lands profitable and to see his religious legislation through parliament. It was a pivotal time in the Anglo-Irish relationship. The varied and vital information on Ireland contained in the Hatfield Compendium offered a means for Tudor officials, such as the royal commissioners, to begin to understand the country that was emerging as an important part of the new Tudor state being fashioned by Henry VIII.

of the British Academy, 21 (1935), 47–73; Rebecca Brackmann, The Elizabethan invention of Anglo-Saxon England: Laurence Nowell, William Lambarde and the study of Old English (London, 2012), p. 12.

THE TEXT OF THE
HATFIELD COMPENDIUM

Hatfield House Archives, Hertfordshire,
Cecil Papers MS 144, fos 1–16.[1]

1   **Editorial Notes.** The transcription that follows preserves the original spelling, capitalization and punctuation of the anonymous manuscript that resides among the Cecil Papers in the library at Hatfield House where it is neatly bound into a guard book. Abbreviations have been expanded and marked within square brackets. Gaps and illegible words, or parts of words, in the text appear as [.....]. Words in the text which we are uncertain of, but think likely, appear in brackets with a question mark: [e.g. their?]. In certain instances we have provided in Arabic numerals the sum totals of numbers given in Roman numerals, and have indicated where each folio page ended: these interpolations in the text appear in curly brackets {e.g. 100} and {e.g. **end fo. 1**}. We have also attempted to retain the placement on the page and the spacing of headings and paragraphs as they were laid out in the original manuscript.

3 The first page of the Hatfield Compendium.

A breviate of the gettyng of Irelande
and of the decaye of the same

1 The lande of Irelande of olde tyme had fyve kynges whiche devyded all the lande in fyve porcions, that is to say Leynyster contaignyng fyve counties, that is to say, the cou[n]tie of Dublyne, Kyldare, Cartherlaghe, Weyxforde and Kylkenye
2 It[e]m twoo porcyons in Mounster one by sowthe the Ryver of Shenyne from Waterforde unto Lym[er]ycke contaynyng fyve cou[n]ties, that is to say, the com[itatus] of Wat[er]forde, Corcke Kyerye Typp[er]arye and Lym[er]ycque. It[e]m the other porcion of Mounster is by weaste the Ryver of Shenyne called O Bryenes countree
3 It[e]m an other porcion Connaght contaignyng dyverse counties
4 It[e]m an other porcion Ullester contaignyng dyverse counties
5 It[e]m the chiefe of the fyve kynges called Monarcha kepte the com[itatus] of Mydthe with hymselfe ad mensam, etc[2]
6 It[e]m the moste parte of Leynester, sowthe Mounster, Connaght Mydthe and Ullester was conquered by kynge Henrye Fytz Empresse[3] and by suche lordes and gentlemen that came unto Irelande by his lycense and com[m]aundement
7 It[e]m the chiefe of the gettyng and conqueryng of Leynest[er] under kynge Henrye Fytz Emprese was Rycharde erle of Strangebowe[4] who maryed Mac Morrowghes doughter wyth whom aswell by the saide Mac Morrowghes gyfte as by conquest he had all Leynester and reduced it to goode ordre and obedyence of the kynges lawes and enioyed it eight yeres duryng the saide Mac Morrowghes lyfe and syxe yeres after duryng his owne lyfe[5]
8 It[e]m the saide erle deyed xiiii yeres after the conquest and had yssue but one doughter whom kynge Henrye Fytz Emprese toke into Englande and maryed her to Wylliame erle Marshall,[6] whiche erle Marshall came into Irelande and enioyed all Leynester in peace lx yeres after the conqueste, and lefte all the same obedyent to the kynges lawcs at his deathe excepte certayne of the bloude and name of Mac Morrowghes, whiche by suffrau[n]ce of the forsaide erle for

---

2 'that is, for the maintenance of his more honorable diet': LPL MS 600, fo. 204.
3 Henry II, king of England (reigned, 1154–89). His mother, Matilda, was first married to the Holy Roman Emperor Henry V.
4 Richard fitzGilbert de Clare [nicknamed 'Strongbow'], second earl of Pembroke (c.1130–76).
5 In 1170 Strongbow married Eva, the daughter of Dermot MacMurrough, king of Leinster. Strongbow, in fact, inherited Leinster following MacMurrough's death (at Ferns) in May 1171 and enjoyed it until his own death five years later.
6 In 1189 William Marshal (c.1146–1219) married Isabel de Clare (c.1172–1220), the only child of Strongbow and MacMurrough's daughter.

allyau[n]ce of their wyves were duellyng under trybute in the com[itatus] of Catherlaghe in a place as it were a baronye called Yepyn[7]

9 It[e]m the saide erle Marshall had yssue by therle Straugbowes doughter, fyve sonnes and v dought[er]s and dyede {*end fo. 1*}

10 It[e]m the saide fyve sonnes were earles and lordes of Leynester everie of them after other and ruled all Leynester in peace and p[ro]sp[er]itie obedyent to the kynges lawes duryng all their lyves whiche contynued to kynge Edwarde the fyrstes daies[8] and deyed all without yssue of their bodyes lawfully begotten[9]

11 It[e]m all these forsaide fyve doughters duryng the lyfe of their fathers and brethren were all maryed in Englande to lordes, who after the deathe of their brethrene made partycion betuxte them of all Leynester in forme followyng: the eldest had the countie of Catherlaghe; the seconde the com[itatus] of Wexforde; the thirde the cou[n]tie of Kylkenye; the fourthe the cou[n]tie of Kyldare; the v[th] had the mano[ir] of Downamase in Leys[10] with other certayne landes in the cou[n]tie of Kyldare[11]

12 It[e]m the forsaide lordes housbou[n]des to the forsaide ladyes havyng great possessions in Englande of their owne, regarded lytle the defence of their landes in Irelande but toke the p[ro]fyites of the same for a whyle as they coulde and some of them never sawe Irelande. And when their revenues of the same began to decaye, then he that had Downamase in Leys retayned an Irishman one of the Mores to be his capytayne of warre in Leys in defence of Irishmen upon that bordours

13 It[e]m the other ii lordes that had Catherlaghe and Wexforde retayned one of the Keavauneghes that remayned in Ydronee to be capytayne of warre for their defence and toke no regarde to dwelle themselfes in the p[ro]pre parsones upon their landes so that wythin xx[tie] yeres after or theraboute in the begynnyng of kynge Edwarde the secou[n]des dayes[12] the saide Moore that was capitayne of Leys kept that porcion as his owne and called hymselfe O More and the saide capytayne of the Keavennaghes kepte a great porcyon of the cou[n]ties of Catherlaghe and Wexforde wherin he was capitayne as his owne and called hym-

---

7   The barony of Idrone in Co. Carlow.

8   Edward I, king of England and lord of Ireland (r.1272–1307).

9   William Marshal (*c.*1190–1231), fifth earl of Pembroke; Richard (*c.*1191–1234), sixth earl of Pembroke; Gilbert Marshal (*c.*1194–1241), seventh earl of Pembroke; Walter Marshal (*c.*1196–1245), eighth earl of Pembroke; and Anselm Marshal (*c.*1198–1245).

10   Dunamase in Co. Leix.

11   Following Anselm's death in 1245 Leinster passed to the Marshal heiresses: Matilda (Maud) Marshal (1192–1248) who married Hugh Bigod, third earl of Norfolk; Isabel Marshal (1200–40) who married Gilbert de Clare, fifth earl of Gloucester, and then Richard, first earl of Cornwall; Eva Marshal (1203–46) who married William de Braose, Lord of Abergavenny; Sibyl Marshal (*c.*1206–45) who married William de Ferrers, fifth earl of Derby; and Joan Marshal (*c.*1208–*c.*1234) who married Warin de Munchensi, Lord of Swanscombe.

12   Edward II, king of England and lord of Ireland (r.1307–27).

selfe Mᶜ Morroughe, and so wythyn lytle space after, the saide Mᶜ Morrowghe
growyng in strenghte ryse up the Byrnes and Tohylles in his ayde so that hitherto
they have kepte all the countreye betwxte Catherlaghe and theaste seae as their
owne whiche is xxxᵗⁱᵉ myles and more and so began the decaye of Leynester

14 It[e]m the successour of the saide Mᶜ Morrowghe beyng in greate strengthe
in the later ende of kynge Edwarde the iiiᵈᵉˢ dayes¹³, the kynge gave hym wadges
lxxx marckes yerelye out of theschequyer¹⁴

15 It[e]m it is to be consydered and true it is that in everie of the saide v porcions that was conquered by kynge Henrye Fytz Emprese and suche lordes and
gent[lemen] as came with hym into Irelande or by his lycense and com[m]-
aim[n]dme[n]t lefte under trybute certayne Iryshemen of the pryncypal bloude
of Irishe nacyon that were before the conquest inhabitau[n]tes {*end fo. 1v*}
wythin everye of the saide porcions as in Leynester the Keavauneghes of the
bloude of Mac Morrowghe somtyme kynge of the same in sowth Mounster the
Machartyes of the bloude of Machartie somtyme kynge of Corcque. In the
other porcion of Mounster by weaste the Ryver of Shenyne wher O Bryene is
whiche as I saide was never conquered ne obedyent to the kynges lawes, O
Bryene and his bloude have contynued ther styll whiche O Bryene bare trybute
to kynge Henrye Fytz Emprese and to hys heyres by the space of an hundreth
yeres and the lorde Gylbarde de Clare erle of Glowchester had one the best
manoⁱʳ in the saide O Bryens countree and dwelled in the same, and in
Connaghte was lefte under trybute certayne of the bloude of O Connoʳ somtyme kynge of the same and certayne of the Kyellies and others

16 It[e]m in Ullester were lefte under trybute certayne of the Neeles of the
bloude of O Neele somtyme kynge of the same and others

17 It[e]m in Mydthe were lefte certayne of the bloude of O Mollaghlyn somtyme kynge of the same and dyverse others of Iryshe nacyons

18 It[e]m all these forsaide Irishemen have ever sythens the conqueste had an
inclynacion to Yrishe rule and ordre waytyng ever when Englyshmen woulde
rebell and dygresse from obedyence of lawes whiche more harme is have fallen
to their purpose as here after shalbe more playnlyer declared

19 It[e]m all the sowthe porcyon of Mounster betuxte Wat[er]forde and
Lim[er]ycke whiche contaigneth fyve counties, that is to saye the count[ie] of
Wat[er]forde Corcque, Kyerrye Typp[er]rarie and Lym[er]ycke were conquered

---

13 Edward III, king of England and lord of Ireland (r.1327–77).

14 This was Art More MacMurrough (*c.*1357–*c.*1416). Such was MacMurrough's power in
    Leinster (and such was royal weakness there) that the government made money payments to
    him in 1377–8 to avoid a direct confrontation. In late 1378, during the reign of Richard II in
    fact, the government appointed MacMurrough as keeper of the king's highway which con-
    nected Carlow and Kilkenny, for which service the populations of the two shires paid him an
    annual fee of eighty marks.

by kynge Henrye Fytz Emprese and suche noble knyghtes as inhabyted the same by his graces lycense and com[m]aundeme[n]t as the Geraldynes the Butlers, Berryes Roches Cogans with many other noblemen whiche countre was Englyshe and obedyent to the kynges lawes by the space of an clx yeres as it appeareth by the kynges recordes

20 It[e]m in kynge Edwarde the iii[thes] dayes Leonell duke of Clarence[15] beyng the kynges lyevtenau[n]t of Ireland p[er]ceavyng not onelye the lordes and gentlemen of Mounster but also in other cou[n]trees begynnyng to enclyne to Iryshe rule and ordre at a p[ar]liament holden at Kylkenye made certayne statutes for the comon weale for p[re]servacion of Englyshe ordre whiche if they had ben kepte thys lande had ben obedyent to the kynges lawes hitherto

21 It[e]m these were called the statutes of Kylkenye[16] wherof the fyrste was that no man shoulde take coyne ne lyveraye[17] upon the kynges subiectes, w[ch] woulde destrue hell yf it were used in the same {end fo. 2}

22 It[e]m an other was that none of the kynges Englishe subiectes shoulde made any allyaunce by alterage or fusteryng[18] with any of Irishe nacion

23 It[e]m an other was that no man of the kynges Englishe subiectes possessed of landes or teneme[n]tes shoulde marye any woman of Irishe natyon, ne noo woman to marye a man of Irishe natyon upon payne of forfayito[r] of all their landes and teneme[n]tes with dyv[er]se other beneficyall statutes for con-tynua[n]ce of Englishe order

24 It[e]m as longe as these forsaide statutes were kepte the lande was in goode p[ro]sp[er]itie and obeyed the kynges lawes but sone after the departure of the saide duke into Englande, the great lordes aswell of Mounst[er] of Leynester then beyng in great wealthe and growyng into greater name and authorytie as Johne FitzThomas late created earle of Kyldare Jeames Butler then created erle of Ormonde and Mauryce Fytz Thomas than created earle of Desmond,[19] havyng dyvysion betwxte themselfes began to make alterage with Irishemen[20]

---

15 Lionel of Antwerp (1338–68), first duke of Clarence, the third son of Edward III, arrived in Ireland in 1361 and died seven years later. Clarence was recognized as earl of Ulster by right of his wife Elizabeth de Burgh.

16 The thirty-six statutes enacted by the lordship's parliament held at Kilkenny in February 1366 – the famous Statutes of Kilkenny – were a codification of the legislation made in Ireland since 1297 and were intended to ensure, inter alia, that English ground, and indeed Englishmen, remained English.

17 'Coign and livery' (Coin-mheadh = billeting; livery = purveyance). This was the general term for the various Irish exactions arising from the free quartering of the chief's dependants on the country. The Statutes of Kilkenny in fact made no direct mention of 'Coign and livery'.

18 Fosterage was the Irish custom whereby the children of the elite were raised by others with the view to develop a political connection.

19 The three earls were so created in 1316, 1328 and 1329, respectively.

20 The fostering of children with Irishmen.

for their strenght to resyst other and disdayned to take punysshement of knyghtes beyng the kynges justyces or deputie for the tyme, by reason of whiche dyvisyon the earles of Ormonde and of Desmonde by strenght of Irishe men on either syde fought together in battayll in Kynge Henrye the syxtes daies[21] in whiche battaylle all the goode men of the towne of Kylkenye with many others were slayne

25 It[e]m never sythens the Geraldynes of Mounst[er] the Butlers ne the Geraldynes of Leynester dyde obedyentlye obeye the kynges lawes in Irelande but contynuallye allyed themselfes with Irishemen usyng contynually coyne and lyverye wherby all the lande is nowe of Irishe rule excepte the lytle Englishe Pale withyn the counties of Dublyne Mydthe and Uryell whiche passed not xxx or xl myles in compace

26 It[e]m in the forsaide maner for lacke of punyssheme[n]t of these greate lordes of Mounster by mynistracyon of justyce they by their extorcyon of coynee lyveraye and other abusion have expelled all the Englyshe freeholders and inhabytau[n]tes out of Mounster so that in L yeres passed was none ther obedyent to the kynges lawes excepte cyties and walled townes and so this have ben the decaye of Mounst[er]

27 It[e]m the countie of Mydth was geven by kynge Henrye Fytz Emprese to S[r] Hughe de Lacye to holde of the kynge by knyghtes fees, whiche S[r] Hughe dyde conquere the same and gave moche of it to lordes and gentelmen to holde of hym and as the saide S[r] Hughe was buyldyng the castelle of Dervathe in weaste Mydthe he was traytourslye slayne by a mason of his owne and it is wrytten in the chronycles & ibi cessauit conquestous & c.[22]

28 It[e]m the saide S[r] Hughe had yssue twoo sonnes S[r] Waltier and S[r] Hughe whiche Hughe afterwarde was erle of Ullester as shalbe declared hereafter[23]

29 It[e]m the saide S[r] Waltier had yssue twoo doughters and deyed thelder was marryed to S[r] Theobalde de Verdon the other to Geffroye Genevyle[24] whiche made porcion of all Mydthe betuxte them, so as the mano[ir] of Tryme was alotted to S[r] Geffroye Genevyles porcyon, to whom our sov[er]aigne lorde the kynges highnes is rightfull heyre {end fo. 2v}

30 It[e]m the mano[ir] of Loghsedye in weste Medthe[25] was allotted to S[r] Theobalde de Verdens porcion who had none heyre but doughters whiche were

---

21 Henry VI, king of England and lord of Ireland (r.1422–61; 1470–1).

22 Sir Hugh de Lacy was assassinated, at Durrow, in 1186 and, according to the Dublin chronicler, 'et ibi cessavit conquestus' [and thereupon the conquest ceased]: *Chartularies of St Mary's abbey, Dublin; with the register of its house at Dunbrody, and annals of Ireland*, ed. J.T. Gilbert, 2 vols (London, 1884), ii, p. 305.

23 Walter de Lacy (d.1241) and Hugh de Lacy (d.1242).

24 It was, in fact, this Walter de Lacy's granddaughters, Margaret and Matilda, who married John de Verdon (d.1274) and Geoffrey de Geneville (d.1314).

25 Loughsewdy.

maryed i[n] Englande to the lorde Ffournyfall and others who duelde styll in Englande and toke suche p[ro]fytes as they coulde gett for a whyle and sende smale defende for their landes in Irelande,²⁶ so as withyn fewe yeres after all their porcions were loste, excepte certayne manoirs withyn the Englishe Pale, whiche Thomas baron of Slane and Sʳ Robarte Holywodde²⁷ and Sʳ Johne Cruce and Sʳ Johne Bellowe purchased in kynge Richarde the secoundes daies.²⁸ And so this have bene the decaye of halfe of Mydthe whiche dyde not obeye the kynges lawes theis iᶜ yeres and more

31 It[e]m as concernyng the porcion of Connaght Gylbarte de Clare erle of Glowchester whiche maryed the secou[n]de doughter of Wylliame erle Marshall²⁹ Sʳ Wylliam de Burcke and Sʳ Wylliam Brynghehame of Amorye under kynge Henrye Fitz Emprese were the pryncipall conquerours of Connaght,³⁰ who with their complyces dyde enhabyte the same and made it Englishe and obeye the kynges lawes from O Bryens countree to Sleyggo, in lenghte above lx myles and more whiche contynued so in prosp[er]itie iᶜ lx yeres to kynge Edwarde the thirdes daies. The decaye wherof shall appeer in the nexte treatyse of Ullester

32 It[e]m Sʳ Johne Coursye³¹ under kynge Henrye Fitz Emprese was the chiefe conqueroʳ of Ullester who aboute the gettyng of the same had vii battaylles wᵗʰ Irishemen wherof he wanne fyve and loste twoo. Nevertheles he gate it and reduced it to Englishe rule and ordre and contynued so aboute xxᵗⁱᵉ yeres unto suche tyme as kynge Johne³² havyng hym in dyspleasure for certayne evyll reportes³³ he shoulde have made by the saide kynge Johne for the kyllynge of Arthure sonne to Geffroye elder brother to the saide kynge Johne wrote into Irelande to Sʳ Waltier de Lacye and to his brother Sʳ Hughe to have the saide Sʳ

26 Theobald de Verdon (1278–1309) was the son of Theobald de Verdon (d.1309), son of the above mentioned John de Verdon. He first married Matilda (d.1314), daughter of Edmund Mortimer; his second wife was Elizabeth de Clare (1294–1360), daughter of Gilbert de Clare, earl of Gloucester and Hertford (1243–95), widow of John de Burgh (d.1313) and mother of William de Burgh (d.1333), third earl of Ulster, whom the Irish annalists referred to as the 'brown earl'. De Verdon's two marriages produced four daughters: Isabella, Elizabeth, Margery and Joan. Thomas, second lord Furnival (d.1334), married Joan de Verdon.

27 Thomas Fleming, second baron of Slane (1358–1435), and Robert Holywoode (d.1384), chief baron of the exchequer.

28 Richard II, king of England and lord of Ireland (r.1377–99).

29 Isabel Marshall (d.1240) married Gilbert de Clare (c.1180–1230), fifth earl of Gloucester.

30 William de Burgh (1157–1206).

31 John de Courcy (c.1219).

32 John, king of England and lord of Ireland (r.1199–1216).

33 Harris added: 'The reasons of the king's displeasure against earl Courcey were the bold, though generous speeches, which he cast out against King John, in relation to the murder of his nephew Arthur, the right heir to the crown, which earl Courcy suggested, was effected by the king's command'.

Johne Coursye taken and sende into Englande to execution. Wherfore the saide S[r] Hughe de Lacye wente wyth an hooste into Ullester and had battayll with the saide S[r] Johne at Dwnne[34] in whiche battaylle was many slayne on bothe sydes and the saide S[r] Johne p[re]vaylled at that tyme

33 It[e]m the saide S[r] Hughe had made practyse with certayne of the saide S[r] Johne Coursyes men so as they promeysed to betraye their m[aste][r] for money. Whereupon the goode Fryday nexte ensuyng the saide S[r] Hughe toke the saide S[r] Johne goyng aboute the churchyarde of Downne and that done, the saide S[r] Hughe payed the saide S[r] Johnes men such sum[m]es of money as he p[ro]meysed them, and in contynent[35] dyde hange them all for their falshede for the betrayng of their maister etc {*end fo. 3*}

34 It[e]m for the forsaide acte Kynge Johne gave unto the forsaide S[r] Hughe the erledome of Ullester who enioyed the same duryng his lyfe and had yssue one doughter and deyed

35 It[e]m the saide Hughe de Lacyes doughter was maryed to S[r] Waltier de Burke lorde of Connaght whiche S[r] Waltier was erle of Ullester and lorde of Connaght and had them bothe then beyng obedyent to the kynges lawes duryng his lyfe and had a so[n]ne S[r] Wylliame de Bourke who enioyed the saide erledom of Ullester and lordeshipp of Connaght in p[ro]sp[er]itie duryng his lyfe and had yssue S[r] Richarde de Bourke whiche was erle of Ullester and lorde of Connaght and mought dyspende yerelye by the same x[m] libr[e] sterlyng and above whiche Richarde had yssue Wylliame whiche Wylliame had yssue but one doughter and was traytourslye slayne by his owne men[36]

36 It[e]m the forsaide Wylliame erle of Ullesters doughter and heyre was maryed to Leonell duke of Clarence secounde sonne to kynge Edwarde the iii[de] who came into Irelande, as is afforesaide and was the kynges lyevtenau[n]t of the same and had all Ullester and Connaght in rest and peace obedyent to the kynges lawes as longe as he taryed in Irelande whiche was not veraye longe

37 It[e]m after the departure of the duke of Clarence into Englande, he leavynge behynde hyme smale defence for his landes in Ullester and lesse defence for his landes in Connaght, then in kynge Richarde the secoundes dayes certayne knyghtes of the Bourkes brethren and kynnesmen of the forsaide Wylliame late erle of Ullester who duryng their lordes lyfe had the rule of Connaght in their lordes absence consyderyng themselfes farre from punysshement of the kynges lawes, and their naturall lorde out of the lande usurped all that countree to themselfes makyng dailye allyau[n]ce and frendshipp wyth Irishemen and fell to Irishe ordre, so that from the deathe[37] of the saide duke of Clarence his heire

---

34 At Down in east Ulster.
35 Incontinently = without delay.
36 For the Burkes, see below, pp 97–8.
37 Here, at the top of fo. 28v, in TCD MS 842, is added 'and soe cont'nuing w[t] out looking on

never after had any ['thynge' *is crossed through*] revenues out of Connaght and so contynuyng without lokyng on and goode defence for the saide dukes landes in Ullester aswell as in Connaght before kynge Edwarde the fourthes daies[38] who was veraye heire to the forsaide erles of Ullest[er] boothe it and Connaght was all loste, so as at this daye our sov[er]aigne lorde the kynge hath in effecte no more p[ro]fycte out of all Ullester but the mano[ir] of Carlyngforde[39] and in this forsaide man[er] for faulte of goode defende was the dekaye as well of Con[n]aght as of Ullester[40] {*end fo. 3v*}

38 It[e]m consyderyng that in the p[re]misses the man[er] of the gettyng and decaye of this lande is somewhat shewed wee must beseche allmyghtie God that some causes may be shewed to our sov[er]aigne lorde the kynge for reformacion of the same

39 It[e]m some men have the oppynion that this lande is harder to be refo[r]med nowe than it was to be conquered at the fyrste conquest consyderyng that Irishemen have more hardynes and pollicye in warre and more harneyse and artyllerye then they had at the conqueste

40 It[e]m this oppynion may be shortelye aunswered, for surelye Irishemen have not suche wysdome ne pollycie in warre but Englishmen when they sett themselfes therunto excede them farre and as towchyng harneys and artyllerye Englishemen excede them to farre and as for hardynes I have seene thexp[er]ience that in all my daies never hearde, that i[c] foote men ne horsemen of Irishemen woulde abyde to fyght with so manye Englishe men, whiche I reporte me to the duke of Northfolke[41] and other greate capitaynes that have ben here and knoweth thexp[er]ience of the same

41 It[e]m besydes all this, Englishemen have a greate advauntage to gett this lande nowe whiche they had not at the conquest, for at that tyme ther was not

38 Edward IV, king of England and lord of Ireland (r.1461–70; 1471–83).

39 'Which is scarce worth 100 mark by the year': LPL MS 621, fos 92–6.

40 The contents of two paragraphs which appear at this point in LPL MS 621, fo. 95, but are omitted in the present manuscript are given here: 'The said earl Richard had many knights and gentlemen of his name and kin, dwelling in Connaught, who, after his death, made alliance and alterage with the Irish, fell to Irish ordre, and usurped all the said lordship of Connaught betwixt two of them, of whom the chief was called McWilliam Oghter, the other McWilliam Eighter, and so do continue to this day as Irish as the said O'Brien. At the Conquest, certain men of name and condition were suffered under tribute, as Irishmen, in every of the said five portions; which Irishmen have been enemies to good order, unless compelled thereto; and therefore they were glad to aid Englishmen when they fell to disobedience, which at length turned to the confusion of the English, as appears now in Leinster, Munster, Connaught, Meath and Ulster'.

41 Thomas Howard (1473–1554) became third duke of Norfolk upon the death of his father, and namesake, in 1524. The earl of Surrey, as Howard then was, served in Ireland as Henry VIII's lord lieutenant, 24 May 1520 until 21 Mar. 1522.

in all Irelande out of cyties fyve castelles ne pyles and nowe ther be v^c castelles and pyles etc

42 It[e]m the iiii saynctes, that is to saye, saynte Patrycke sayncte Columbe, saynte Braghan and saynte Molynge whiche many hundreth yeres agone made prophecye that Englishmen shoulde have conquered Irelande, saide that the saide Englishemen shoulde kepe the lande in p[ro]sp[er]itie as longe as they shoulde kepe the^r owne lawes and assone as they shoulde leave their owne lawe and fall to Irishe ordre, then they shoulde decaye, thexperynce wherof is prowed true. Therfore whensoever our sov[er]aigne lorde shall extende the reformation of Irelande he muste reduce the lordes and gentlemen of this lande whiche be of Englishe natyon to due obedyence of his graces lawes whiche is veraye harde to doe onles the kynge with an armye represse Irishemen upon the bourdo^rs to tribute in a goode confourmytie

43 It[e]m firste our sov[er]aigne lorde the kynge shoulde extende his gracyous power for the reformation of Leynester whiche is the keaye and highe waye for reformation of the remanent, and is sytuated in an angle betuxte Wat[er]forde and Dublyne wherin no moo Irishemen dwelle but the Kievaunaghes of whome Mac Morrowghe is capytayne whiche can not make horsemen passe cc and the Byrnes and Tohylles whiche can not make i^c horsemen besydes the Irishe inhabytau[n]tes of their countree whiche be but naked men, as kierne whiche were not in this hundreth yeres and moo febler to be conquered than they be nowe

44 It[e]m to helpe therunto the kynge hath on thoone syde of them the cou[n]tie of Weisforde wherin dwell many goode Englishe gent[lemen] which woulde be veray glade to ayde therunto {*end fo. 4*}

45 It[e]m upon the other syde the countie of Kyldare and Dublyne. It[e]m^{42} at the weaste ende of their cou[n]tie is the cou[n]tie of Kylkenye and at the easte ende the seae

46 It[e]m they can have no succour of Irishemen excepte it be throughe the counties of Kyldare or Kylkenye whiche is lyghtlye to be stopped

47 It[e]m to allevyate the kynges chardges to this reformation of Leynest[er] ther be dyv[e]^{r}se abbayes adioynyng to this Irishe men whiche do more ayde and supportacion to these Irishe men than to the kynge or his subiectes, parte agaynste their wylles, as the abbeye of Down[n]brathye in the countie of Weixforde the abbaye of Tyntarne in the same, the abbaye of Dowske in the cou[n]tie of Catherlaghe the abbaye of Grane in the cou[n]tie of Kyldare the abbaye of Balkynglasse in the same, whiche may be suppressed and geven by our sov[er]aigne lorde the kynge to younge lordes knyghtes and gent[lemen] out of Englande, whiche shall dwelle upon the same besydes other dyverse mano^rs pyles and castelles upon the bordo^rs as here after followeth

---

42   This is not numbered in the MS.

48 ffyrste the kynges grace to geve to one goode Englishe capitayne the forsaide abbaye of Downnbrathy with certayne landes adioynyng to the same

It[e]m to an other the abbaye of Tynterne wyth a baronye adioyng to the same

It[e]m to an other olde Rosse with the ffassaghe of beantrye, wch is a lyvyng for a lorde

It[e]m to an other the castell of Leighlyne with a barony adioynynge etc

It[e]m to an other the castell of Catherlaghe with a baronye adioynyng to the same

It[e]m to an other the mano^rs of Rathvyllye and Clonemore with a baronye etc

It[e]m to an other the lordeshipp of Weixforde

It[e]m to an other the castell of Ffernes with a baronye adioynyng to the same

It[e]m to an other the abbaye of Dowske by the ryver of the Bearrowe with etc

It[e]m to an other the abbaye of Balkynglas whiche is a lyvyng for a lorde

It[e]m to an other the abbaye of Grane with a baronye

It[e]m to an other castell Kevyne with a baronye adioynyng to the same

It[e]m to an other the mano^rs of Rathedowne and Pouerscourte with a baronye

It[e]m to an other the castell of Wyckloo with a barony ioynyng to the same

It[e]m to an other the castell of Ardckloo with a baronye

It[e]m to an other the castell of Athye and Wodstocke with the baronye of Rebane to be a stoppe betuxte the cou[n]tie of Kyldare and O Moore

It[e]m to an other the mano^ir of Ratheannegan with a barony to be a stoppe betuxte the cou[n]tie of Kyldare and O Conno^r

49 It[e]m besydes all this the castelles and pyles in Mac Morrowghes cou[n]tree and the Byrnes cou[n]treye with all their landes to be devyded at the kynges pleasure betuxte thies forsaide capytaynes

50 It[e]m the wourste of thiese forsaide capitaynes by the divysion forsaide shall dispende yerelye ii or iii hundreth marckes besydes certayne landes to be geven by everye of them to freeholders under them

51 It[e]m that all thies forsaide capytayns shall holde all their landes of the kynge by roiall servyce {*end fo. 4v*}

52 It[e]m suche lordes and gent[lemen] to whom the kynge shall geve these landes afforesaide shoulde have no greate possessions in England, so as they shall not have an eye to returne in to Englande for suche lyke hath bene the greate decaye of this lande as is afforesaide

It[e]m[43] shuche [*sic*] lordes and gent[lemen] to whom the kynge shall geve these forsaide landes shoulde not for awhyle coveyte easye beddes ne goode fare but shoulde followe thexample of the noble lordes knygthes and gentlemen that conquered this lande under kynge Henrye Fitz Emprese the whiche regarded not easye lyghyng delycate fare ne pompeous apparaille, but ever their myndes were

43 This is not numbered in the MS.

to wynne and attayne the honour that have and shalbe spocken of them to the worldes ende and I beseche God to sende to our sov[er]aigne lorde the kynge that shall begynne this entrepryse and his capitaynes lyke and more honour[44]

53 It[e]m consyderyng that these lordes and gent[lemen] to whom our sov[er]aigne lorde the kynge shall geve these forsaide landes shall not be hable of themselfes to recover the landes, that the forsaide Kievaunaghes Byrnes and Toohylles occupie ne to bannyshe them out of their cou[n]trees without our saide sov[er]aigne lorde the kynges ayde, the kynge of his aboundant grace muste fynde an armye so as everie of these forsaide capytaynes may have certayne men for their defen[n]ce for ii or iii yeres, unto suche tyme as they shalbe settled and the lande tylled and inhabyted

54 It[e]m as concernyng inhabytau[n]tes ffor almost as it is toughte daungerous for o[r] sov[er]aigne lorde the kynge to depeople his realme of Englande this lande may be well inhabyted with Irishemen as it was at the fyrste conqueste, for ther be no bett[er] labourres ne earthtyllers than the poore comon people of Irishemen ne soev[er] woulde be brought to goode frame if they be kepte under lawe

55 It[e]m our sov[er]aigne lorde the kynges highnes shoulde not pon[n]der the greate coste that is grace hath had for the defence of his subiectes in this poore lande consyderyng, it is his owne inheritau[n]ce, no man havyng right therunto but onelye his maiestie therfore whatsoever cost his grace shall do for the reformatyon of the same the hono[r] that his highnes shall gett therbye shall recompense his chardge

56 It[e]m I beseche almyghtie God to put in the kynges mynde by this meane or a better to refourme this forsaide countree betuxte Dublyne and Wat[er]forde ffor then his grace shall have revenues to kepe the same contynuallye in goode ordre and to resyste the malyce of Irishemen, therunto adioynynge[45] {*end fo. 5*}

---

44 The version of the 'breviate' in the 'Book on the state of Ireland', *c*.1575, TNA, SP 63/54/29, fo. 96 reads: 'Item these lordes and gentillemen unto whome the kinges grace shall geve these landes must not regard good fare of meat and drink ne softe lynge in fetherbedds for lyvinge a yeare or two but must followe the wayes of noble kingship and gentillemen that conquered this lande under King Henry ffitzempresse w[ch] regarded not during a greate while dilacat fare pompouse apparrell ne soft lying but regarded the honno[r] and prayse that they should have by writing unto the worlds ende: And I beseach almightie god to sende like & more honore to my said soverayne w[ch] I trust shall accomplish the premisses and to his lordes, knights, and gentlemen that shall p[er]forme the same'.

45 TNA, SP 60/2/7, fo. 24 continues (and concludes): 'wyche did hawe bene and wylbe enymes to good ordre and lawe onles they be kept ther unto by compulsion etc. God saue the kyng. Patricke Ffynglas baron'.

A discruption [*sic*] of the power of Irishemen

It[e]m ther is none of this lande of Irelande whiche do obeye the kynges lawes but a parte of the iiii shyres whiche bene called Medthe Uriell Dublyne and Kyldare the whiche iiii shyres of their owne power and strenght be not scau[n]t able to beare the warre of iii Irishemen greate capitaynes next adioynny[n]g to them in any waye

It[e]m ther be in the saide lande fyve portions called kvyeghes[46] and hath ben severed and devided of olde tyme, whiche ben called Leynester both Mowesters (Desemonde and Tomonde) Connaght and Ullester. ffyrste I shall speake of Leynester[47]

It[e]m Mac Morrowghe is prynce and lorde of Leynester,[48] and he and his kynnesmen of his name wylbe ii^c men on horsbacke well harneysed a battaylle of galloglas and iii^c kierne

It[e]m O Bryne is lorde of hys cou[n]tree[49] and wylbe lx horsmen a battayll gallowglas and viii^{xx} kierne

It[e]m O Toohyll is lorde of Ffercullyn and Imayll[50] and wylbe xxiiii horsmen and lxxx kierne

It[e]m Arte mac Donoghe is lorde of Ikynsele[51] and wylbe xvi horsmen and lx kierne

It[e]m Redmonde mac Shyane[52] is lorde of Gowyllranell and wulbe viii horsemen and xl kierne

It[e]m O Morrovghe is lorde of Iphelyme[53] and wylbe xvi horsemen and xl kierne

It[e]m O Novlane is lorde of Ffoghwtye[54] and wylbe xii horsmen and xx^{ti} kierne

It[e]m O Brenane is lorde of Idowghe[55] and wylbe xl kierne

It[e]m O Moore is lorde of Leyse[56] and wylbe lx horsmen and a battayll and ii^c kiearne

---

46 From the Irish, *cúige*, literally a fifth part of Ireland.
47 For each lord named below we have attempted to provide an English rendering of their surname, and the lordship over which they ruled, which is more recognizable to the modern reader.
48 Mac Murrough, lord of Leinster.   49 O'Byrne, lord of Crebranagh.
50 O'Toole, lord of Fercullen.
51 Art MacDonogh MacMurrough, lord of Hy Kinsellagh.
52 Redmund MacShane O'Byrne, lord of Culraynell.
53 O'Murrough, lord of Ifelymye.   54 O'Nolan, lord of Forth.
55 O'Brennan, lord of Odogh.   56 O'More, lord of Leix.

It[e]m O Riane is lorde of his cou[n]tree[57] and wylbe xii horsmen & xxiiii
kiearne

It[e]m Mac Guyllepatricke is lorde of Osserie[58] and wylbe xl horsmen a battaylle
and lx kiearne

It[e]m Mac Morishe is lorde of Ieery[59] and wylbe syx horsemen and xxiiii
kiearne

It[e]m O Doviune is lorde of Ireegan[60] and wylbe viii horsmen and ii[c] kiearne

It[e]m O Dempcye is lorde of Klynvallyre[61] and wilbe xxiiii horsmen & i[c]
kiearne

It[e]m O Conno[r] is lorde of Opallye[62] and wylbe xl horsemen and a battayll and
ii[c] kiearne

Sum[m]a horsemen v[c] xxvi [526]
Sum[m]a gallogasse v battailles [5]
Sum[m]a kiearnes i[m] v[c] xiii[th] [1,513][63]

It[e]m also ther is in Leynester the coun[n]tie of Wexforde and wylbe lx horsmen and ii[c] kiearne and they be so envyrouned wythe Irishemen that they can
not au[n]swere the kynges deputie nether helpe hym and they be not of power
to keepe themselfes from their ennemies. And ther is nothyng saweth them but
they paye yerelye trybutes to Irishemen {*end fo. 5v*}

It[e]m ther is in Leynester beforesaide the countie of Kylkenye wherin parte of
the Buttlers dwelleth and they wylbe lxxx horsmen ii battaylles and ii[c] kiearne
and they be so envyrou[n]ed with Irishemen, and yerelye debate betuxte them
and the ['Geraldynes' *is crossed through*] awarre of the Geraldynes of Mownster
that scantly thei can kepe themselfes, so as lytle they can helpe the kynges
deputie

It[e]m ther is in Leynester afforsaide a parte of the coun[n]tie Catherlaghe, w[ch]
therle of Kyldare dyde conquere on Irishemen and but latelye inhabyted and
they be so sett aboute with Irishe men that without ayde of the kynges deputye
they can not be saved ne kepte

Desmonde

It[e]m Mac Charthy more is prynce and lorde of that portion[64] and wylbe of his
own[n]e name and kynne xl horsmen ii battailles and ii[m] kierne

---

57 O'Ryan.
58 MacGillapatrick, lord of Ossory.
59 MacMorish O'Connor, lord of Irry.
60 O'Dunne, lord of Iregan.
61 O'Dempsey, lord of Clanmaliere.
62 O'Connor, lord of Offaly.
63 The given sum does not tally: the number of kerne should be 1,548.
64 MacCarthy More.

It[e]m Mac Chartie revghe is lorde of Carrebre[65] and wylbe lx horsemen a battaylle and ii[m] kierne

It[e]m Donoghoe oowge mac Chartie is lorde of Ahallye[66] and wylbe xxiiii horseman a battayll and ii[c] kiearne

It[e]m Mac Teyge mac Cormeghe is lorde is [sic] Mowscrye[67] and wylbe xl horsemen a battayll and ii[c] kiearne

It[e]m O Kiewe is lorde of his cou[n]treye[68] and wylbe xii horsmen and i[c] kiearne

It[e]m O Crowlye is lorde of his cou[n]treye[69] and wylbe viii horsemen and lx kiearne

It[e]m O Downeghvan is lorde of his cou[n]treye[70] and wylbe vi horsmen & lx kiearne

It[e]m O Dryscoylle is lorde of Cortlaghe and Ballytymore[71] and wylbe vi horsemen and ii[c] kierne and they use longe galleys

It[e]m O Mahonne is lorde of Unheraghe[72] and wylbe xvi horsmen & vi[xx] kierne

It[e]m O Solyvan is lorde of Heraghe beare and Bentrye[73] wylbe xvi horsmen and ii[c] kierne

It[e]m O Donoghowe Moore is lorde of Loghleene[74] and wylbe xii horsme[n] & ii[c] kierne

It[e]m O Donoghowe Glanslyghe[75] wylbe vi horsemen and lx kierne

It[e]m Mac Gyllyroddye is lorde of his contreye[76] and wylbe xl kiearne

It[e]m Conogho[r] Kierye[77] wylbe xxiiii horsemen and vi[x] kierne

It[e]m a septe of the Bryenes dwelleth at the mano[ir] of Carrigghogenlen[78] and ther aboute and wylbe xx[ti] horsemen and lx kiearne

It[e]m an other parte of that bloude dwelleth at Haerrelaghe[79] and wylbe viii[th] horsemen and xxiiii kierne

It[e]m more of them dwelleth in the Combraghes[80] and wylbe vi horsemen and xxiiii kierne

---

65 MacCarthy Reagh, lord of Carbery.
66 Donough Oge MacCarthy, lord of Duhallow.
67 MacTeige MacCormac (MacCarthy), lord of Muskerry.
68 O'Keefe.   69 O'Crowley.
70 O'Donovan.   71 O'Driscoll, lord of Baltimore.
72 O'Mahony, lord of Fonn Iartharach.
73 O'Sullivan, lord of Kenmare and Bantry.
74 O'Donoghue More, lord of Lough Lene.
75 O'Donoghue Glenflesk.   76 MacGillycuddy.
77 O'Connor Kerry.   78 O'Briens of Carrigogunnell.
79 O'Briens of Aherlow.
80 O'Briens of the Comeragh Mountains.

Sum[m]a horsemen iii^c iiii horsemen[n] {304}[81]
Sum[m]a gallogasse v battaylles {5}
Sum[m]a kiearnes v^m vi^c lxviiith {5,668}[82] {*end fo. 6*}

It[e]m ther is in the saide Mounster therle of Desmonde and his kynnesmen lordes and servau[n]tes and hath of landes unde^r his domynion and lordshipp vi^{xx} myles and wylbe iiii^c horsmen viiith battaylles gallowglas a battaill of crosbowmen and go[n]n[er]es and iii^m kierne and his cou[n]treis ben so longe and so envyrou[n]ed with Irishe men and for the more parte ever at warre with his kynnesmen and hattethe the kynges lawes, so as he geveth no ayde ne assistance to the lorde deputie

It[e]m ther is also in that Mounster a parte of the Bourkes called the Bourken countreye[83] and wylbe xxiiii horsemen on horsbacke a battayll and ii^c kierne and they be so envyroned with Irishmen and dyssevered themselfes that they can not helpe ['yor' *is crossed through*] the deputie

It[e]m ther is ther also the countie of Typp[er]rarie wher parte of the Butlers dwelleth and wylbe iii^{xx} horsemen ii battaylles and ii^c kierne and they ben severed in three bandes and porcions and eache of them hateth thother and ben ennemyes so as they can not helpe the lorde deputie, and also they be sett nyghe Irishemen whiche ben stronge and ben their daily en[n]emyes

Thomonde

It[e]m O Bryen is lorde of that porcyon[84] and wylbe ii^c horsemen and ii battayls gallowes and v^c kierne
It[e]m Mac Nemarrye is lorde of Clynzellan[85] and wylbe ii^c horsemen and a battayle of gallowglas and vi^c kierne
It[e]m Mac Mahoune is lorde of Corkewasknye[86] and wylbe xx^{tie} horsemen & lx kierne
It[e]m O Conno^r is lorde of Corkenray[87] and wilbe xxiiii horsmen and i^c kierne
It[e]m O Daa is lorde of Iferraghe[88] and wylbe viii horsmen and xxiiii kierne
It[e]m O Logheryn is lorde of Borryn[89] and wilbe xx horsmen and i^c kierne

---

81 The sum here does not tally: the number should be 316 horse.
82 The sum here does not tally: the number should be 5,608 kerne.
83 The baronies of Clanwilliam in Tipperary and Limerick.
84 O'Brien.
85 MacNamara, lord of Clancullen.
86 MacMahon, lord of Corca Baiscinn.
87 O'Connor, lord of Corcomroe.
88 O'Dea, lord of Ifearmaic.
89 O'Loghlen, lord of Burren.

It[e]m Mac Bryenarrhye of the Breynes is lorde of Arrye[90] and wylbe xl horsemen a battayll of gallowglas and an c kierne

It[e]m O Molryan is lorde of Hoenye[91] and wylbe xxiiii horsmen and i[c] kierne

It[e]m Mac Bryen a septe of the Bryenes is lorde of Iconnaghe[92] and wylbe xvi horsemen and xl kyearne

It[e]m Mac Teyge is lorde of one of the Ormondes[93] and wylbe xxiiii horsmen and lx kierne

It[e]m O Kynnedye is lorde of thother Ormonde[94] and wylbe lx horsemen a battayll and vi[xx] kierne

It[e]m O Kearroule is lorde of Elye[95] and wilbe iiii[xx] horsmen a battayll & viii[xx] kierne

It[e]m O Maghyr is lorde of Ikyrrye[96] and wylbe xvi horsmen and i[c] kierne

It[e]m O Dwyre is lorde of Kylnemanaghe[97] and wylbe xii horseme[n] and i[c] kierne

It[e]m Mac Teyge M[c] Phelypp is lorde of Kyllenalongorte[98] and wylbe vi horsemen and xl kierne {*end fo. 6v*}

Sum[m]a horsemen vii[c] l {750}
Sum[m]a gallowglas vi battailles {6}
Sum[m]a kierne ii[m] i[c] xliiii {2,144}[99]

Connaght

It[e]m O Con[n]ogho[r] is prynce and lorde[100] of that porcyon and wylbe of his name and kynne vi[xx] horsemen ii battaylles gallowglas and iii[c] kierne they ben severed and ennemyes

It[e]m O Kiellye of Imanny is lorde[101] and wylbe ii[c] horsmen ii battaylles and iiii[c] kierne

It[e]m O Fflahertye is lorde of Yarckonnagh[102] and wylbe xiiii horsemen & iii[c] kierne

It[e]m O Mailye is lorde of Owylemale[103] and wylbe xvi horsemen and ii[c] kierne and used longe galleyes

90 Mac-I-Brien, lord of Arra.   91 O'Mulryan, lord of Owney.
92 MacBrien, lord of Coonagh.   93 MacTeige, lord of Ormond.
94 O'Kennedy, lord of (Lower) Ormond.
95 O'Carroll, lord of Ely.   96 O'Meagher, lord of Ikerrin.
97 O'Dwyer, lord of Kilnamanagh.
98 This may refer to O'Fogarty.
99 The sum here does not tally: the number should be 2,204 kerne.
100 O'Connor.   101 O'Kelly, lord of Hy Many.
102 O'Flaherty, lord of Iar-Connacht.
103 O'Malley, lord of Owles.

It[e]m O Garee is lorde of Kowlowyne[104] and wylbe xiiii horsmen & i[c] kierne

It[e]m O Harye bwye is lorde of Lynee[105] and wilbe vi horsemen & iii[c] kierne

It[e]m O Dowde is lorde of Terhereghemoy[106] and wylbe xx horsmen & iii[xx] kierne

It[e]m O Shaghenysse is lorde of Kynnalehe[107] and wilbe xii horsmen & xl kierne

It[e]m O Maddey is lorde of Shylnauneghe[108] and wylbe xiiii horsemen & vi[xx] kierne

It[e]m Mac Donoghe is lorde of Tryveris[109] and wylbe xl horsmen a battayll gallowglas and viii[xx] kierne

It[e]m Mac Dermothe is lorde of Moilorge[110] and wylbe xl horsmen a battayll & ii[c] kierne

It[e]m Mac Mawni Ikongho[r] is lorde of Carrbre[111] and wylbe xl horsmen a battayll and i[c] kierne

It[e]m O Rorke is lorde of one of the Brenese[112] and wilbe xl horsemen a battayll and iii[c] kierne

It[e]m Magranell is lorde of Montyrolishe[113] and wylbe viii horsmen & iii[c] kierne

It[e]m Magaurean is lorde of Tallyagha[114] and wylbe vi horsmen and ii[c] kierne

It[e]m M[c] Kyrnane is lorde of Tallaghkengho[r][115] & wilbe vi horsmen & ii[c] kierne

It[e]m O Ffaralle is lorde of the Annall[116] and wylbe iii[xx] horsmen a battaylle and iii[c] kierne and be severed and ennemyes

It[e]m O Raghley is lorde of thother Brenee[117] & wilbe iii[xx] horsmen a battayll and iiii[c] kyearne

English man.

Sum[m]a horsemen viii[c] lxviii[th] {868}[118]

Sum[m]a gallowglas x battailles {10}

Sum[m]a kierne iii[m] vii[c] xl {3,740}[119]

It[em] Mac Wylliame Bourke is lorde of Clynrykarde[120] in that porcyon of Connaght and wylbe vi[xx] horsmen ii battaylles & iii[c] kierne, and now severed

---

104 O'Gara, lord of Coolavin.   105 O'Hara Boy, lord of Leyny.

106 O'Dowd, lord of Tireragh. This entry is omitted from the copy in the British Library.

107 O'Shaughnessy, lord of Kinelea.   108 O'Madden, lord of Silanchia.

109 MacDonagh, lord of Tiraghrill.   110 MacDermot, lord of Moylurg.

111 MacManus O'Connor (O'Connor Sligo), lord of Carbury.

112 O'Rourke, lord of (west) Brefny.   113 MacRannell, lord of Munterolis.

114 Magauran, lord of Tullyhaw.

115 MacKiernan, lord of Tullyhunco.

116 O'Farrell, lord of Annaly.   117 O'Reilly, lord of (east) Brefny.

118 The sum here does not tally: the numbers given here amount to 716 horse.

119 The sum here does not tally: the numbers given here amount to 3,980 kerne.

120 MacWilliam Upper [Uachtar], lord of Clanrickard.

It[em] Mac Wylliame Bourke called Mac Wylliame eghteraghe is lorde of Kenykekelye[121] and wilbe ii[c] horsmen iii battaylles and iii[c] kierne

It[em] the lorde Bremyngham is lorde of Konnykedonuere[122] and wylbe xiiii horsemen and xl kierne

It[e]m Nangle is lorde of Clyncostele[123] and wylbe xii horsemen and xl kierne

{end fo. 7}

It[e]m M[c] Shiertane called depetur is lorde of Gallyn[124] and wilbe xii horsmen & iii[xx] kierne

It[e]m M[c] Kemylee is lorde of Kera[125] and wilbe vi[xx] kierne

It[e]m Mac Davye of the Bourkes is lorde of Clynkene[126] & wilbe xxiiii horsmen & xl kierne

It[e]m Mac Phelypbyne Bourke is lorde Oyell[127] & wylbe xl kierne

It[e]m bothe the saide lordes Bourkes called either of them M[c] Wylliame be mortall ennemyes and the saide Irishemen be severed with them, and with the Irishmen in bandes and ben all no better condicyons then Irishmen and weareth their habytes and ben so frended and allyed with them that thei take their parte agaynst the kynges subiectes and hateth the kynges lawes and geveth no ayde ne assistance to his deputie

Ullester

It[e]m O Neille is prince and lorde[128] of that porcyon and wilbe of his bloude and kynnesmen ii[c] horsmen iii battaylles and iii[c] kierne

It[e]m Conn mac Hue bwye is lorde of Clanybwy[129] and wilbe ii[c] horsmen iii battaylles and ii[c] kierne

It[e]m O Kahane is lorde of Iraghe Ikahane[130] and wilbe iii[xx] horseme[n] a battayll and i[c] kierne

It[e]m M[c] Honee is lorde of the Glynns[131] and wilbe xx horsmen and i[c] kierne

It[e]m M[c] Hulme is lorde of the Rute[132] and wylbe xx horsmen and i[c] kierne

---

121 MacWilliam Lower [Íochtar]. This MacWilliam is referred to as lord of 'Connyke Ghowle' in the 'State of Ireland and plan for its reformation': *SP Hen. VIII*, ii, p. 7.

122 Bermingham, lord of Conmaicne of Dunmore.

123 Nangle, lord of Clan Costello.

124 MacJordan, originally De Exeter, lord of Gallen.

125 MacAveely, originally Staunton, lord of Carra.

126 MacDavy Burke, lord of Clanconway.

127 MacPhilbin Burke, lord of Oyell.

128 O'Neill.

129 Conn MacHugh Boy O'Neill, lord of Clandeboy.

130 O'Cahan, lord of Irraght Ichan.

131 MacEoin, lord of the Glens.

132 MacQuillan, lord of the Route.

It[e]m Mc Gunnesse is lorde of Iveaghe[133] and wylbe iii^{xx} horsmen a battayll & ii^c kierne

It[em] Mc Kartane is lorde of Kynnalertye[134] and wilbe vi horsmen and iii^{xx} kierne

It[e]m O Hawlene is lorde of Orrey[135] and wylbe xxiiii horsmen and iii^{xx} kierne

It[em] Mac Mahone is lorde of Ffernye[136] and wylbe xl horsmen a battayll and iii^c kierne

It[em] Macgwyre is lorde of Ffermannaghe[137] and wilbe xl horsmen and a bat-taylle and iii^c kierne

It[e]m Mc Kynna is lorde of the Trughys[138] and wylbe x horsmen and xl kierne

It[e]m Mc Kawell is lorde of Kynnalarde[139] and wylbe viii horsemen and xl kierne

It[e]m O Donell is lorde of Tyrkonyll[140] and wilbe i^c horsemen iiii battaylles and iii^c kierne

It[e]m in this porcyon dwelleth Sawaghe an Englishman[141] and dwelleth in the Arde and wylbe xxiii horsmen a battayll and iii^{xx} kierne. And he is so environed with Irishmen that he is nerehande expulsed out of his landes

Sum[m]a horsemen viii^c xi {811}

. Sum[m]a gallowglas xv battailles {15}

Sum[m]a kierne ii^m i^c lx {2,160}

It[e]m in Mythe whiche is oone of the iiii shires that obeyeth the kynges lawes ther ben theis many Irishemen as here ensueth

It[e]m O Mollaghlyn called hymselfe prynce of Mythe and is lorde of Clynkeneon[142] and wylbe xxiiii horsemen and i^c kierne {*end fo. 7v*}

It[e]m O Molmoy is lorde of Ffercall[143] and wilbe xx horsmen and i^c kierne

It[e]m Maggoghegan is lorde is lorde [*sic*] of Kynnaliaghe[144] and wilbe xxiiii horsmen and iiii^{xx} kierne

It[e]m Synnagh is lorde of Montyrhagan[145] and wilbe vi horsme[n] and xl kierne

It[e]m Macgawbee is lorde of Kalrye[146] and wilbe iiii horsmen and xxiiii kierne

It[e]m O Brynne is lorde of Brahone[147] and wilbe iii^{xx} kierne

It[e]m Mac Koghlan is lorde of Doltyn[148] and wylbe viii horsmen[n] and vi^{xx} kierne

133 Magennis, lord of Iveagh.   134 MacCartan, lord of Kinelarty.
135 O'Hanlon, lord of Oriel.   136 MacMahon, lord of Farney.
137 Maguire, lord of Fermanagh.   138 MacKenna, lord of Truagh.
139 MacCawell, lord of Kinel-Farry. 140 O'Donnell, lord of Tyrconnell.
141 Savage.   142 O'Melaghlin, lord of Clonlonan.
143 O'Molmoy (O'Molloy), lord of Fircal.
144 Mageoghegan, lord of Kineleagh.
145 Fox (Sionnach), lord of Monthycagan.
146 Magawly, lord of Calrige.   147 O'Breen, lord of Brawney.
148 MacCoughlin, lord of Delvin.

Handwritten margin notes (top left): Points / Just tell these people / what they / are like

Sum[m]a horsmen lxxxvi {86}
Sum[m]a kierne v^c xxiiii {524}

1 It[e]m a battayll of gallowglas ben iii^{xx} or iiii^{xx} harneysed men on foote with a certayne weapon called a sparre and everie gallowglas hath a knave to beare his harneys and some hath speares and some hath bowes

2 It[e]m everie kyernaghe hath a bowe a shieve or three speares called [dar]tes and a swearde and a skyene and ben without any harneys and everie ii kierne hath a ladde to beare their gere

3 It[e]m everie horsman hath ii horses some iii horses a iacke well harneysed for the more parte, a swearde a skyen a greate speare and a darte

4 It[e]m everie horse hath his knawe [knave], and their beste horse shalbe alway leade and one of his knawes ryde alwaye and beare his harneys and speares if he have harneys

5 It[e]m the forsaide men for the more parte ben goode and hardye men of warre and lyve full hardely and can suffre great myserie and payne and thei wyll ventyr them verye well on their ennemyes when thei see their tyme and thei can wake well by nyght and ben as goode men of warre in the nyght as ben men of other landes in the daye light

6 It[e]m all the forsaide Irishmen hateth the kynges lawes and s[u]biectes mortally and what gyftes is geven them and what othes they make unto us for their trouthe, when thei see their advauntage thei then do the beste they can on the kynges subiectes to their destruction

7 It[e]m thei use many wayes to be powerable and stronge all their tenau[n]tes and servau[n]tes goodes thei take it when thei nede as their p[ro]pre goodes

Handwritten margin note: ?des. Use in essay.

8 It[e]m when any of the lordes of the forsaide cou[n]treis dye, then is the strongest and best man in all that cou[n]treye then made lorde, and the best and wysest capytayne and ['falsest' *is crossed through*] seldome is any of their heires lordes successyve after their father

9 It[e]m moreover thies use many women besydes [their?] wyfes and p[ro]create many children and everie of their sonnes children and all their {*end fo. 8*} fathers p[ro]pre landes ['enheritance' *is written above the line*] purchase and fermes shalbe indifferentlye devided betuxte them everie of them in lyke muche ^{+ wms}

[88]

10 It[e]m also all their men children shall lerne to be a man of warre fro xvi yere
of adge forthe and shall dailye use the feates of the same

11 It[e]m also they have meanes to be stronge, all the benefyces of their
cou[n]treis shalbe geven to the saide lordes sonnes and p[ro]vided from Rome,
thoughe one of them scau[n]te can his pater noster, and they spende the
p[ro]fyites of the same on their kynnesmen to make them well apparoulled to
the warre agaynste us Englishemen

12. It[e]m God do p[ro]vide for the kynges subiectes here that he sendeth dailye
dissencions amonge the saide Irishemen, so as more then three of the saide capitaynes loveth not other and make mortall warre dailye on thother so as thei
cannot loke on us the kynges subiectes ne p[er]ceyve our debylite ne strenghte

Havens of this lande of Irelande

Loghsonell
The Banne
Wolderfrythe
Cragfergus
Strangforde
Ardeglasse
Logheven
Karlyngforde
Kilkele
Dundalke
Kyleloghir
Droghedaa
Holmepatricque
Rushe
Malahide
Howth
Dublyne
Dalkee
Wycklowe
Arcklowe
Wexforde
Waterforde
Downgarvan
Yowghyll

Corcke tomabegge
Kynsale
Kierye
Rosse Iller
Dorrye
Ballytymore
Downnenore
Downesheade
Downneslonnge
Arttannan
Croghan
Downbwye
Ballyneskyllyge
Dangyn Iyons
Tralye
Shenyn
Cassane
Kylnewyne
Lymericke
Innyskace
Beloclem
Aryne Neweyve
Glanenaghe
Ballyweyham

Rynwarre
Dowrys
Weran
Roskam
Galway
Kylly[n]kyllye
Innesbosyn
Burske
Bellaclare
Rathsylbene
Byerwers oure
Durwers zare
Ardue makow
Rosbare
Kylgholyn
Ballalee
Rabran
Strone
Burwers nowe
Zaltra
Kalbaly
Ardcuacke
Ardcowse
Slygaghe {*end fo. 8v*}

[Sir William Darcy's articles to the King's council]

Here ensueth such artycles as S[r] Wylliame Darcye knyghte put in before the kynges counsell of Inglande at Grenewyche the xxiii daye of June the vii[th] yere of the raigne of kynge Henrye theight[149]

1 It[e]m coyne and lyveraye and dailye coyne borne

2 It[e]m wylfull warre made by the kynges deputie wythout thassent of the lordes and kynges counsell

3 It[e]m cartyng cariages and other unlawfull imposicions sett on the kynges subiectes

4 It[e]m the lordes and gentlemen fallyng to Irishe ordre and Irishe habytes

5 It[e]m maryages and nowrishynges dailye makyng with the kynges Irishe rebelles

6 It[e]m cuddyes called nyght sowpers[150]

The causes of the sore dekaye of the kynges subiectes of his lande of Irelande

1 It[e]m Jeames erle of Desmonde graundfather to therle that nowe is and it [lit]tle above L wynters sythens he deyed[151] and he was the fyrste man that ever put coyne and lyverie on the kynges subiectes. There is the counties of Waterforde Corke Kierye and Lym[er]ycke wherin dwelled dyverse lordes knyghtes esquyers and gentlemen and ware the Englishe habyte and kepte goode Englishe ordre and rule and the kynges lawes ther well obeyed and the kynge had in the saide iiii shyres then above ii[m] markes a yere of landes rentes and custcomes and the forsaide earle had but one parte of one of the saide iiii shyres and before he deyed he put by the saide extorcyon of coyne and lyverye the saide iiii shyres under hym and his heires, so as nowe the kynges lawes be not used the kynge ne his deputie not obeyed, the kynge have lost his rentes and revenues the lordes and gentlemen of the same be in no better case then the wylde Irishe, for thei use Irishe habyte and Irishe tongue and where the saide erle had not of yerclyc rentes then, past v[c] libr[e] a yere nowe his heires as they receave, everie thynge accompted may dyspende x[m] libr[e] a yere

2 It[e]m the cou[n]ties of Kylkenye and Typp[er]arie were Englishe and kepte the Englishe order and rule and the kynges lawes obeyed ther wythin this L yeres and ther dwelled dyverse knyghtes esquyers and gentlemen and ware the

---

149   23 June 1515.

150   *Cuid Oíche*, literally a night's portion, was the hospitality that a lord and his retinue were entitled to claim from his inferiors.

151   James FitzGerald Fitzgerald, sixth earl of Desmond, died in 1462; his grandson, Maurice FitzThomas Fitzgerald (*d.*1520), the ninth earl, was earl when Darcy's articles were drawn up.

Englishe habyte and kepte goode ordre, and the Butlers dwellyng in the saide ii shieres and their seyng the late demeano^r of the forsaide erle of Desmonde and of his conqueste then thei began the same ordre of coyne and lyverie and used it sythens, so as by the same thei have put thes ii shires clerelye under their rule and the kynges lawes be not obeyed and all the kynges subiectes ben in no bett[er] case then the wylde Irishe

3 It[e]m therle of Ullester mought dispend a year in the lande above xxx^m markes and had fyve shyres besydes dyvers lordeshippes and man[n]ers as the {*end fo. 9*} wryter hereof can shewe and declare thies ben the saide fyve shires the counties of Towlroch An[n]tryme Cragfergus Newtoune and Lekale and the last erle called Wylliame had but one doughtyre she was maryed to Leonell duke of Clarence and they had but one doughter was maryed to therle of Marche^{152} and so fowrthe to the howse of Yorcke and thies forsaide greate estates had so moche landes in the this [sic] realme of Englande and tymes vexed and trowbled that h[e] toke no hede to the forsaide erledome ne put kepyng on the same so as by that meanes Irishemen hath near hande conquered the saide fyve shyres

4 It[e]m the iiii shyres ther whiche shoulde obeye the kynges lawes called Mythe, Lowthe, Dublyn and Kyldare the forsaide abhomynable ordre of coyne and lyverie was began on within lytle above L yeares by Thomas erle of Desmonde, sonne to the forsaide Jeames; and he was then the kynges deputie ffor the whiche ordre and presidence he was put to execution and then the saide ordre shortelye began and renued within this xxx^{ti} yeres bene cuddies carttyng cariages io^{r}neyes and other imposicions farre hostynges and io^{r}neyes and wylfull warre began synce that tyme the deputies wyves goo to cuddyes and put coyne and liverie ['at their plea' *is crossed through*] in all where. Many of his kynnesmen do put coyne and make wylfull warre at their pleasure and do styrre greate warre that now by the forsaide extorte meanes and presidentes all the kynges subiectes of the saide foure shyres be nerehande Irishe and weare their habyte and used their tongue, so as they are cleane goone and decayed and ther is not viiith of the lordes knyghtes esquyers and gentlemen of the saide iiii shires but ben in debte and their landes be made waste and wythout briefe remedye be had thei must sell their landes other leave them and [depar]te unto some other landes^{153}

5 *It[e]m in many paraches that men myght fynde in some vi^{xx} bowes and some i^c wy[nches?] [.....]^{154} the saide season of xxx yeres [now]e is there not one bowe and in the substance of the saide iiii shyres goode housbondmen they ware thEnglishe habyte and kepte goode Englishe ordre and rule and lordes and gentlemen in lykewyse, nowe*

<hr/>

152 See below, p. 97.

153 The better-known version of these articles in LPL, MS 635, fos 185–7, entitled the 'Decay of Ireland' (*Calendar of Carew MSS*, i, pp 6–8), is an Elizabethan copy and ends here.

154 Parts of the right-hand edge of this folio are damaged: some words are lost altogether, while others are now illegible.

scau[n]tlye shall [have?] iiii gownes worne in a paroche and in many no gownes and speke all the Irishe tongue and thoone halfe of the saide foure shyres obeyed not the kynges lawes and ben worse then they were wythin the saide xxx^{ti} yeres by xl thowsande markes

6 It[e]m ii thowsande markes wyll not repayre the kynges castelles and maners ther

7 It[e]m in the saide foure shyres the kynges revenues ther were not so goode to [.....] this iii^{xx} yere as they be thes xxiiii yeres and notwythstandyng all the forsaide ungracyous ordre and presiden[n]ce ben dailye used

8 It[e]m who dothe put or use coyne and lyverie on the kynges subiectes other arysere is made highe treason by authorytie of parlyament in that lande, and for[.....]se they be not put in execution no man regardeth them

Artycles for the reformation of Irelande

1 That the deputie of the lande of Irelande alway be an erle or some noble man of [Eng?] lande the Chann[celor] a[.....] lorde of Englande, the theasaurer a wyknyght[155] B[.....] and the iii chief [jud]ges and m[aste][r] of the rowles to be men of England

It[e]m {*end fo. 9v*}[156]

A betaghe towne[157] contaigneth ix[c] lx {960} acres arrable lande or tyllynglande besydes woddes moores and pastures & etc
Irelande is devided in porcions, that is to say Ulester Leynester both the Mownesters (Desmonde and Thomonde), and then Connaght
The saide Ullester contaigneth xxxv {35} cantredes whiche is a M & L {1,050} betaghtownes[158]
Leynester contaigneth xxxi {31} cantredes whiche is a ix[c] xxx {930} betaghtownes
Desmonde contaigneth xxxv {35} cantredres w[ch] is a M & L {1,050} betaghtownes
Thomonde contayneth xxxv {35} cantredes whiche is a M & L {1,050} betaightownes

155 This may be a mistake for viscount, or perhaps a 'wyse knight'.
156 The following folio, or folios, is lost. What immediately follows here is headed in other documents 'The reveniwes of Irelande': see, for example, TNA, SP 63/214, fo. 8.
157 A betagh, from the Irish *biatach* – one who gives food – was an unfree (and almost invariably Irish) tenant of equivalent status in the late medieval period to an English villein. As noted above, a ballybetagh, or ballibetagh, was derived from *baile biatach*, that is a 'food, or victualler's, town'. Writing in 1607 to Robert Cecil, the earl of Salisbury, concerning the state of Ireland, John Davies explained: 'every ballibetagh, which signifieth, in the Irish tongue, a town able to maintain hospitality, containeth sixteen taths; every tath containeth three-score English acres or thereabouts: so as every ballibetagh containeth nine hundred and sixty acres': *Historical tracts: by Sir John Davies*, p. 242.
158 A ballybetagh was thus a thirtieth part of a cantred, or a *triocha céad* in Irish.

Connaght contaigneth xxx {30} cantredes whiche is ix^c {900} betaghtownes
Both Breynes that is to saye Breyne Iroyrke and Breynes Yreyle[159] were not accompted with Connaght at that tyme whiche doth contaigne iii^c {300} betaghetownes
Mydthe contaigneth xviiith {18} cantredres wch is v^c and xl {540} betaghtownes and Mydth was at that tyme fro the wat[er] of alesse to the wat[er] of down-dongen

S[u]m[m]a totalis the betaghtownes of Ireland v^m ix^c xx^{tie} {5,920}[160]

The forsaide description and dyvision was made longe before thincarnacon of Christe,[161] so as sythens woddes be fallen and cast downe and tyllynglande ther of made the whiche is not comp[re]hended in the saide description
The kynges grace receyvyng one penye out of everie acree of tyllyng lande of subsydie yerelye wyll come to the sum[m]e of xxiii^m & ix^c libr[e]
All the dignyties and benefyces of this lande to pay the kynges grace of subsydie by the yere of x yeres xiid out of everie libr[e] whiche theye may dispende of sp[irit]uall possessions by the yere. S[u]ma
The sp[irit]ualtie of the iiii obedyent shyres hath payed of yerely subsydie hith-erto out of everie marcke taxed xiid
The archebysshes of this lande to be bou[n]de to levye the forsaide subsydie in this fourme followyng[:] their suffregans to make collectours under them in their dioceses and they to be [ac]comptable to ['yor' *is crossed through*] the kynges offi-cers yerelye and if thei lacke power to levye the same the lorde lieutenau[n]t and armye to mantaygne them to levye the same
Everie ploughlande whiche shoulde be but vi^{xx} acres tyllyng lande was ceassed vi*s* viii*d* of subsydie in Edwarde the iii^{des} dayes whiche is above a penye an acre and everie ploughlande within the iiii obedyent shyres beareth nowe yerelye above i*d* ob the acree, the kinges chiefe rentes reserved of all his grau[n]tes to be made of his conquestes lyke as affore
The feefermes and customes of all cyties and townes of this lande and like cus-tomes to be receyved as is receyved in Dublyng and Droghedaa
All the forsaide matters to be enacted in the fyrste parlyame[n]t holden [.....]nde
{*end fo. 10*}
The rentes and profyttes of the kinges mano^{irs} and landes here by the yere, his esthate and casualties by the yere

159   That is, Breifne O'Rourke and Breifne O'Reilly. These lordships were shired as Leitrim and Cavan, respectively, during Elizabeth's reign.
160   The number of betaghtowns listed here adds up to 5,820.
161   In the later, Elizabethan, copies this section reads, and concludes, 'before the English mens commynge wherefore nowe it is more, one pennye of ev[er]y acre of land yearely amoun-teth the sume of 24900li.': see above, p. 50.

It[e]m I dyde delyver a boke of the kyngs mano^{rs} and landes to his co[m]mys-sion[er]s at their beying here[162] let the same be kepte for if I were goen the same woulde not be lyghtlye gotten agayne

The forsaide boke was sende to the kynge with the chiefe justyce of the kynges benche[163] of Irelande in the xviiith day of September anno x[v?] Henrici octavi

---

162   Three royal commissioners – Dr James Denton, Sir Ralph Egerton and Sir Anthony Fitzherbert – visited Ireland (June–Aug. 1524) to compose differences between the earls of Kildare and Ormond and to reform government in the English Pale.

163   Patrick Bermingham (c.1460–1532) was appointed chief justice of the king's bench, 2 Dec. 1513.

The petygrewe of the Bourkes

Wylliame Aldelmi filis otherwyse called Aldelmson had yssue Richarde and Richarde whiche Richarde the form[er] had yssue Waltier fyrste erle of Ullester and Wylliame.[164] the saide Waltier had yssue Richarde called Redde erle which had yssue Johne the saide Johne had yssue Wylliame called erle donne and was kylled by his servauntes the theegaundvyles by treason[165] whiche Wylliame had yssue Elysabeth whiche was maryed to Leonell second sone to Edwarde the iiide and the saide Leonell had yssue Phylippa maryed to Roger erle of marche whiche had yssue Edmonde and he had yssue Ellyano[r] whiche was maryed to the erle of Cambrydge whiche had yssue Richarde duke of Yorcke father to kynge Edwarde the fourthe[166]

Mac Wylliame Bourkes petygrewe

The forsaide Wylliame brother to the erle Walthier had yssue S[r] Wylliame whiche had yssue Edmonde albunaghc and he had yssue Thomas whiche had yssue Waltier, Edmonde, Thomas Shane and Richarde. Of these iiii all the best men of Konnylkonly ben come[167]

---

164 William FitzAdelm Burke (d.1206) was the first lord of Connacht. He had three sons: Richard (the second Richard in the text is a mistake), Hubert and William. The oldest, the Richard named here, died in 1243. He was father to Walter, first earl of Ulster (d.1271), Richard (d.1248) – he may account for the confusion surrounding the second Richard in the text – and William (d.1270). The descendants of this William Burke are sketched in the following paragraph.

165 Richard Burke (c.1259–1326), second earl of Ulster and lord of Connacht, referred to by the Irish annalists as 'an t-iarla ruadh' [the red earl]. His second son, John de Burgh (d.1313), married Elizabeth de Clare (d.1360) – their son William Burke (d.1333) was third earl of Ulster, referred to here as 'erle donne' [the brown earl]. He was murdered by his own servants, among whom the Mandevilles (rendered 'theegaundvyles' here) were prominent.

166 William Burke's heir Elizabeth (d.1363) married Lionel of Clarence (1338–68), the son of Edward III. They too left a single female heir, Phillippa (d.1378), who married Edmund Mortimer (III) (1352–81), third earl of March. The reference to Phillipa marrying Roger earl of March is incorrect: Roger (1374–98), fourth earl of March, was Phillipa's son. He, in fact, married Eleanor Holland, daughter of Thomas Holland, earl of Kent. That union produced Edmund (V) (1391–1425), fifth earl of March. This Edmund died childless, so the Mortimer inheritance passed to Roger and Phillipa's daughter, Anne Mortimer, who married Richard of Conisbrough (1385–1415), fourth earl of Cambridge, father of Richard, duke of York (1411–60), and grandfather of King Edward IV.

167 This section traces the ancestry of the Lower [that is the more northerly Burkes centred round Mayo] MacWilliam branch of the family descended from William Burke (d.1270),

Mac Wylliame Clanryckerdes petygrewe

Richarde seconde sonne to the forsaide Aldelmeson whiche had yssue Wylliame leghe and he had to son[n]e Richarde whiche had Oyllycke and he had yssue Oyllyecke whiche had yssue Oyllycke father to the vii sonnes that now ben[168]

The forsaide Richarde called the Redd erle was lorde in demeane and s[er]vice for the more parte fro Shewaghtyn to Belasamye whiche is i^c myles a[nd from] Norbriughe by the sea syde to Balinaskanlan by Downdalke and also from Lim[er]ycke to Waterforde besydes all his landes in the iiii shyres and in the counties of Kylkenye andTypp[e]rarie {*end fo. 10v*}

younger brother of the first earl of Ulster. This William was father of William 'Liath' [the grey] (*d*.1324) – referred to here as Fitzwilliam – whose son, Edmund 'Albanach' [the Scot] (*d*.1375), was father to Sir Thomas Burke (*d*.1401), who was father to: Walter (*d*.1440), Edmund (*d*.1458), Thomas (*d*.1460), Richard (*d*.1473).

168 This section, more briefly and less accurately, traces the ancestry of the Upper [that is to say, the southern Burkes centred round Galway] MacWilliam branch of the Burkes. The progenitor of this line was in fact Sir Ulick Burke (*d*.1343), son of William 'Liath', who was the grandson of the 'Aldelmeson' named here.

Ordynau[n]ces and provisions for this lande of Irelande

1 It[e]m[169] *that the deputie shall see that the kinges lawes be duelye put in execution and that all the kynges offycers and mynistres of the same be mantaygned and assysted by hym to execute the same lawes*

2 It[e]m that no deputie do sende pryvate seale l[ett]re myssyve ne com[m]andeme[n]t to any of the kynges iudges in lettyng of the kynges lawes to p[ro]cede and if ther come any suche com[m]andeme[n]t to them that then the saide iudges or iudge to disalowe the same and to p[ro]ceade in the matter before them com[m]enced accordyng the lawe

3 It[e]m that the deputie do his endevo[r] to see that the churches of the iiii shyres be repayred, also to cause the mynistres of the same to be of goode rule and goode ordre and that no man of Irishe nacyon be p[ro]moted to any dignytie or benefyce upon payne contaygneth in the statute theron made

4 It[e]m that all the statutes of provision be duely put in execution

5 It[e]m that all the statutes made beyng benefyciall for this lande be duelye put in execution, and that none of them be broken excepte it be for a bett[er] entente and that onely by thadvyse of the lordes and kynges cou[n]sayll

6 It[e]m in avoydyng thabomynable extorcyon of cou[n]tye and lyverye that the deputie for the tyme beyng have in contynuall wadges and retynue i[c] goode tall yemen and xx[tie] gonn[er]s, everye yeman havyng his bowe, shiefe iacke sallet either stoule[170] *and an horse some of them havyng ii horses and weapon and to have amonge them x pavyces,*[171] *everie gonner to have his horse brestplate other brygundyse*[172] *his stoule or sallet, everie of them takyng for his meate drynke and wadges and horse fyndyng by the yere vi libr[e] xiiis iiiid and the capitayne to have a yere xx[tie] libr[e]   Sum[m]a viii[c] and xx[tie] libr[e]*

7 It[e]m also to have vi[xx] goode galloglasse everie of them to be harneysed receyvyng by the yere for his meate drynke and wadges ii libr[e] vis viiid   Sum[m]a iiii[c] libr[e]

8 It[e]m also to have ii[c] goode kierne everie of them to have a yere for his meate drynke and wadges xxxiiis iiiid   Sum[m]a ii[c] libr[e]

9 It[e]m to have xl goode horsmen well appoynted everie of them takyng by the day for meate drynke and wadges horse fyndyng and boyes xiid

10 It[e]m the forsaide chardges can not be borne untyll the revenues be encreased

11 It[e]m that the deputie ryde never without his standarde and trompett

---

169   The entries in italics do not appear in TCD MS 842, fos 25–36.
170   A jack was a sleeveless leather tunic; a salet was a light helmet which was widely used in fifteenth-century Europe; a 'stoule' would appear to have been some similar form of helmet.
171   A pavyce, or 'pavice', was a type of shield.
172   Body armour comprised of iron plates or rings sewen into fabric.

12 It[e]m that no deputie make warre upon no man but by assent of the kyngs cou[n]sayll and by thassent of everie of the iiii shyres and that the lordes and gentyls of everie of the saide shyres shall goo to election ones everie yere and to electe suche men as they shall thynke best to geve their advyse and consaill of the warre and peace of that yere, the nu[m]bre of ii out of one shyre and also for p[ro]visyon of all other good ordynau[n]ces and this election to be cont {*end fo. 11*} uwed yerely and that all men have xiiii dayes warnyng by wrytt to goo to any suche hostyng excepte it be for a greate nede

13 It[e]m in all matters whiche shoulde drywe the iiii[or] shyres or any of them to any chardge that then fyrste the same matter to be concluded by the kynges cou[n]sayll and to saide p[er]sones of everie shyre so chosen or by the more parte of them and duryng the tyme of the saide conclusion in the premisses that the deputie be not present wyth them in concludyng the same

14 It[e]m wheras the greate custome called the pou[n]dage[173] whiche was grau[n]ted to fynde a garde of bowes to adtende upon the kynges deputie wherfore fro hensforwarde that the saide custome to be bestowed upon tall yemen yerelye to attende yerely upon the deputie accordyng to the saide grau[n]te and as is before specyfyed

15 It[e]m that [no] man of the iiii[or] shyres do make warre or reyse warre eith[er] make preye upo[n] any Irishman but by thadvyse and assent of the deputie and kynges counsayll

16 It[e]m that no Englishman of the lande weare overlypp Irishe coate and hoode on payne of i[cs] totiens quotiens[174]

17 It[e]m if the deputie sende for any Irisheman to come speake wyth hym either if any of them come wythout sendyng for that then none of them have any coyne either lyverie but that they be styll on theire p[ro]pre costes other the deputies costes tyll they returne

18 It[e]m that all lordes and gentyls and wyddowes of the iiii[or] shyres shall sende an able man well appoynted for warre for everie xx[tie] libr[e] that they may dispende yerely to goo wyth the deputie to an hostynge wyth iackes and salletes bowes and arrowes and who can not dyspende xx[tie] libr[e] togetthre to be cessed aft[er] that rate

19 It[e]m that everie gentleman dwellyng in any marches shall sende an horseman well appoynted to goo wyth the deputie to any hostyng for everie ten marckes that he may dyspende a yere

20 It[e]m yf any that gothe to the felde be not an able man appoynted as he ought to be and this to be examyned by the deputie or the greate capytayne that then his m[aste][r] to furfeite a m[er]cymen[n]t competent as if the saide man had not appeared to the sayde hostyng

21 It[e]m that the cytie of Dublyne and the towne of Drogheda and the towne of Down[n]dalke do goo wyth the kynges deputie when they are requyred to hostyng

173   12*d.* in the pound levied since 1474 on imported and exported goods.
174   *Totiens quotiens* = in any case whatever.

in consydaracion that their custumes and pou[n]dages is fergeven them yerelye

22 It[e]m that no Englishman[n] dwellyng wythin maughre grou[n]de[175] do take no spere w[th] hym to the felde excepte he hath a bowe or pavyce upon payne of furfeite of vis viiid and losyng of his spere totiens quotiens

23 It[e]m that assone as the hostyng is concluded that ['they' *is crossed through*] then the gentyls of shyres of Mydth and Dublyne shall goo togetthre and electe them a captayne to be captayne and their barone at that hostyng and if it shoulde fortune hym to be taken in the fielde, then his rampson to be cessed upon xx[tie] libr[e] lande accordyng the chardge of the yomen of his shyre {*end fo. 11v*}

24 It[e]m that no lorde ne gentleman be chardged to goo to the fielde in their p[ro]pre p[er]sones but suche as wyll goo for the deputies pleasure

25 It[e]m that no yoman ryde to the fielde but everie vi yemen to take an hack-eney a ladde to beare their iackes stoulles bowes and arrowes, and all bowmen to go on foote except the greate capytayne

26 *It[e]m that the capitayne of the bowe men have a bannyer boughte on the deputies costes and the capytayne of the countie of Dublyne in lykewyse*

27 It[e]m that the maio[rs] of Dublyne and Drogheda be not chardged to goo in their propre p[er]sones to the fielde excepte it be within the iiii[or] shyres but one of the sheryfes of Drogheda to goo with xxiiii bowes with a banner of footemen and all the bowes of the cou[n]tie of Louthe to goo and wayte on that banner and that bann[er] to goo styll with the bann[er] of Mydthe

28 It[e]m that ther be newe capitaynes elected agaynst everie hoostyng

29 It[e]m that the gentyles chardged with the speres of the iii shyres shall goo assone as the wryttes of the hoostynges come fourth to electe a capytayne for the speres of their shyre and that the saide capytayne have a bannyer and that all the speres of the shyre wayte on that capytayne and bann[er] and thorderyng of that capitayns and bann[er]s of the com[itatus] of Kyldare be ordered by the deputie so that ther be xl men on horsbacke at the lest attendyng on oone bann[er]

30 It[e]m that all gentyles of the marches of Mydthe shall cesse on their m[ar]che landes vi[xx] kierne of their own[n] kyerne to be indyfferentlye cessed to everie hoostyng and a capytayne to be elected for them, and that capytayne to have a lytle bann[er] and all the kierne to followe the same of that shyre and to be alwayes redye togetthres

31 It[e]m the shiere of Uriel to cesse xl kierne the countie of Dublyne xl kyerne the counties of Kyldare and Catherlaghe vi[xx] kyerne and their capitaynes to be elected and everie capytayne their lytle gytton[176]

32 It[e]m that the hooste goo not a daye past xv myles

---

175 'Maghery', a transliteration of the Irish word *machaire*, meaning 'a plain', refers to the inner-most districts of the English Pale where conditions approximated most closely to those in lowland England.

176 A small ensign or standard.

33 It[e]m and of the forsaide p[er]sones of the saide shyres upon payne of highe treason and that no pardon helpe in this cace and that it [be] lawfull to the kynges subiectes next adioynyng to the Irisheman[n] upon whom any suche praye shoulde be made to do the best that they can to reskewe and let the saide praye and to see it restored to the owners

34 It[e]m if the deputie drawe any Irisheman to goo wyth hym to any hoostyng oth[er] io[r]neye that they have lyverie one nyght goyng and an other com[m]yng and wher they be lyv[er]yed to goo to their lyverye next nyght xii myles, and that none dwellyng wythin the iiii shires have any lyverie goyng nether comyng

35 It[e]m that at any suche coyne or lyverie every cheife horse to have but xii shieves of otes and everie hackney oth[er] bearyng horse viii[th] shieves & that ther be but i boy for an horse

36 It[e]m that all suche so lyveried shall take suche meate and drynke as the housbandman[n] hath unto whom he is lyveried so that it be competent mete and drynke {end fo. 12} and if they wyll not receyve such ['receyve suche' is crossed through] meate and drynke as thei fynde, then everie horsman[n] to have for a meale but iid everie galloglas kyerne and boye id and if it be a fleshe day to have but one man[er] of fleshe soddan without any rooste and but breade and butter and ale to boyes and footemen excepte the Sondaye

37 It[e]m if any so lyveried take pledges of them otherwyse then is ordered abovesaide that for everie daye that the housbondm[en] or his s[er]vau[n]tes do followe suche as have the pledge, that the pledge taker to paye xxd a daye to the saide housbondm[en] or his servau[n]t and to restore the same pledge and also to forfeicte to the deputie xxs totiens quotiens

38 It[e]m whensoever the deputie with his garde either retynue come within any of the iiii shyres then they to be lyveried in the countree and in the bor-oughetownes by the kynges herbynger[177] payng for everie yeman horseman and kiearnes meale iid, and for everie boye id a meale and for everie vi shieves otes id everie pecke[178] of oates vid a gallon ale iid and that they shall take suche meate and drynke as the housbondm[en] hathe on whom he is lyveried and to take one mann[er] fleshe sodden wythout rooste, nether to drywe hym to buye none ale ne ther victualles and that they playe no ryote ne evyll ordre on payne of their lyves

39 It[e]m that ther be none herbeng[er] withyn the iiii shyres but onely the kynges herbenger and that he sende ne byll but suche as shalbe sealed with the sygne of the horse heade and that everie byll do contaygne the best man[n]s name w[ch] shall goo wyth the same byll and that the herbenger do regyster the saide bylles and names in his boke and the daye and yere upon payne of forfei-ture vis viiid totiens quotiens

177   The harbinger was a royal officer responsible for purveying lodgings for the army.
178   A unit of capacity for dry goods equal to approximately a quarter of a bushel.

40 It[e]m that ther be no towne in any paraishe free from lyverie by the kynges byll but suche as hath alwaye ben free from the conquest or suche as is made free by the kynges deputie for some goode consyderation

41 It[e]m if the herbenger take rewarde ether brybe in executyng his offyce to forfeite to the kynge for everie groote[179] so taken vis viiid and if he be fou[n]de in three defaultes such to be then put out of his offyce

42 It[e]m when the kynges deputie shall fortune to ['be' *is crossed through*] parte or int[er]comen with any Irisheman adioynyng to any of the iiii shyres, at whiche tyme the sheryfe of that shire to have notyce a sevennyght tofore for to warne the gentyls next adioynyng to tende upon the saide deputie on payne of am[er]cyment aswell as thoughe it were by the kynges wrytte to them whiche make defaulte

43 It[e]m that none do put coyne ne lyverie on any ma[n]ns landes excepte it be on his owne in the marches upon payne contaigned in the statutes to the restraynght made of the same and over this to forfaicte x libr[e] totiens q[u]°tiens and forfeiture of their horses and har[n]nese thoone halfe to the kynge and thother {*end fo. 12v*} to hym on whose landes the saide lyvrie is made and that it be lawfull to any man[n] so greved wyth coyne or lyverie to sue in any courte whiche the kynge hath for thone halfe of the saide x libr[e]

44 It[e]m that the deputie and the cytie of Dublyne and the towne of Drogheda shall have their caryages borne to hostynges on the kynges landes and also suche landes as be in the kyngs handes & i[n] all other landes of wch thown[er]s be not bou[n]de to goo wyth hostynges

45 It[e]m that the deputie put by p[ro]meyses and bandes upon everie Irisheman adioynyng his power to come wth hym to all hostynges with a c[er]tayne sum[m]e of horsmen and kierne on thei^r propre costes

46 It[e]m that no bannyer ne getton be rered ne displayed in the fyelde but suche as shall be appoynted by by [sic] the deputie and that the saide deputie suffer but feawe bann[er]s ne gyttons reared wyth hym in the fielde

47 It[e]m from the tyme the deputie approched with his hooste to his enemyes cou[n]tree then he or his marshall shall appoynte a forwarde myddlewarde and rerewarde and if they be of power to appoynte twoo myddlewardes and that no man[n] departe from his warde ne bann[er] tyll they be cleane come out of their enemyes cou[n]tree upon payne of forfeiture of horse and harneyse

48 It[e]m that the hooste be redye everie daye at sonne rysyng and the saide wardes to goo forwarde as they shalbe appoynted and that none of the saide wardes goo ferre from other, so as ther be none awoydau[n]ce betuxte them and if they come to any dau[n]ger or fastnes or pase that then assone as the forwarde is departed out of their fastnes they to tarye with the myddlewarde and so they

---

179   A groat was English specie worth 4*d*.

lykewyse to tarye with the rerewarde to tarye with the rerewarde, and if nede be they all to abide and tarye

49 It[e]m that oone of the deputies marshialls shall take and appoynte a grou[n]de for the hoost to lodge by syxe of the clocke after none and in that grounde shall appoynte the deputies lodgyng and after that all others to take their lodggynges place as nyghe as they can aboute that lodgyng, so that thoone lodge ioyne with thother and so to lodge throughout all the hooste so as all the hooste lodge as nyghe as they can possible

50 It[e]m that none goo to make foerge[180] but ther as it shalbe appoynted by the deputie or his marshiall upon payne of forfeiture of his horse and harneyse and that ther be certayne gyttons of horsmen and bannyers of footemen appoynted nyghtlye upon the forragers to wayte, so as they shall take no hurte

51 It[e]m he that may be fou[n]de lodged loose out of the hooste to ferfeite xx[tie]s tocie[n]s q[uo]tiens thone halfe therof to the deputie and thoth[er] halfe to the fynder

52 It[e]m that the watche everie nyght be appoynted by the deputie or his marshiall and they so appoynted to watche aboute the hooste all nyght and this watche to goo by course nyghtlie upon all the hooste duryng their bydyng in the felde

53 It[e]m who so ever make a fraye in the hooste or mantayne or take partye with the same to forfeite his lyfe or a grevous fyne at the deputies discrecion

54 It[e]m who soever may be fou[n]de with thefte or with thefte prowed on hym in the hooste {*end fo. 13*} to be hanged or who may be founde w[th] receipte of thefte in the hooste to be hanged

55 It[e]m who taketh any vyctuall co[m]myng to be solde in the hooste either to any man[n] in gyfte and int[er]upte the bryngers to forfeite a grevous fyne totiens quotiens

56 It[e]m that everie shyre with their stau[n]dardes lodge roundelye togetthre by themselfes in one quart[er] of the fyelde and that the standardes of Dublyne the cou[n]tie of Dublyne and the countie of Kyldare goo togetthre and the stan-dardes of Droghedaa Mythe and Uryel do goo togetthres

57 It[e]m if *the deputie essue hostages of Irishemen for peace that then the saide hostages be not delyv[er]ed by no man[n] but by the deputie and advyse of the kynges* cou[n]saill and the persones before named of everie shyre or by the more parte of them

58 It[e]m if the deputie be drywen that he must have a battayll or battaylles of galloglasse goyng to any hostyng or iourney that they be lyveried by the kynges herbyng[er] by bylles after the fourme as is affore in the lyverye of Irishmen that shall come to hostynges or io[r]neyes

59 It[e]m that the justyces of peace shalbe made in everie shyre and they to make wardeynes of the peace in everie baronye and constables in everie

180 i.e., to forrage.

paraiche, and that they kepe ['mynisters' *is crossed through*] mustres ones everie quarter of the yere

60 It[e]m everie man havyng foure libr[e] of free goodes and so upwarde unto x libr[e] is wourthy to have his bowe some arrowes or a byll and fro x libr[e] is wo^rthy to have his iacke sallet bowe arrowes and a byll upon payne of vis viiid as often as he be founde wythout the same

61 It[e]m that shootyng be used in everie parishe within thEnglishe Pale everie holydaye so that the weather be fayre on payne of iiis iiiid

62 It[e]m that everie housbondman havyng a ploughe wythin thEnglishe Pale shall sett by the yere xii asshes in the dytches and closses of his ferme upon payne of iis

63 It[e]m whersoever any crye be rered in any place that all these that are adioynyng nexte unto the same place where such cryes be made shall aunswere to the same crye in their most defensible araye upon payne of iiis iiiid that make defaulte totie[n]s q[u]otiens

64 It[e]m that no man take pledges withyn thEnglishe Pale excepte it be for his ren[n]te upon payne conteyneth in the statutes therupon made and forfeture of v libr[e] totiens quotiens theone moytie[181] to the kynge and thother moytie therof to hym upon whom the saide pledges be made and that it be lawfull to hym to sue in any courte that the kynge hath for the same moytie

65 It[e]m also if the lande be in debate by severall tytles, then the distresses to be put in the heade towne of the baronye wher the saide lande is and ther to be kepte in pound were tyll they be repleved, upon payne of i^cs

66 It[e]m that ther be no horsman ne kiernaghe dwellyng wythin the Englyshe Pale upon payne contayned in the statutes ther upon made, and over that to forfett all their goodes and also that none wythin thEnglyshe Pale have horsboye of Irishe natyon upon payne of forfeture of xls totiens quotiens {*end fo. 13v*}

67 It[e]m that all men shall au[n]swere for the offences of their servau[n]tes and boyes excepte treason murther and manslaughter

68 It[e]m if ther be any warre wyth Irishmen made upon any of the iiii^or shyres that then the lordes and gentyls shall goo dwell on their landes next adioynyng to the saide warres and ther to contynue duryng the contynua[n]ce of the saide warres so that ther be a castell upon the same landes

69 It[e]m if any man[n] be slayne in the kyngs servyce with the deputie he in the felde, he holdyng his landes of the kyng or of any other by knyghtes servyce, then they of whom the lande is holden to take none advau[n]tage of their tenurye as to have the warde of the landes and maryage of the bodyes duryng the nonage of the heyres but that their next frendes ['of' *is crossed through*] so kylled shall kepe their landes and the profyctes of the same as gardeynes in soccage

181 Half.

70 It[e]m that no Irishe mynistrelles rymours shannaghes[182] ne bardes messengers come to deasyre any goodes of any man[n] dwellyng wythin the Englishe Pale upon payne of forfeiture of all their goodes and their bodyes to be prysoned at the kynges wyll

71 It[e]m who so ever geve unto his lorde or m[aste]r any nyghtes lodgyng or a cuddye, that he shall fynde duryng that season with hymselfe or on his p[ro]pre tenau[n]tes all horses boyes and men upon payne of ten libr[e] totiens quotiens

72 It[e]m that no Irisheman compell any man[n] to buye his alterage upon payne of x libr[e] totiens quotiens and the penaltie of the statutes theron made

73 It[e]m yf any nacyon Irishe or Englishe dwellyng within any of the iiii shyres buye alterage of any man[n] that then he that buye or he of whom it is bought shall rere no pounge of the saide buyers nacyon without that they geve it wythe their own[n]e freewylles wythout any dystresse or pledge therfore taken upon payne of v libr[e] totiens quotiens

74 It[e]m that ther be no coyne in this lande but suche as shalbe currau[n]t in Inglande and thEnglishe groate to goo for vd, and golde after the same rate

75 It[e]m that the coyne stroken in this lande be uttered and eschau[n]ged out of this lande wythin a twelve moneth after the p[ro]clamacion made ther upon

76 *It[e]m that ther be no coyne strucken in this lande upon payne of highe treason*

77 *It[e]m that no man havyng a plough of his own[n]e by any corne upon payne of forfe-ture of the same corne if it may be founde, and if not, then to forfeite xiid agaynst everie pecke that he so buye untyll his own[n] corne be all spente*

78 It[e]m that no man[n] lade corne out of this lande if the pecke wheat be above the valo[r]e of xiid and malte above the value of viii[th]d upon payne of for-feiture of the same and that no lycense be geven to any man of suche ladynge

79 It[e]m that noo m[er]chau[n]t by no corne in shiefe upon payne of forfeiture of the same

80 It[e]m that no m[er]chau[n]tes wyfe use any taverne or sellyng of ale upon payne of xxs totiens quotiens as often as any of them do the contrarye but let the[m] be occupied in makyng of wollen clothe and lynnen clothe

81 It[e]m that ther be none ale solde above iid the gallon upon payne of vis viiis totiens quotiens {*end fo. 14*}

82 It[e]m that the statutes of the Spanyshe wynes be put in execution: that is that no hydes be geven for any man[er] wares excepte it be for wheate salte yron or smale wynes upon payne of forfeture of the same or the valo[r] and all men sen-dyng any hydes out of this lande shall fynde suerties to the customers that the returne of the saide hydes shall come in such wares as is afforsaide

83 It[e]m that the saide statute be put in execution in all townes and creakes fro Down[n]garvan unto the water of the Banne

---

182   In early modern Irish society, a *seanchaí* was a custodian of tradition, or a historian.

84 It[e]m no man[er] man buye any hyde above the value of xvid upon payne of forfeiture of the same hyde or the value

85 It[e]m that no mercha[n]t do sende any man[er] of wares amonge Irishmen to be solde upon payne of forfeiture of the same or the value

86 It[e]m that no m[er]chau[n]t nether his serwau[n]te shall goo out of the cytties and townes wherin they dwelle to thintent to buye or sell any man[er] of wares and that thei whiche dwelle in Dublyne and Drogheda shall skerekhe and bar-gayne wares wythin them whiche dwell in the boroughtownes in the cou[n]tree

87 It[e]m that the iiii^th parte of the yarne bought in the cou[n]tre be wrought in clothe or it departe this lande upon payne of forfeiture of the same fourth parte or the value therof

88 It[e]m that the iiii^th parte of all the hydes that shalbe boughte shalbe tanned or thei goo out of this lande on payne of forfeiture of the same or the value

89 It[e]m that no lorde gentleman freeholder or housbondman shall salte any hydes upon payne of forfeiture of the same or the value

90 It[em] that no shipp ne pycarde breake bulcke fro the heade of Wycklowe to the Leystowne Excepte onely in Dublyne Drogheda and parte in Down[n]dalke at the discretion of the town[n]e of Droghedaa upon payne of forfeiture of all theire goodes

91 It[e]m that all m[er]chau[n]tes excepte freemen bryngyng any wares to be solde within any of the saide iiii parties if the saide wares be no bought of the so withyne xl dayes after their com[m]yng that then they take their wares freelye out of the saide parte with them

92 It[e]m that the iiii^th parte of salmon herynge and dryefyshe made with them of this cou[n]treye be kepte and solde within the same lande upon payne of the forfeiture of the same or the value

93 It[e]m that no man take any horse or hawke out of this lande to be solde upon payne conteyned in the statutes therupon made

94 It[e]m that all borowghetown[n]es have goode lodgyng to lodge the kinges {*end fo. 14v*} subiectes therin and that the kynges offycers of the same townes see that the people be well lodged and that they shall have victualles plentyefull for their money and that goode cheape and that they shall have vi shieves of oates for a penye and a pecke of oates for vd

95 It[e]m that the borowghe townes be made sure amd faste and the customes yerely be well bestowed upon the walles and dytches of the saide townes and that ther come a man out of everie house of the saide townes on their p[ro]pre costes vi dayes in the moneth of marche everie yere from hensforwarde to repayre and make faste their walles and dytches

96 It[e]m that none buye any caples[183] or kyne of any suspecte p[er]son[n]es in the marketes upon payne of forfeiture of the same or the value

183   From the Irish word for horse(s): *capall/capaill.*

97 It[e]m that ther be no wheate malte made in this lande upon payne of forfeiture of the same or the value therof

98 It[e]m that ther be but one maker of aquavite in everie borovghe towne
upon payne of vis viiid totiens quotiens as many as do the contrarie

99 It[e]m that no wheate ne malte goo to any Irishmans cou[n]trey upon payne
of forfeitur of the same or the value excepte onlye breade ale and aquavytie

100 It[e]m the deputie to have pledges contynuallye of the capitaynes of
Irishmen next adioynyng the Englishe Pale for the peace

101 It[e]m that no blacke rente be geven or payed to any Irishman[n] upon any
of the iiii shyres from hensforwarde and any blacke rent whiche they had affore
this tyme that it be not paied unto them forever

102 It[e]m that the lordes and the kynges cou[n]saille shalbe bou[n]de to do their
dylegen[n]ce that the premysses shalbe put in execution

103 It[e]m that the iudges of the kynges courtes and the iustyces of the peace in
everie shyre shall have authorytie to enquere for the transgressours and
offendours of the premysses and to punyshe suche as shalbe culpable in any article afforsaide

104 It[e]m that the lordes and the kynges cou[n]sayll shall adde correcte and
amende all that is contaigneth in thys boke after their discretions

105 It[e]m that the kynges revenues be not grau[n]ted to none nor nor parcell
of his revenues in Irelande

106 It[e]m that the deputie receave the halfe feeferme and customes of the cytie
of Wat[er]forde and halfe the feeferme of Corcke Yowghyll Lym[er]ycke and
Galwaye and thother halfe to goo to the reparacons of their walles and to their
defen[n]ce

107 It[e]m it is a greate abusion and reproche that the lawes and statutes made in
this lande are not observed ne kepte after the makyng of them viii[th] dayes w[ch]
mattier is one of the destruction of Englishmen of this lande and dyverse
Irishmen doth observe and kepe suche lawes and statutes whiche they make
upon hylles in their cou[n]treys fyrme and stable without breakyng of them for
any fawure or rewarde {*end fo. 15*}

108 It[e]m if the deputie for the tyme beyng may lyverye at his pleasure lordes and
gentlemen landes, let never the saide lordes ne gentlemen call that lande theirs at
leynghte, but call it the deputies landes, and take ensamble therof at Mounestere

109 It[e]m that the deputie shall cause all the kynges subiectes nexte adioynyng
to Irishmen of all this lande to fynde good suerties and to be bou[n]de by greate
ban[n]des of recognisau[n]ce to observe the kynges lawes and to kepe their
alliegeau[n]ce truelye and to be forth com[m]yng to aunswere to all suche mat-
tiers as shalbe laied to their chardges by the deputie

110 It[e]m that the deputie be viii[th] daies in everie som[er] cuttyng paases of the
woddes nexte adioynyng the kynges subiectes whiche shalbe thoughte moste
nedefull

The paases names here ensueth

Downe Callyver; the Newedytche; the paases goyng to Poverescourte; Glangkrye; Ballaghmore in Foderth; Barnedareghe goyng to Fernes; Leroge; Strenogloraghe; Pollemontie; Bran Wallehangry; Mortereston; twoo paases in Feemore in O Moryes cou[n]trey; the paases of Fferrynobeghan; Kyllemarkellye; Belanower; Toghrnefyn; twoo paases in Rymaleghe; the paases goyng to Moyele; twoo paases in Kalrye; the paase of Brahon Juryne; Kylkorkye; the Lagh[agh] and Belatrae; Karrykonall and Ballaghmore; three paases on Orore oone by Dongele an other by Ffaghirt and the thirde by Omee; Bellaghkyne on [sic] and Ballaghnere {*end fo. 15v*}[184]

---

184 There follows another folio page. It is blank, apart from its designation as folio 16 – printed in the upper right-hand corner – and, just discernible on 16v, what appear to be the words 'A breviate of the getting of Ireland and the decay of the same' written (faintly) in a later hand.

PART II

Discovery and reform

For as I suppose that deasire in your noble progenitors to reforme all Irlande at oon instante hath bene thoccasion that it is soo ferre out of order and frame as it is; for, as I have lerned, these 250 yeres together the same hath decaied, from tyme to tyme, alwaais differing [=deferring], and expecting tyme to reforme all, wherby the lande hath soo decaide, from oon tyme to another, that ever, either for other outwarde busuines of your Realme of Englande, for lak of preparacion, or sume other thing, tyme never served.

– John Alen, the master of the rolls, to Henry VIII (1536)

2.1

Discovery and the origins of Tudor reform

Ireland was but one of the many responsibilities of kingship about which Henry VII had immediately to learn upon his accession to the throne of England. The ideal way for the new king, the first of the new Tudor dynasty, to acquaint himself with Ireland and the political and socio-economic conditions in his lordship was to do what he did in England: live there and move deliberately and widely with his court through the country and among its people.[1] Yet Ireland was an outlying territory of secondary importance – he could not afford even to visit the country, still less to make an extended progress through it, or base his court there. Ireland was thus a subject that Henry VII would have to come to understand by different means. Of 'the strong bent of that country towards the house of York' he must, like his later biographer, have been aware;[2] and though it is now impossible to ascertain how much, if any, written material on Ireland was available to the king at his accession, or whether he would have cared to consult it, Henry was more than likely familiar with the broad outlines of the English crown's perceived relationship with the lordship: that Ireland rightfully belonged to the crown of England; that the island's keeping was essential to England's safety; that it had once been, and could be again, a territory from which the crown might profit; and that two kinds of people lived there – English subjects, some of them loyal, some of them not, and the king's 'Irish enemies' with whom the king's loyal subjects had been at war for centuries. Such was the kind of information on the lordship of Ireland that had been set down centuries earlier by the author Gerald of Wales [Giraldus Cambrensis] in his *Topographica Hibernica* (c.1187) and his *Expugnatio Hibernica* (c.1189) – both texts enjoyed a wide circulation in manuscript form in England (and beyond) throughout the late medieval period. More recently, information about Ireland was included in the well-known political poem 'The Libel of English Policy' (c.1437).[3] Should

1 Steve Gunn, *s.v.* 'Henry VII', *ODNB*.
2 Francis Bacon, *The history of the reign of King Henry the Seventh*, ed. F.J. Levy (Indianapolis, 1972), p. 26 (quotation). In his history of England, Polydore Vergil explained that the Oxford priest who famously trained Lambert Simnel to impersonate the earl of Warwick, Edward IV's nephew, chose to send him to Ireland because he had heard that 'that land ... always uniquely loved King Edward's name and stock': *The Anglica Historia of Polydore Vergil, A.D. 1485–1537*, ed. Denys Hay (London, 1950), ch. xxvi. Indeed, in 1474, the Irish parliament in an address to Edward IV explained to the king that he was 'reputed here in prophesyes the whyte lyon and sextus Hib[ernie] which by the sayd prophesies shall wyn this land and many other realmes': TNA, C 47/10/29 (printed in Bryan, *The great earl of Kildare*, pp 18–22).
3 S.J. David, 'Looking east and west: the reception and dissemination of the *Topographia Hibernica*

the young king have sought out current administrative documentation to better acquaint himself with conditions in Ireland he would have found a statement, lately prepared for Richard III, of the extents of the Irish revenues. The revenues, the extent showed, yielded a small surplus barely sufficient to cover the normal operation of the government of Ireland, and so could not, in their present state, make any significant contribution to the crown's revenues.[4] More explicit themes of danger, decay and decline were evident in the addresses of the Irish parliament that had been made to Henry VII's royal predecessors. The assembled members of the parliament held in Ireland in 1421, for instance, had written to the crown, then worn by Henry V, that his lordship was 'for greater part devastated and destroyed' and that, 'within a short time', the king's subjects there would be 'quite utterly ruined and destroyed for ever'. The situation had allegedly become so dire that the parliament held out hope that the Pope would sanction a crusade against the Irish enemies. More recently, in 1474, the parliament of Ireland had written to their king Edward IV of the 'pitiose decay' and the 'myserable state and desolacyon' of Ireland and the king's true subjects there.[5]

Still, the age in which Henry VII lived and acted was a deeply personal one, where society and the exercise of power was based on vast interconnected networks of personal relationships. The acquisition of knowledge was an extension of this reality: information was best communicated and obtained face-to-face. The surest way to learn about a thing was first-hand through direct personal experience of it; but it was still far better to learn about a thing from a person who had personal experience of that thing than from an inherently limited source like a book, manuscript or letter. The written word, after all, could neither answer questions, nor provide additional or tangential information. It is tempting to see this as symptomatic of the influence of the Renaissance humanist preference for experience in the world over derived or abstract knowledge.[6] But this

and the *Itinerarium ad partes orientales* in England, 1185–*c*.1500' (PhD, St Andrews, 2009), pp 132–4; Bradshaw, *The Irish constitutional revolution*, p. 46; Hiram Morgan, 'Giraldus Cambrensis and the Tudor conquest of Ireland' in Hiram Morgan (ed.), *Political ideology in Ireland, 1541–1641* (Dublin, 1999), pp 22–44; *The Libelle of Englyshe Polycye: a poem on the use of sea-power, 1436*, ed. George Warner (Oxford, 1926), pp 185–90. The inventories of the books owned by Henry VII, the first king of England to have a library, did not include any material relating to Ireland: S.B. Chrimes, *Henry VII* (Berkeley, 1972), p. 307.

4 D.B. Quinn (ed.), 'Guide to English financial records for Irish history, 1461–1558, with illustrative extracts, 1461–1509', *Analecta Hibernica*, 10 (1941), 17–27.

5 *Statutes and ordinances, and acts of the parliament of Ireland, King John to Henry V*, ed. H.F. Berry (Dublin, 1907), p. 563; Bryan, *The great earl of Kildare*, p. 18. Cf. Elizabeth Matthew, 'Henry V and the proposal for an Irish crusade' in Brendan Smith (ed.), *Ireland and the English world in the late Middle Ages: essays in honour of Robin Frame* (London, 2009), pp 161–75.

6 T.A. Noble, 'Scripture and experience' in P.E. Satterthwaite and D.F. Wright (eds), *A pathway into the Holy Scripture* (Grand Rapids, 1994), p. 286; William Bouwsma, *The waning of the Renaissance, 1550–1640* (New Haven, 2002), p. 37.

4 Henry VII, unknown artist, 1505, NPG 416.

impulse was almost certainly a continuation of an older emphasis on the importance of personal connections to people and to places. The anonymous author of 'The Libel of English Policy', for example, declared with pride that some of the key information on Ireland included in his poem was based on what he had personally heard from the earl of Ormond whom he described as 'a lorde ful of grete astate' in Ireland.[7] This desire for personal interaction and direct experience was expressed in a different way in the respective appeals of the Irish parliaments of 1421 and 1474 to Henry V and Edward IV. The former noted that Ireland 'has fallen so greatly into decline that your said land will never have relief ... without your most sovereign and most gracious presence'; King Edward was later exhorted 'to come personally unto his said land for the relief of the same'.[8]

Thus the question for Henry VII in 1485 was: to whom, rather than to what, could he turn for more current information on conditions in his lordship of Ireland? There was Thomas Butler, seventh earl of Ormond, a committed Lancastrian who now sat on the king's council. Butler was born in Ireland and held an Irish peerage rooted in his family's ancestral lands in north Munster; but Ormond was by this stage an old man and had, in any case, lived most of his life in England. Apart from Butler, there was not a single man on Henry VII's newly assembled (and otherwise large and heterogeneous) council with direct experience of Ireland. So, when Gerald Fitzgerald, eighth earl of Kildare, who had for long governed Ireland for the Yorkist kings of England, sent his client John Estrete over to England to explain that the earl wished to continue as the king's deputy, but that he would not come before his new king without a guarantee of safe conduct, Henry had Estrete sworn to his council. This was an unusual move: Estrete was already a member of the king's council in Ireland. But as a native of Dublin and a man well versed in the working of English government in the lordship – he was the king's serjeant-at-law and had also deputized as chief baron of the exchequer – Estrete was possessed of the specialist knowledge of Ireland that Henry and his councillors in England so sorely lacked.[9]

The political situation was delicate: Kildare commanded a broad and militarized following in Ireland; the earl was also a stranger to the Tudor king. Kildare

7   *The Libelle of Englyshe Polycye*, p. 189.
8   *Stat. Ire., John to Henry V*, p. 563; Bryan, *The great earl of Kildare*, p. 18. This was a well-worn request: in 1385 the Great Council of Ireland predicted the 'conquest of the greater part of the land of Ireland' and appealed to the king because they could conceive of no 'other remedy except the coming of the king, our lord, in his own person': quoted in J.F. Lydon, 'Richard II's expeditions to Ireland', *JRSAI*, 93 (1963), 136.
9   We know practically nothing of Estrete's life, but see the information gathered in F.E. Ball, *The judges in Ireland, 1221–1921* (London, 1926), p. 187; Ellis, *Reform and revival*, pp 35, 222, 224.

had had a relationship with King Edward, having travelled to court in 1479 to consult with him on Ireland.[10] A personal relationship between king and magnate was important. Richard III, though a Yorkist and the king's brother, knew nothing of Kildare and less of Ireland. When he came to power in 1483, King Richard retained Kildare as deputy of Ireland and had it communicated to the earl that he did so principally 'in consideracion of the good fame and noble disposicion that [he] Thomas Fitzgerard erle of Kildare is reported to be of'. Except the earl with whom the king sought to establish a relationship was Earl Gerald; Gerald's father, the seventh earl, was Thomas, and had been quite dead since 1478. The following year, King Richard had a series formulaic letters – in which the intended recipient's name was simply inserted at the top, though some of them were left entirely blank – drawn up for a number of English lords across Ireland thanking them for their continued loyalty.[11] Henry VII was more careful and precise – hence his cultivation of Estrete whom the king subsequently employed as his messenger. Estrete was sent back to Ireland armed with knowledge of the king's mind and carrying his written instructions: Kildare was commanded to present himself at court forthwith and without a safe conduct. Kildare's past Yorkist affiliations notwithstanding, Henry VII was desirous 'to here thadvise' of the earl on Ireland 'considering that for the long rule that he haith borne there, ther can no man therin better counsaill his grace than he'. The king, according to his instructions, would 'as benignely, tendrely and largely take him into the favour of his grace as ever did King Edward the iiij[th]' and hoped 'that upon mutuall sight and communication' he and the earl would forge a personal relationship which would allow them to work together to 'conclude and devise for the bringing of the said land of Irlande into pleyn obeissaunce and such estete, welth, and prouffitte as it hath been in tyme passed'.[12]

Yet Henry VII's use of John Estrete as an intermediary with Kildare, and between the crown and Ireland's political elite more generally, failed. Not only did Kildare not go to court, he and most of the lordship's political establishment helped to launch the unsuccessful Yorkist effort to overthrow the Tudor king and place a pretender on the throne. Henry VII easily defeated the Yorkist force that crossed into England from Ireland and which included a sizeable contingent of Irish kerne raised by Kildare; but the weakness of the Tudor position whence

10 Ellis, *Ireland in the age of the Tudors*, p. 78.
11 *Letters and papers illustrative of the reigns of Richard III and Henry VII*, ed. James Gairdner, 2 vols (London, 1861–3), i, pp 43, 76–8.
12 King's instructions to John Estrete, BL, Cotton MSS, Titus B XI, i, fo. 23 (*L. & P. Rich. III and Hen. VII*, i, pp 91–3). The instructions carried to Ireland by Estrete are undated, leading some historians to conclude that they were the work of Richard III: A.J. Otway-Ruthven, *A history of medieval Ireland* (London, 1980), p. 401. However, Richardson and Sayles offer convincing evidence in favour of a *c.*1486 date: H.G. Richardson and G.O. Sayles, *The Irish parliament in the middle ages* (Philadelphia, 1952), p. 328.

the attack came was clearly exposed for all of the king's enemies to see.[13] King Henry, whose claim to the English throne was extraordinarily weak, was largely unknown in Ireland and bore the surname of an obscure Welsh family. The pretender, by contrast, who appeared in Ireland in early 1487, was accepted as being Edward, earl of Warwick, the son of George, duke of Clarence, Edward IV's brother. Clarence had been born in Dublin Castle in 1449 during his father's successful lieutenancy, and was baptized at St Saviour's Church where the earls of Desmond and Ormond stood as his godparents. He twice served as lord lieutenant of Ireland and was rumoured to have secreted his young son to Ireland in 1478 for safekeeping before his own execution that year. Of Henry Tudor's accession to the throne an Irish annalist who lived through these events recorded: 'Richard III was slain ... and the son of the Welshman [mac Breatnaigh] ... was made king. And there lived not of the race of the blood royal that time but one young man, who came, on being exiled the year after, to Ireland'.[14] This 'young man' of the blood royal was Lambert Simnel the Yorkist pretender whom Kildare saw crowned king of England (and Ireland) in Dublin at Christ Church Cathedral in 1487.

Henry VII desperately needed to bolster support in Ireland for his still-unfamiliar dynasty. It was recorded that in mid-May 1488 a messenger on behalf of 'divers Lordes of Ireland' came before the king's council in England. But the messenger was upon his arrival instructed to 'put all his desires and requestes' in writing: 'all thinges shalbe accomplished accordinge' he was told.[15] Rather than engage in another round of detached negotiations with his subjects, Henry VII resorted to what would over the next century become a common strategy for the Tudors: he despatched into Ireland an Englishman, trusted and well regarded at court, but who was possessed of neither experience nor knowledge of the neighbouring country. His choice in late May 1488 was Sir Richard Edgecombe. A member of the king's council and the comptroller of the royal household, Edgecombe had fought beside Henry at Bosworth. He was also with his king at Stoke Field where the royal army had defeated the Yorkist pretender and cut Kildare's Irish host to pieces.[16] Edgecombe was made a special royal commissioner and placed in command of some 500 troops; his mission: to administer a new oath of allegiance to, and exact bonds of recognizance from, Kildare and other leading members of the English political establishment in Ireland. Edgecombe's undertaking was a qualified success: he secured recognition for Henry VII from the English political nation in Ireland, including from Kildare; however he failed to bind the earl and

---

13 Ellis, *Ireland in the age of the Tudors*, pp 85–6.

14 *AU*, s.a. 1485.

15 *Select cases in the council of Henry VII*, eds C.G. Bayne and W.H. Dunham (London, 1958), p. 18.

16 J.L. Kirby, 'Sir Richard Edgcumbe [Edgecombe]', *ODNB*.

the other lords over in the potentially crippling bonds that the first Tudor was to use to such great effect in England.

Richard Edgecombe's mission to Ireland is of significance beyond the political settlement he achieved.[17] Edgecombe wrote a detailed account – a 'book' as it was called – of his voyage to Ireland.[18] Why Edgecombe, who may well have written the document himself, or perhaps instructed his secretary to do so, should have chosen to record the daily details of his voyage to Ireland is a mystery.[19] He had served as the king's ambassador to Scotland the previous year, but (so far as we know) did not write an account of that mission. Nevertheless his book represents the first written account of Ireland to be penned by an Englishman in Tudor times. Though the oral relation of Edgecombe's experiences in Ireland – something that he doubtless would have conveyed to his king and his fellow councillors upon his return to England – would have counted for more, any words he may have spoken concerning his mission are now irretrievable. The information preserved in his account survives, however – as it was meant to: Edgecombe's account allows the historian a means with which to gauge the extent of Tudor knowledge of Ireland at the outset of the reign of Henry VII.

The overriding impression that one gets from Edgecombe's account is that the king's representative was an outsider in Ireland with no evident knowledge of the place. He did not travel the length and breadth of the king's lordship as one might have expected of a newly arrived royal commissioner. Rather, he visited several English settlements on the south and east coast by ship. Edgecombe made no effort to journey into the island's interior where the king of England's writ, be he a Yorkist or a Tudor, barely ran; that most of the lordship lay under the political control of dozens of independent Irish lords is only evident from Edgecombe's apparent refusal to stray too far from his ships (his means of egress). Even allowing for the fact that Edgecombe's concern was, above all, to secure the allegiance of as many men as possible to Henry VII and to make a record of their promises and oaths by committing their names and the terms of their submissions to paper, Ireland still comes across as an unknown and uncomprehended backdrop to the royal commissioner's single-minded pursuit of recognition for the

17 For the terms and significance of the settlement, see Ellis, *Ireland in the age of the Tudors*, p. 86.

18 'The Voyage of Sir Richard Edgecombe', 1488, BL, Cotton MSS, Titus B XI, ii, fos 282–98 (printed incompletely in Harris, *Hibernica*, i, pp 59–77). Representations of this document may be found in Trinity College, Dublin: TCD, MSS 664 and 842.

19 Richard Polwhele, *The history of Cornwall, civil, military, religious, architectural, agricultural, commercial, biographical, and miscellaneous*, 7 vols (London, 1816), iv, pp 48–51. James Ware made the following observation while on the subject of 'foreign writers who had preferment in Ireland': 'Sir Richard Edgecomb, a Cornishman, was sent into Ireland by King Henry VII ... He writ a book of the success of that employ, which is in manuscript': Ware, *The antiquities and history of Ireland*, p. 41.

new Tudor regime. Still, the lists of the names of those men who swore allegiance to the crown which were recorded at the end of Edgecombe's book amount to a virtual 'who's who' of Ireland's English political community in the 1480s, precisely the kind of information that the famously detail-orientated king in England could pore over and refer back to. If Edgecombe was struck in any way by the physical, political, economic or social structure that confronted him in Ireland he did not remark upon it as he carried out his mission. It may be said that an additional worth of the book is in what it does not say.

Edgecombe's mission bore fruit the following year when, if the account in the *Book of Howth* (and repeated by Sir James Ware) is to be accepted, Kildare and some of the leading temporal nobility of Ireland came before Henry VII at his riverside palace at Greenwich outside London.[20] The king could at last look upon the assembled nobility of his lordship with his own eyes and establish the personal bonds of loyalty that he had, to this point, been denied. To that end, he interviewed the lords in an effort to understand why they had supported the pretender and, satisfied with their response and having shown them their previous faults, the king licensed Kildare and the rest to return to Ireland.

But neither Edgecombe's 'book', nor the meeting at Greenwich addressed the basic fact that the king's lordship of Ireland was, by all accounts, in a decayed state. With no one to turn to in England on how best to address the situation, Henry VII again looked to Kildare, ordering him to return to court. The summons came within a year of the earl's last visit.[21] Historians have typically approached this interaction between the king and the earl within the context of a monarch trying to curb an 'overmighty' subject, or a regional magnate seeking to preserve his (or indeed his country's) autonomy within a suddenly changed political dispensation.[22] Yet the evidence, though it is meagre, can also be interpreted as the king's tentative attempt to confront the longstanding problems in his lordship, and who better to counsel him on this subject than Kildare. On this occasion Kildare did not leave Ireland; but the earl's letter of excuse, in which he refers to the king's instructions to him (now lost), offers a window on Henry VII's thinking on Ireland. Henry, according to Kildare, sought to have 'plenary [by which he meant, full and complete] communicacion' with him 'in alle such thynges as mought concerne the wele' of Ireland, so that his subjects there 'may be reduced to a good and lafull ordyr and obeisaunce'.[23]

---

20 *Cal. Carew MSS (Book of Howth)*, v, p. 190; Ware, *The antiquities and history of Ireland*, p. 15.

21 *Calendar of the patent rolls, Henry VII, 1485–94* (London, 1914), p. 316.

22 Bryan, *The great earl of Kildare*, pp 160–70; G.O. Sayles, 'The vindication of the earl of Kildare from treason, 1496', *IHS*, 7 (1950–1), 39–40; Agnes Conway, *Henry VII's relations with Scotland and Ireland, 1485–1498* (London, 1932) pp 61–3.

23 *L. & P. Rich. III & Hen. VII*, i, p. 380. Two letters to Henry, from the parliament of Ireland and from the earl of Desmond, contain identical wording to Kildare's letter.

This was, to be sure, a rudimentary understanding of the situation. There is no mention, for instance, of the Irish population and the myriad political, social and economic problems that they posed for a crown which claimed lordship over all of Ireland. Instead, the king's concern was focused more narrowly on Ireland's English population. Much of this understanding can be attributed to Henry's ignorance of politics and society in Ireland. But it stemmed also from the prevailing Renaissance apprehension of time as repetitive and cyclical.[24] King Henry's use of the word 'reduced', by which he meant 'to bring back, or to restore', is significant and must be understood within this context. It reveals how the king, and English people in England and Ireland, conceived of the Anglo-Irish relationship at the dawn of the Tudor period: the English Conquest's accomplishments in terms of establishing English 'civility' in Ireland some three hundred years earlier had been undone by the late fifteenth century and now needed to be restored. To put it another way, one golden age needed to be recovered so as to usher in another.[25] Something in England (or indeed any-where else) might equally be 'reduced' or restored to its former state, but in an Irish context 'to reduce' also touched on what was believed to have been the achievement of the English Conquest of Ireland. It is hard to gauge the extent to which the king, or his councillors, was familiar with the details of the twelfth-century conquest, or whether they understood what Henry II had actually achieved in Ireland so many years before. While a sense of anachronism was evi-dent in early Tudor historical thought, the king and his councillors would nev-ertheless have apprehended the gulf of time that separated the late twelfth century from the late fifteenth century as one marked by continuity rather than discontinuity, by closeness rather than remoteness.[26] Thus, for Henry VII in 1490, it was Kildare, with his personal experience and expert knowledge of Ireland, who was best suited to assist him and his council in formulating a policy that would restore what had once been (or was thought to have been) and so contribute immediately to the security of the fledgling Tudor dynasty.

But Kildare's refusal to repair to England, coupled with the appearance in 1491 of another Yorkist pretender in Ireland – this time Perkin Warbeck who was presented as Edward IV's son, Richard, duke of York – forced the king to abandon any thoughts of a broad restorative engagement with the English of Ireland in favour of a less ambitious interventionist strategy intended to preserve the status quo. The king was scarcely in a better position by then to intervene in Ireland than he was at the time of his accession. Immediate action from England

24 On this point generally, see L.B. Campbell, *Tudor conceptions of history and tragedy in 'A Mirror for Magistrates'* (Berkeley, 1936).

25 Euan Cameron, 'The power of the word: Renaissance and Reformation' in Euan Cameron (ed.), *Early modern Europe: an Oxford history* (Oxford, 2001), p. 63.

26 F.J. Levy, *Tudor historical thought* (San Marino, 1967), p. 36.

was necessary, however: while Kildare was not openly supporting Warbeck, the earl was making little effort to expel the pretender. The king's only councillor with recent experience of Ireland – Richard Edgecombe – had died in 1489 (Estrete died c.1491), so Henry looked to the Butlers. The king had called upon Thomas Butler, earl of Ormond, his only Irish-born councillor, to counsel him on Ireland before. Years earlier, when Simnel landed in Ireland, the king had written to Ormond, commanding the earl to attend upon him so that he might avail of his 'advice and counsel' on how best to suppress the rebels.[27] Yet, as in 1487, Ormond was either unable – he served as an ambassador to Charles VIII in 1492 – or unwilling to serve the king in any capacity in Ireland. So, as a means to thwart Warbeck, Henry VII turned to James Butler, alias Ormond, Earl Thomas' illegitimate nephew. He made Ormond a royal commissioner and placed him at the head of the small expeditionary force which he sent to Ireland in late 1491. That Henry should entrust to Ormond so important a mission reflects the emphasis that the king placed on employing men with personal experience and knowledge of Ireland: though James Ormond had lived in England for most of his life, and though he was not possessed of any discernible military or administrative experience, his Irish birth and Irish connections – his father had been the sixth earl of Ormond and his mother was an O'Brien – were enough to earn him the command. The notice of the Irish annalists of James Ormond's arrival, when they had entirely ignored the presence in Ireland of Richard Edgecombe, spoke to the importance of the Butlers there and would seem to have validated the king's choice of Ormond as his representative.[28] But Henry VII was nothing if not cautious: Ormond was to share his command with the experienced English administrator Thomas Garth.[29]

The Ormond-led expedition was a success in so far as it undercut support for Warbeck, who fled to the Continent, and facilitated the steady replacement in the following two years of a Geraldine-dominated administration with a Butler-dominated administration nominally under the control of Earl Thomas at court. Yet this sudden alteration of the lordship's political terrain revived a feud between the Butlers and the Fitzgeralds, which had lain dormant for decades. Kildare's dismissal and James Ormond's rapid political advancement – he was elevated to Henry's council, was appointed joint governor of Ireland for a time before being made treasurer in a new government headed by Walter Fitzsimons, the archbishop of Dublin – led to violent clashes between adherents of the two houses. At one point, in early 1493, Kildare briefly took Garth prisoner and hanged Garth's son, prompting the king to dispatch a force of 300 soldiers to

27 Henry VII to Ormond, 13 May 1487, BL, Cotton MSS, Titus B XI, fo. 24.
28 The annalists noted that James Ormond had come to Ireland after a long time in England [do teacht i n-Erinn iar m-beith athaidh foda h-iSaccsaibh]: *AFM*, s.a. 1492.
29 Conway, *Henry VII's relations*, pp 49–51.

Ireland led by Sir Roger Cotton and then to appoint trusted English servants – Garth and Thomas Wyatt – as special royal commissioners to restore order.[30]

This politically destabilizing feud, and the fear that Warbeck would soon launch another invasion, ultimately moved the king to summon Ormond, Kildare and other prominent government officials to court for discussions in 1493. Kildare and Ormond used their time in England to defend their conduct and to hurl further allegations at one another. So much is well known. But before either arrived at court, Archbishop Fitzsimons, having been replaced as governor by Robert Preston, Viscount Gormanston, had made his way to court. There, Fitzsimons declared to King Henry in full 'the state affairs of Ireland'. His testimony may have included allegations of Kildare's misrule, but Ware recounts an exchange between the archbishop and the king, which suggests that the discussions on Ireland held at court in late 1493 addressed the lordship's problems in terms much broader than the Butler–Fitzgerald feud:

> The king among several discourses with the archbishop, asked him the question: my lord, I do much admire at my subjects of Ireland, why they do so oft rebel against their prince, and that they have not improved my lordship there all this while, since our ancestors conquest there; the country being, as is reported, a fruitful soil, and a place for good trading?[31]

This fits well with what is known of Henry VII. The king was practical. He was prepared to pardon men who were useful to him, even those who had rebelled against their prince – the king had, just five years earlier, pardoned Fitzsimons himself for the archbishop's conspicuous support of 'Edward VI'. But the king was also exceedingly apprehensive, and it is clear that the support the latest pretender had received in Ireland weighed on him.[32] His remarks on Ireland were detached and depthless, in keeping with a king who knew little about conditions there – one might have formulated the question which Henry posed to Fitzsimons after a cursory reading of a 'Libel of English policy'. It was Fitzsimons' reply to his king that was more revealing. Rather than articulating an oral response before the court, Fitzsimons referred the king to a letter, which he had sent him in advance of his coming to England. That letter is now lost, but Ware relates some of its contents:

---

30   For this see, BL, Additional MS 4791, fo. 135; S.G. Ellis, 'Henry VII and Ireland, 1491–1496' in James Lydon (ed.), *England and Ireland in the later middle ages: essays in honour of Jocelyn Otway-Ruthven* (Dublin, 1981), p. 240. For a more general discussion of feuding in Ireland in this period, see now Peter Crooks, 'Factions, feuds and noble power in late medieval Ireland', *IHS*, 35 (2007), 425–54.

31   Ware, *The antiquities and history of Ireland*, p. 26.

32   Chrimes, *Henry VII*, p. 81.

The greatest and chiefest thing that not only impoverisheth this your highnesses lordship of Ireland, as also causeth so many stirs and jars with them (is idleness;) for if the father have an estate, and dies, though he have never so many children, they all hanker on that name, who is prince or chief of them, rather than to take an employment or trade, supposing it a disgrace so to do; their fathers afore them having acquired an estate. This is the custom of the countrey, which your highness subjects have learned of the natives, filling their panches [stomaches], care not for any other than brawling, and plotting. There are so many straglers, and poor, that it is more charity to put them to work, then to succour them with victuals.[33]

The archbishop's comments represent the first known attempt in the Tudor period to identify for the crown the causes of the problems that beset its lordship of Ireland. Fitzsimons, a Palesman whom the sixteenth-century chronicler Richard Stanihurst later described as 'a famous clerke and exquisitelie learned both in philosophie and divinitie', drew special attention to the phenomenon of Englishmen disregarding the law of primogeniture in favour of the Irish custom whereby any member of a four-generation agnatic kinship group – known as the *derbhfine* – might succeed to land and political and social distinction.[34] Of the many differences between English society and Irish society, nothing set the two apart more than these conflicting modes of succession. It comes as small surprise that later Tudor commentators would list chronic succession disputes as one of the greatest evils of Irish society. However the root of the problem, according to Fitzsimons, was idleness. This language of social control, which the archbishop employed, was something which the king of England could understand and which he wrestled with in his own kingdom.

To judge by the tenor of the question that Henry VII put to Fitzsimons, the king had not yet engaged in any meaningful way with the problems facing his subjects in Ireland, which the archbishop had sought to highlight in his letter. Nevertheless, the winter of 1493–4 represented a pivotal point in the development of Henry VII's understanding of conditions in Ireland. The traffic between Dublin and the royal court was increasing: Fitzsimons had been a part of a delegation that had attended upon the king at Kenilworth that summer.[35] But, by early 1494,

---

33   Ibid.

34   Raphael Holinshed, *The ... chronicles of England, Scotlande and Irelande ...* (London, 1577) (ed.), Henry Ellis, 6 vols (London, 1807–8), ii, p. 41. For a discussion of succession in Irish society, see Nicholls, *Gaelic and Gaelicized Ireland in the later Middle Ages* (2nd ed. Dublin, 2003), pp 28–31.

35   A sum was paid out of the exchequer to Henry Wyatt to cover the costs of passage from England to Ireland of Thomas Garth, Alexander Plunkett, the lord chancellor, Thomas Butler,

Fitzsimons, Kildare, Garth, James Ormond, Lord Deputy Gormanston, Archbishop Octavian del Palagio of Armagh, Edmund Lane, the bishop of Kildare, Nicholas Turner, chief justice of the commons pleas, half a dozen Pale gentlemen and several Limerick merchants had all joined their king (and Earl Thomas Ormond) at court.[36] Kildare is said to have gone to the king 'with great retinue and splendour'; he and his household stayed in England for a full year.[37] In January, the visitors from Ireland attended a royal feast at Westminster where, we are told by the London chronicler, King Henry knighted 'ii Iresshemen of therlis of Kildare' before the dinner in the king's chamber – the chronicler was referring to the knighthoods bestowed upon the Pale peers, Nicholas St Lawrence, Lord Howth and Christopher Fleming, Lord Slane.[38] All told, this was the largest gathering in England of the political community of Ireland in well over a century.[39] The king used this opportunity to compose the differences between the Butlers and Fitzgeralds. But Kildare and the leaders of Ireland's English political community also made use of their nearness to the king and his sustained interest in Ireland. They prevailed upon Henry VII to initiate a policy that would establish a lasting political settlement in Ireland.[40] With Warbeck in Vienna seeking the support of Emperor Maximilian, the time seemed right to secure Ireland against a Yorkist invasion and, in the process, to address the lordship's longstanding problems, which were doubtless communicated to the king during the winter of 1493–4. Not for nothing did Henry VII instruct his ambassador in August 1494 to inform the king of France that he had determined to put Ireland in order, in particular the 'Irlandois sauvaiges', so that they might live under the same law as the English and the Irish of the country who had adopted the English language. Charles VIII learned that it was the principal men of Ireland, men like Kildare and Fitzsimons who had lately come to the English court for consultations, who convinced Henry VII to act. An army, which was to be led by distinguished soldiers, and complemented by men distinguished in their knowledge of English law, would, the king declared, be ready to leave for Ireland in September.[41]

the master of the rolls, Christopher Dowdall, the archdeacon of Meath, and Archbishop Fitzsimons. Conway reckoned that Fitzsimons and the rest were at court for consultations with the king sometime in early summer 1493, prior to the opening in late June of that year of the parliament which Fitzsimons presided over: *Henry VII's relations*, p. 56.

36 Ellis, 'Henry VII and Ireland', p. 241.
37 *AU, s.a.* 1493.
38 Conway, *Henry VII's relations*, p. 58; *Chronicles of London*, ed. C.L. Kingsford (Oxford, 1905), p. 200 (quotation); *The knights of England*, ed. William Arthur Shaw, 2 vols (London, 1906), ii, p. 28.
39 In early 1376 two proctors from each diocese, two knights from each shire and two burgesses from each borough were elected in Ireland and travelled to court to consult with the king: Richardson and Sayles, *Irish parliament*, pp 83–5.
40 Chrimes, *Henry VII*, p. 262; Ellis, 'Henry VII and Ireland', pp 241–2.
41 Instructions to Richmond, King of Arms, 10 Aug. 1494, BL, Cotton MSS, Caligula D VI, fo.

The expedition reached Ireland in October 1494, led by Sir Edward Poynings, deputy to Prince Henry, the nominal lieutenant, and accompanied by the earl of Kildare and James Ormond, plus a handful of skilled lawyers and administrators. Poynings was an experienced military commander, having lately served as deputy-lieutenant of Calais in France. He brought with him a further 400 archers which, together with the English troops still in Ireland (chiefly the retinue of Thomas Garth, since appointed constable of Dublin castle), gave him command of a small army of 653 men. This was not much more than the force disposed by Edgecombe in 1488, although the aims of Poynings' expedition were certainly more ambitious. As previously at Calais, his overriding priority was to deny Ireland as a base to Warbeck; but beyond that, with Kildare's connection defending the borders of the English Pale, Poynings' army could also be deployed as a strike force against the Irishry. In the event, Poynings immediately marched into Ulster, accompanied by Kildare and Ormond with their retinues. The earldom of Ulster – or the coastal remnants of it, which was all that now survived – had been annexed to the crown in 1461; and sometime in 1494 two south Ulster lords, MacMahon and O'Reilly, had routed a force of *Gaill*, reportedly killing sixty and imprisoning many others.[42] But the urgency with which Poynings pressed this late autumn campaign would suggest that his main aim – as English sources suggested – was to counter the intrigues there of Warbeck and James IV, the king of Scots. The Ulster Irish mostly submitted, surrendering pledges to keep the peace, while those who refused had their lands destroyed.[43] Very soon, however, the expedition's military aspects began to unravel after Poynings misinterpreted Kildare's negotiations with O'Hanlon for his surrender as treasonable. Following the earl's arrest and removal to England, the governor was preoccupied in the spring and summer with the siege of Carlow castle, seized by Kildare's brother, and then the threat from Warbeck, culminating in the siege of Waterford.[44] Hopes thus evaporated of penetrating further into the Irish interior and recovering lands to which the king held title.

This did not, however, prevent the administration from laying the groundwork for a forward policy. The king had, in preparation for this, initiated in August–September 1494 what proved to be almost a clean sweep of the top posts in the Dublin administration. The political backbone for this remodelled administration were provided by Poynings himself and the treasurer, Sir Hugh Conway, both of whom had been closely associated with the king since Buckingham's rebellion in 1483. Legal expertise was supplied by Thomas

---

19 (printed in *L. & P. Rich. III & Hen. VII*, ii, pp 295–6); Conway, *Henry VII's relations*, pp 61–2; Ellis, 'Henry VII and Ireland', p. 242.
42   *AU, s.a.* 1494.
43   Conway, *Henry VII's relations*, pp 78–9; *Cal. pat. rolls, 1485–94*, p. 461.
44   Conway, *Henry VII's relations*, pp 79–86; Ellis, 'Henry VII and Ireland', p. 243.

Bowring and John Topcliffe, appointed chief justices of king's bench and common pleas respectively, plus Walter Yvers, chief baron of the exchequer. And the new lord chancellor, heading the lordship's chief writing office with associated equitable jurisdiction, was Henry Deane, bishop of Bangor and the future archbishop of Canterbury, supported by John Forster, clerk of the hanaper and of the crown in chancery. By 1496, Deane had replaced Poynings as governor as the military threat from Warbeck receded; and Conway's financial role had in effect been superseded the previous June by a triumvirate of William Hattecliffe, undertreasurer, John Pympe, treasurer of the wars, and the return of Henry Wyatt, as commissioner and auditor. They were also supported by Hugh Blagg, appointed chief chamberlain and chief engrosser.[45]

By this date, the focus of the regime was more on raising additional revenues so as to balance the books; but from the outset the search for additional sources of revenue had included a close scrutiny of the revenues that had formerly been available to the crown in Ireland, which the new Tudor regime had precious little knowledge of. This was backed by a sweeping act of resumption, passed by Poynings' parliament, of all the king's lands and rights alienated since the reign of Edward II. Another statute, relating to the king's title to lands and revenues in the earldom of Ulster and the lordships of Trim and Connacht now annexed to the crown, ordered the return of all the records, rolls and inquisitions held 'in the treasury of Trym' which had of late been 'taken and embesilled by diverse persons of malice prepensed'.[46] The hope was that a thorough investigation of the crown's feudal rights – a typical device of the new Tudor regime – would uncover concealed sources of income, notably in outlying parts of the lordship beyond the normal reach of the Dublin administration. Parliament also granted the king a double subsidy, and in preparation for this levy, the regime instituted further searches that revealed the levy of a subsidy, based on an early-fifteenth-century extent, including small sums received from districts outside the English Pale – from Co. Wexford, the clergy of Ferns and Waterford and Lismore dioceses, the city of Waterford, and the town of New Ross.[47] Thus, the decidedly optimistic estimate of receipts now due at the exchequer following the act of resumption passed by parliament in winter 1494–5 included the feefarms of the cities of Cork (£53 6s. 8d.), Limerick (£73 6s. 8d.) and Waterford (£66 13s. 4d.), plus the manors of Ballymergy and Bray in the south Dublin marches. Ballymergy, recently worth £5 a year, now lay 'wast. in defectu tenencium'. Bray had long lain waste, but a search of the records revealed that it had once been valued £40 8s. 6d. a year, and that it was still worth £7 1s. 8½d. annually

---

45 Ellis, *Reform and revival*, pp 220–3; Conway, *Henry VII's relations*, pp 63–6, 83–4.
46 Statute roll, 10 Hen. VII c. 29 (*Stat. Ire.*, i, 51–2 (c.14 in printed statutes)); Conway, *Henry VII's relations*, pp 204–9.
47 BL, Royal MS 18C, XIV, fo. 108.

as late as 1349. Further searches revealed that the value of other manors belonging to the king in the south Dublin marches was now only around half what it had been in the late thirteenth century.[48] In the 1470s, the Irish parliament had hoped to reverse this decline through renewed colonization. Invoking a statute enacted in a parliament at Leicester [1426], parliament had asked King Edward IV in 1474 to issue a proclamation that 'all maner persons of Irland byrth ... dwelling w'in England' should return to Ireland 'to enhabit such contries as shall [be?] conquered' by an army of 1,000 archers which they also asked the king to send for 'the relief and adepcyon of the sayd land'.[49] It may be that a similar request to Henry VII in connection with Poynings' expedition had prompted the general inquisition recorded in a contemporary London chronicle:

> Also in the said moneth of September [1495] was a generall Inquisicion made thrugh oute England, and specially in the Citie of London, for all men, women and children born w[th]in the land Ireland, and dwellyng w[th]yn this realme of their namys, agis, and ffaculties; which were certified in to the Kynges exchequyr at Westm'[inster]'.[50]

These searches were intensified under the new undertreasurer, William Hattecliffe, who found among the records of the liberty of Meath evidence of a local subsidy granted to the earl of March in 1413–14 of 6s. 8d. a ploughland on each of 342 ploughlands in sixteen Meath baronies.[51] In early Tudor times, moreover, scutage (called 'royal service' in Ireland) was still occasionally levied in the English Pale, and so Hattecliffe also scrutinized the records for the amounts previously owed by military tenants throughout Ireland. He extracted lists of scutage owed by tenants in the Pale counties, and Cork, Kilkenny, Limerick, Tipperary, Waterford and Wexford, plus the lordships of Connacht, Trim and Ulster. Some of these went back to 1297–8, but the Wexford returns appear to be for a service in c.1415.[52] Hattecliffe outlined his strategy here in memoranda concerning the office of treasurer. The clerk of the pipe should search the pipe rolls for every shire, city, and borough within the land to know 'the demesnes and fermes certain belonging to the king in right of his lordship', 'the values and extents of the same in the best yeres of pease', and also 'the grenewex of issues, fynes, and amercimentes' charged to every sheriff 'in most comon yeres', and thus to 'se what is lesse answerd nowe in every of the premises, and for what cause resonable'.[53]

---

48 BL, Royal MS 18C, XIV, fos 111, 113v, 116; TNA, E 101/248, no. 17.
49 TNA, C 47/10, no. 29 (printed in Bryan, *The great earl of Kildare*, pp 18–22).
50 Kingsford, *Chronicles of London*, p. 207.
51 BL, Royal MS 18C, XIV, fo. 108v.
52 Ibid., fos 159–65. Cf. S.G. Ellis, 'Taxation and defence in late medieval Ireland: the survival of scutage' *JRSAI*, 107 (1977), 5–28.
53 BL, Royal MS 18C, XIV, fo. 231 (*L. & P. Ric. III & Hen. VII*, ii, 64).

Overall, the Poynings regime was evidently very efficient in collecting and increasing the king's revenues in Ireland. In the year 1495–6 the exchequer accounted for no less than £3,055 15s. 7¾d. in moneys received or assigned, which was almost double the amount that had normally been available for most of the fifteenth century.[54] Yet the costs of government were also much larger under Poynings so that, even after various economies had been made in winter 1495–6, the administration was still running a deficit of more than £1,000 a year. Of the various additional sources of revenue identified by the exchequer, moreover, almost nothing had been collected from outlying parts of the lordship hitherto beyond the normal reach of the Dublin administration. In that sense, the search instituted by the regime for concealed sources of income based on the crown's feudal rights had proved fruitless. Even so, what the experience of the Poynings regime had perhaps highlighted to the cluster of English-born officials inserted into the Dublin administration to spearhead reform was that the crown's rights extended over large parts of the island outside the English Pale. What was needed, therefore, was to devise how the system of English law and administration based on these crown rights might be more fully restored in the lordship's southern shires, as well as in the earldom of Ulster and the lordship of Connacht now annexed to the crown.

In summer 1496, however, Henry VII decided to revert to traditional methods of governing Ireland and reappointed the earl of Kildare as deputy, granting him the Irish revenues without account in lieu of a salary. There is no sign thereafter that the king took any further interest in the Irish revenues or the reform of the Irish exchequer. Most of the English-born officials serving under Poynings departed when the remaining English troops were discharged, although the two chief justices stayed on. Hattecliffe apparently left in late autumn,[55] bringing with him his books of accounts which, since they ended up in the Royal Manuscripts now housed in the British Library, were presumably scrutinized initially by Henry VII. There is no indication, however, that Hattecliffe's activities in 1495–6 had influenced the direction of Tudor policy when the crown next mounted an expedition to Ireland, under the earl of Surrey in 1520. Indeed, as we shall see, the knowledge gained about Ireland by Englishmen, though they were often careful enough to preserve in it written form, was for all intents and purposes lost to subsequent generations of officials through the careless storage of records and the crown's regular reversion to long periods of rule through local magnates.

Kildare's restoration as governor in 1496 has often been viewed as marking the effective end of Henry VII's involvement in Ireland. After all, it heralded a

---

54 Calculated from BL, Royal MS 18C, XIV, fos 22–89v. Cf. Ellis, 'Henry VII and Ireland', p. 245.

55 Conway, *Henry VII's relations*, p. 77.

return to aristocratic delegation, the beginning of a 'Kildare ascendancy', which secured the lordship for the Tudor dynasty and allowed the English crown to recede into the background of Irish affairs for another two decades.[56] At the same time, however, there is evidence to show that the crown maintained an interest in Ireland and was prepared to play a more active role in assisting Kildare in the defence of the lordship from the Irish. In spring 1496 the king heard a detailed petition from the prior of St Patrick in Holmpatrick, Co. Dublin. He learned that pirates regularly availed of the many havens that dotted the coast of the nearby island of Lambay – the spot of Richard Edgecombe's landing near Dublin a decade earlier – to threaten the priory's interests along the coast. The king granted the priory and convent the licence (and the local customs revenues) necessary to construct a fortified harbour and wall between Lambay and the mainland for 'the common advantage and defence of the king's subjects'.[57] Later, but probably in the months following Warbeck's capture in October 1497, the king commanded John Wise of Waterford, a former chief baron of the exchequer in Ireland, to furnish him with information on Ireland. In April Wise wrote to the earl of Ormond at court informing him how he had

> written to the Kinges grace of thorde and maner of this his lande in euery thing accord[ing] to his formo^r comaundementes and if his grace move of the same vnto you for the love of God dispose you *to reforme* the abusyon of the same by yor wisdome and powere that the land may the better be remedyed by you as it dyd sumtyme by yor noble auncesters.[58]

Certainly for Wise, King Henry's request for information of 'this his lande in euery thing' was a sign that the king was considering the 'reforme' of Ireland. Wise's letter represents the first known reference to the reform of Ireland in Tudor times. The idea, as we have seen, was not new. To write, as Henry VII had a decade earlier, of his desire to see his subjects in Ireland 'reduced to a good and lafull ordyr and obeisaunce' was as much as to state his intention to 'reform' them. In the English of the early sixteenth century, 'to reduce' and 'to reform' both meant the same thing: to restore something to a previous (positive) state or condition. In a land that was invariably described as being in a state of decay – or in this case 'abusyon' – having retreated from the glories of the original conquest the need for reduction and reform was self-evident.[59] But, while there was

---

56 S.G. Ellis, 'Tudor policy and the Kildare ascendancy in the lordship of Ireland', *IHS*, 20 (1977), 235–71.

57 *Rotulorum patentium et clausorum cancellariae Hiberniae calendarium*, ed., Edward Tresham (Dublin, 1828), p. 271/17.

58 John Wise to earl of Ormond, 30 Apr. 1498, TNA, SC 1/52/64, fo. 67 (our italics).

59 *Oxford English dictionary* (eds), John Simpson and Edmund Weiner (2nd ed. Oxford, 1989), *sub* 'reduce' and 'reform'.

a clear recognition that reform was necessary, how, exactly, reform was actually to be carried out was far from clear. Reform, as we shall see, was an elastic concept with no agreed meaning, though the evidence would suggest that reform, when applied to fifteenth-century Ireland, entailed a military conquest of the Irish, and any rebel English, followed by an overhaul of government and society in English areas. The king had not, to this point, explicitly written of the need (or his intention) to reform Ireland in a broad socio-political sense (though his reference to his decision to put Ireland ['pais dIrlande'] in order ['mectre ordre'] in his communication to the king of France Charles VIII came close); but as is evident from the repeated declarations issued by the parliament of Ireland in the fifteenth century, the reformation of Ireland was a well-established political theme which must have been broadly familiar to the Tudor king. In 1455, the parliament of Ireland held in Dublin agreed to despatch a message that was to communicate to Henry VI, and to his lieutenant the duke of York, 'the great eminent danger that rests in this land, by the which this said land is likely to be finally destroyed, unless the most speedy remedy be had out of England for the reformation [*reformacion*] thereof'.[60] Here, as in 1421 and later in 1474, the English of Ireland sought to show the desperate condition of the lordship and urged the crown, in the most formal way available to them, to save them from the Irish and thereby restore Ireland to its former state. It is within this tradition that this first Tudor reference to reform must be situated.

But before any reform of Ireland could begin, if indeed that is what Henry VII intended at all, the king clearly sought information. After more than a decade on the throne, Henry VII had gained some knowledge of Ireland and was better equipped to rule it. He had in that time welcomed to his court a variety of his subjects from across the Irish Sea. He had fashioned a strong personal bond with Kildare in whom he placed his trust as his representative and to whom he might always turn for counsel on Ireland; the bond between Henry and Earl Gerald grew closer still when in 1503 Kildare visited court to celebrate the occasion of his son's marriage to Henry's kinswoman. In England, the earl of Ormond continued to be an active royal councillor whose influence and connections in Ireland remained valuable; and after 1495 the king could count Poynings as a councillor who could lay claim to recent military and administrative experience of Ireland. Wise, however, could speak directly to the growing threat from the Irish in Munster. James Ormond, marginalized and embittered since Kildare's restoration, had been killed in 1497, but not before he had introduced his O'Brien kinsmen into the Butler lands in Kilkenny and Tipperary. Wise was then engaged in defending these English districts from the growing power of the O'Briens: the day of his writing to Earl Thomas, Wise claimed to

60 *Stat. rolls Ire., Hen. VI*, pp 356–8; above, p. 116.

have travelled to Carrick-on-Suir in Co. Tipperary 'for to byld a place in the same to resist all the Irishemen in this land'.[61] The situation was serious. Kildare wrote to Ormond that O'Brien, 'with the assistance of all Irishmen', intended to make war on the Butler lands in Kilkenny and Tipperary and on 'all the king's subjects here'. According to Kildare, O'Brien was 'a mortal enemy of all Englishmen', who had only allied with James Ormond 'to destroy Englishmen'; the earl was compelled to ask Henry VII to send over an army of 300 archers and 60 gunners.[62] Wise, Ormond's client, was thus well-positioned to furnish the king with information on a subject about which Henry and his councillors knew little – the Irish. As suggested above, in section 1.2, it is possible that the information that Wise sent on to the king formed the basis for what we know as 'A description of the power of Irishmen'. In any event, Henry VII did not begin the reformation of Ireland; and it is unclear whether the king ever sent Kildare the troops he had requested.

But O'Brien's stunning defeat of the Butlers in 1499, in which engagement the sovereign of Kilkenny was killed and '16 score corslets [320 breast-plates]' were carried off, served as a telling reminder of the danger posed by the Irish, and by O'Brien in particular.[63] Even after Kildare won his famous victory over O'Brien and his allies at the Battle of Knockdoe outside Galway in 1504, O'Brien remained beyond the earl's effective control. When O'Brien erected a bridge over the river Shannon in 1506 to carry his power into the English areas round Limerick, Kildare again turned to the king for help.[64] Only two years before, Fitzsimons was at court trumpeting the earl's success at Knockdoe; now Kildare sent Lord Slane to court to convey the seriousness of the situation and to plead for a substantial English intervention in Ireland. The king's surprising response appears in the records of his council:

> My Lord Chauncellor by the Kinges Comaundement shewethe that uppon suche sondes and messages as have been sent to the Kinges grace from the Lord of Kildare of the Rebellion of Ireland and of the warr moved continued by Ebren [O'Brien] of the wilde Irishe his grace fore-seeinge that littell advantage or proffitt hath growne of such Armyes and Captaynes for the Conducte of the same as the Kinges grace hathe divers tymes send into the land of Ireland for the Reduccon of the same there-fore his grace entendythe god willinge to make a viage personall in his moste noble personn for the represse of the wilde Irishe and redresse and sure reduccon of all the said land For which Cause the Kinges grace wil-

61 John Wise to earl of Ormond, 30 Apr. 1498, TNA, SC 1/52/64, fo. 67.
62 *Ormond deeds*, iv, p. 336.
63 Ware, *The antiquities and history of Ireland*, p. 39; *AU, s.a.* 1499.
64 *AFM, s.a.* 1506.

leth his Counsell to comen and treate by ripe advisement of Convenient provision for the said voyage And Firste what number of people shalbe necessarye for the same.

The expedition was discussed at a thinly attended council meeting in early December: Slane was there; Ormond and Poynings were not. The king's council made the following resolution:

> ... yt is thought by the Lordes nowe assembled that Sixe Thowsand persons of well Chosen men and noe lesse over and above those that be and shalbe of the Kinges howshoulde besydes those that shall Convaye the cariages shalbe a Convenient and meete number for this voyage.
> Item they thinke that three greate peeces of gunnes four hundred Hargeboshes threescore Fawkyns fyve hundred handgonnes. Tercio Decembris [22 Hen. VII].[65]

In many respects, King Henry's decision to come to Ireland at the head of the largest English army to cross the Irish Sea in over a century may be seen as the logical culmination of his interaction with Ireland over two decades. The imposition of an Englishmen in Ireland had secured Ireland for the dynasty against the Yorkists. Aristocratic delegation had, at last, proved an effective and relatively inexpensive means of ruling Ireland. But neither had brought about Ireland's 'sure reduccon' as O'Brien's actions were making clear. The consumption of treasure in vain was an important factor in shaping the king's thinking: he had despatched smaller armies to Ireland with Edgecombe, James Ormond, Roger Cotton and Poynings with limited success; he had spent nearly £20,000 sterling on the lordship during the short period of Poynings' administration alone.[66] But the king had also to this point relied on other men to rule Ireland and to communicate to him information about his lordship. Estrete, Edgecombe, Kildare, Ormond, Garth, Fitzsimons, Poynings and Wise all acted on the king's behalf in Ireland in this capacity. Now the first Tudor king of England would travel to Ireland to do and to see and to experience for himself first hand.

Only the expedition failed to materialize: Henry VII never saw his lordship. The expedition, as projected, would have been an undertaking of massive financial and logistical proportions. Richard II's expedition to Ireland of 1394 was of a similar size and it required 500 seafaring vessels and a parliamentary subsidy to see it through.[67] Henry VII, aged 50 years in 1506, was also old (beyond his years

65 *Select cases in the council of Henry VII*, pp 46–7; Ware, *The antiquities and history*, p. 48.
66 Ellis, 'Henry VII and Ireland', pp 242, 247, 250.
67 Lydon, 'Richard II's expeditions to Ireland', 142; P.R. Cavill, *Henry VII and his English parliaments, 1485–1504* (Oxford, 2009), p. 180.

it was said) and his health, if not his mental strength, was beginning to fail.[68] At this stage of his life the king lacked the single-mindedness necessary to transform political aspiration in England into thousands of boots on the ground across the sea in Ireland. And besides, Kildare showed himself, in the months and years after his despatch of Slane to court, quite capable of containing the threat posed by O'Brien and the Irish more generally: like so many of his predecessors the king reasoned that Ireland's reform could wait. Henry VII's death, in 1509, meant that the task of reducing Ireland would fall to some other Tudor king.

By the end of his reign Henry VII had developed a basic understanding of Ireland and how to rule it. He had acquired this knowledge primarily through his efforts to secure both the recognition of his dynasty in the lordship and royal control over the island's English districts: the information yielded by Edgecombe's journey and Poynings' administration and the information communicated to him at court by the representatives of English political society in Ireland were all means to this end. Yet Henry VII had done little to foster a greater or more precise knowledge of Ireland at his court. The king's request for information from Wise may have represented a first step toward creating a written record of current information on Ireland, something that might have outlived the reign and been of use to his successors; but more typically Henry VII established himself as the repository of information on Ireland and placed greater emphasis on cultivating personal relationships with his subjects in the lordship, and with Kildare above all others. The result was that when the old king died, much of what had been learned of Ireland at court died with him.

---

68   Sean Cunningham, *Henry VII* (London, 2007), p. 114.

2.2

'To attayne to the knowledge off the state and maner of this londe'

Henry VIII inherited the council and court of his father, and so also the old regime's lack of expert knowledge of Ireland. This ignorance was mitigated somewhat by the presence on the new king's council of Sir Edward Poynings, the former governor, and the earl of Ormond who, though very old, continued to maintain regular correspondence with his clients in Ireland.[1] Young King Henry could also count among the groomsmen of his privy chamber William Wise, the Waterford-born son of John Wise who, a decade earlier, had furnished Henry VII with written information on Ireland.[2] But Henry VIII had no immediate need for expert or precise knowledge of that part of his inheritance. His father had bequeathed to him an Ireland exorcized of its Yorkist demons and dominated by the earl of Kildare who, over the previous twenty years, had emerged as a loyal supporter of the Tudor dynasty. And, in marked contrast to the start of the previous reign, the Geraldines were no strangers to the new king. Henry VIII would have remembered Kildare from the magnate's several visits to court, and recalled from his own abbreviated boyhood his time spent with the earl's son and heir, Gerald, Lord Offaly. Kildare would govern Ireland for Henry VIII just as he had for Henry VII. It was just as well. The young king expressed no interest in his lordship. His ambitions lay in the south, with his inheritance in France: it was there where the second Tudor king of England planned to make his mark on the world.

There can be little doubt that the new regime's 'habitually passive' regard for Ireland contributed to a renewed expression for reform in the lordship.[3] Within a decade of Henry VIII's accession to the throne, three works of writing appeared that sought to impart information about Ireland to the new king and his ministers. In the case of one of these works, the anonymous treatise entitled 'The State of Ireland and Plan for its Reformation', King Henry was offered a detailed programme setting out how Ireland's reform might be achieved. 'The State of Ireland' – endorsed only with the words 'J[es]us m[er]cy' – was the longest, the most sophisticated in its social and political analysis of conditions in

---

1   *Ormond deeds*, iv, pp 356–73.
2   Maginn, *William Cecil, Ireland, and the Tudor state*, pp 19–20.
3   Bradshaw, *The Irish constitutional revolution*, p. 33.

5 Henry VIII, unknown artist, 1520, NPG 469.

Ireland and much the most informative of the three.[4] Another anonymous (but never published) version of this treatise survives in a later sixteenth-century copy. Its author claimed that his work was merely a 'little abstract in thenglishe tonge' out of a longer book written, seemingly in the form of a poem, by the mysterious author 'Pandar', called 'Salus populi', which, he maintained, had been 'directed to the kinge and his counsell'.[5] The 'State of Ireland' is generally accepted to have been composed about 1515, and so was written around the same time as the two tracts written by Patrick Finglas and William Darcy, which were presented to the king and his council that year and which, decades later, became components of the Hatfield Compendium.[6] Taken together, it has been argued that this 'reform literature' heralded the beginning of a 'mainstream Anglo-Irish political tradition' based on 'the aspirations of commonwealth liberalism', which would become a feature of Irish politics for centuries.[7]

But were these writings evidence of a new form of political discourse in Ireland? On the one hand, as has been demonstrated above, an 'Anglo-Irish reforming milieu' had existed in the lordship for more than a century by the time of Henry VIII's accession. Yet, on the other hand, nothing like these documents survive for earlier periods of Irish history. A comparison between these early

4   State of Ireland, and plan for its reformation, c.1515, TNA, SP 60/1/9, fos 13–28v. The treatise was transcribed and published in extenso in SP Hen. VIII, ii, pp 1–31. Bradshaw's remains the most penetrating analysis of this document: The Irish constitutional revolution, pp 53–6. But see also Fiona Fitzsimons' comments in 'Cardinal Wolsey, the native affinities and the failure of reform in Henrician Ireland', p. 84. Historians' inability to establish definitively the identity of its author limit our understanding of the document's place in early Tudor Ireland. William Rokeby, the English-born archbishop of Dublin, has been suggested as its author: White, 'Tudor plantations in Ireland to 1571', p. 31. However Fitzsimons has more recently argued, pointedly though not entirely convincingly, for John Kite, the English-born archbishop of Armagh's authorship of the treatise: Fitzsimons, 'Cardinal Wolsey, the native affinities and the failure of reform in Henrician Ireland', p. 84. For the similar educational backgrounds of Rokeby and Kite, see D.G. Newcombe, s.v. 'William Rokeby' and 'John Kite', ODNB. It is, perhaps, worthy of noting that Rokeby signed off on a letter to Wolsey, written 12 Dec. 1515, beseeching 'm[er]cyfull J[es]us' to preserve him: TNA, SP 60/1/8, fo. 11.

5   This version of the 'State of Ireland' contains otherwise unknown recommendations for the lordship's reform, such as the suggestion that the king's eldest son 'always be named prince of Yreland as well as of Wales and to dwell w^{th}in the land of Yreland', at a purpose-built English city in the centre of the country at Athlone: BL, Additional MS 4792, fos 107–15v (quotations, fos 107v, 110). Ware classified this 'Pandar', or 'Pandarus', as an Irish writer of the fifteenth century, noting: 'Pandarus, or the author of a book De Salute Populi, flourished in the reigns of Edward IV, Edward V, Richard III and Henry VII; and perhaps also Henry VIII. In that treatise he lays down the causes of the calamities of Ireland, and prescribes remedies adopted to those times': The antiquities and history of Ireland, p. 316. In the Catalogue of the manuscripts preserved in the British Museum, ed. Samuel Ayscough (London, 1782), p. 330, this manuscript is confusingly described as 'Pandarus. Salus Populi, de rebus Hibernicis, temp. Hen. VI'.

6   See above, pp 30–1, 45–8.

7   Bradshaw, The Irish constitutional revolution, pp 32–57, 268 (quotations, pp 33, 37 and 268).

Henrician documents with some of the material copied into Christopher Cusack's commonplace book serves to illustrate the change that had occurred. Among the miscellaneous material in the commonplace book – prayers, historical information and local shrieval records – Cusack included a geographical and economic description of Ireland that, as has been shown, is similar in substance to the section on the 'revenues of Ireland' in the Hatfield Compendium.[8] Cusack's book is dated 1511, but the material in it – some of it written in Latin, some of it written in English – is almost certainly older. Just how old is difficult to say: the description of Ireland refers nostalgically to the landed revenues available to the crown in 'the old erle of March is dayes', but notes that the king of England as 'lord of all Irlande in substaunce hath beside the titill of the crowne that is to say the erledome of Ulster all hole lord[ship] of all Connaght lord of all Myth lord[ship] of iiiith p[ar]te of Leynst^r lord[ship] of the iiii p[ar]te of Mounste$^{r'}$', and so must have been updated after Edward IV's accession in 1461.[9] This description of Ireland in Cusack's commonplace book is also nearly identical to the information contained in a document called the 'Geographical description of Ireland'. This latter document, anonymous and undated, was placed under the year 1514, near to the start of the State Papers, Henry VIII (SP 60). But the orthography is more typical of fifteenth-century practice and there is no evidence, in any case, to suggest a date of 1514.[10] Cusack's description of Ireland notes: 'yf Ireland were reconcilit and English as England is to the king is obeaunce and enabitid and occupied w^t Englis men the king might have ev[er]y yere of comen subsidy of the lande vi^s viii^d of ev[er]y ploweland'.[11] Here, in effect, is an unelaborate and implicit prescription for Ireland's reform. Only this information was not, so far as we can tell, intended for the king, or for a wide audience. Rather, it was information, likely knowledge passed down from generation to generation by Ireland's English community, which Cusack deemed of sufficient importance to copy into his book for his own sake, or for posterity, or perhaps for both. This kind of material is a far cry from the more elaborate historical and reform treatises composed for Henry VIII and his councillors in 1515.

For the modern Irish historian Brendan Bradshaw, it was the influence of Renaissance humanism that moved the English of Ireland, particularly the gentry

8 See above, pp 50–2.   9   TCD MS 594, fo. 36v.
10 A geographical account of Ireland, TNA, SP 60/1/5, fo. 7 (the document is endorsed 'Discriptio Hibernie'). An Elizabethan copy of this document is headed 'out of an old pamflett': BL, Additional MS, Yelverton MS 48017, fo. 76. Historians have generally overlooked the geographical account of Ireland. John Montaño purports to quote from it, but in fact gives evidence from 'The state of Ireland and plan for its reformation': *The roots of English colonization in Ireland* (Cambridge, 2011), p. 227 (quoting *SP Hen. VIII*, ii, p. 8). Another document, a letter from Kildare to 'the king', was originally assigned the date 5 June 1510 and placed at SP 60/1/2. The letter, however, was subsequently deemed to date from Henry VII's reign and was removed from the SP 60 series accordingly.
11 TCD MS 594, fo. 36v.

of the English Pale, to begin lobbying for Ireland's reform early in Henry VIII's reign and to do so in what amounted to a new literary style.[12] It was in their written works, he argued, in his ground–breaking analysis of this material, where the 'new concept' of the 'commonwealth' – that is, their awareness of and interest in the welfare of their community – was first and most clearly expressed.[13] The influence on political thinking of an intellectual phenomenon such as humanism in early modern times is notoriously difficult to demonstrate; its influence in Ireland, where there was neither a royal court nor universities to foster the kind of scholarship and intellectual discourse associated with the phenomenon elsewhere, even more so. It is not enough to highlight the use, early in Henry VIII's reign, of the word 'commonwealth', or 'common wele', as evidence of the new-found influence of humanist ideals. For instance, in a letter to the earl of Desmond, Richard III – a figure not noted for his humanism – wrote that the earl should protect the king's subjects and have due regard for 'the common wele of those parties [that is, south Munster]'. Later, the earl of Kildare, who, as is well-known, was said to have been reared 'without great knowledge or learning, but rudely brought up according to the usage of his country', wrote to Henry VII of all that he had 'done for your honor and the wele of your subjectes of this your land'.[14] In 1508, the earl was reported to have sent his son to England with 'sertain letters and Instrucciones censerynge the Comen wel of this lande of Irland' – this material probably formed the basis for the legislation that was to be considered in parliament later that year.[15] We need not look to the Renaissance and the application of ancient learning to current political discourse to explain King Richard's and Kildare's concern for the commonwealth. Rather, both men employed language that was reflective of an unbroken sentiment that was frequently invoked earlier in the parliaments of fifteenth-century Ireland. The parliamentary statutes, because they were written in Norman French, did not make use of the English word 'common wele'; but they did seek to make laws which were to the 'common advantage of all the people' and the 'common benefit of all the people in the said land' ['p[ro]fit de tout le⁵ people'].[16] Even the author of the 'State of Ireland', a writer who demonstrated both great erudition and a concern for the well-being of the 'comen folke' of Ireland unseen in the works of Finglas and Darcy, was explicit in acknowledging the influence of the writer 'Pandar' and that author's much older ideas about Ireland's reform.[17]

---

12 Bradshaw, *The Irish constitutional revolution*, pp 35–51.

13 Ibid., pp 49–57 (quotation, p. 51).

14 *L. & P. Rich. III & Hen. VII*, i. pp 70, 380; S.G. Ellis, *s.v.* 'Gerald Fitzgerald', *ODNB* .

15 *Ormond deeds*, iv, p 361.

16 *Stat. rolls Ire., Hen. VI*, pp 10–11 (quotation), 26–7 (quotation), 41, 55, 89.

17 The version of the 'State of Ireland' housed in the British Library is more explicitly reliant on Pandar's book: BL, Additional MS 4792, fos 107–15v.

Apart from the influence of humanism, there is another, perhaps more mundane, explanation for the appearance early in Henry VIII's reign of the several written treatises on Ireland. An unintended consequence of Poynings' Law was that it deprived the English of Ireland of their traditional and most formal means of petitioning the king in England: the parliamentary address. Parliament was convened less frequently under the Tudors than in earlier times, thus reducing those occasions when the king's subjects might gather together as a community to make laws and to arrive at a consensus, which formed the basis for the earlier communication to the crown. Members of the English community of Ireland were thus forced to employ a new, more individualistic medium if they wished to communicate their fears, ideas and political aspirations to their king in England.

Still, this does not explain quite why elaborate political tracts do not appear earlier, in the last decade and more of Henry VII's reign for instance. We have already, above in section 1.1, suggested that what occasioned the writing of these several documents was the belief in Ireland (and indeed in England) by 1514 that Henry VIII intended to reform the lordship. The possibility that the young king, whose accession was the cause of so much jubilant expectation in England, would come to Ireland in person, something alluded to in a letter from Archbishop Kite to Wolsey, must have seemed real. It is an expectation evident in the 'State of Ireland'. Here, after outlining a plan for the rapid military reorganization and revitalization of English Ireland, its author held up the arrival of the king at the head of a small army as the final stage in the reform of the lordship: 'nowe is a season for the kyng to come into this land' the treatise read.[18] By 1514, moreover, Henry VIII's war in France was all but over – the only person needing convincing of this fact was the still-belligerent young king. It is conceivable that Wolsey, who had already engineered the appointment of several of his clients to high ecclesiastical office in Ireland and who was throughout 1514 working to conclude a peace with France, identified the lordship's reform as something toward which he might divert Henry's martial energies but which involved much less risk in terms of international diplomacy.[19] The circumstances must, for the first time in Henry's early reign, have appeared favourable for the crown to consider seriously the reform of Ireland. Yet, as is well known, King Henry did not act. The appearance of Francis I on the dynastic scene at the start of 1515 drew the king's attention once again to the labyrinthine world of European war and diplomacy: by May, Henry was receiving intelligence that the dashing young French king was massing his forces near the Italian border.[20] The window to consider a significant royal intervention in Ireland – whether led by

18 *SP Hen. VIII*, ii, p. 27.
19 J.J. Scarisbrick, *Henry VIII* (London, 1968), pp 49–53; Fitzsimons, 'Cardinal Wolsey', pp 84–5.
20 Scarisbrick, *Henry VIII*, pp 56–8; *L. & P. Hen. VIII*, ii, no. 463.

the king in person or by some other means – had closed; Henry's boyhood companion, Gerald Fitzgerald, now the ninth earl of Kildare, was continued as the king's governor of Ireland, the earl's power bolstered following his visit to court in 1515.[21]

Still, an essential function of the written material drawn up in and around 1515 was to educate Henry VIII and his council about Ireland. Together, they painted a picture of the lordship's triumphant English past, its decayed and troubled present and its uncertain future. Finglas' 'Briefe note' made accessible to King Henry a history of English rule in Ireland and its supposed decline down to the reign of the king's grandfather, Edward IV, when the vast inheritance of Ulster and Connacht passed to the crown of England; Darcy's tract covered more recent historical ground, but sought primarily to lay bare before the royal council the difficulties presently facing the English of Ireland, most notably those arising from Irish exactions and military impositions; and the 'State of Ireland', extrapolating from fifteenth-century ideas for Ireland's reform, introduced into Tudor political thinking a comprehensive prescription for the reform of the lordship's English population which would ultimately encompass its Irish inhabitants. The 'State of Ireland', again distinguishing itself from the other two tracts, made explicit reference to its own educative function:

> Percase unto this tyme, yf the King mought pretende anny ingnoraunce in the premisseis, bycause that many colouryd wryteinges and messyngers cometh dayly to hym fro dyverse of the noble folke, shewing otherwyse then the lande is: but nowe, after upsyght hereof, he maye pretende no maner ingnoraunce, for this shewyth to hym all the veraye state of the lande, ayenst the whiche no trewe man wyll saye contrarye.[22]

Ignorance of Ireland in the English government was at the same time being assailed by the visit to Henry's court of the new earl of Kildare and several other high-ranking officials in the lordship's government. A Venetian diplomat reported that Kildare, John Rawson, the prior of Kilmainham and an unnamed archbishop – probably Kite, archbishop of Armagh – were sat with him at his dinner table at Greenwich as part of the king's May Day celebrations in 1515.[23] It would appear that all three men had been summoned to court to discuss Ireland and were almost certainly present, along with William Rokeby, archbishop of Dublin and William Darcy, before the council late the following month when the latter's articles were submitted for consideration.[24] Kildare

---

21 See above, p. 31.
22 *SP Hen. VIII*, ii, p. 14.
23 *Four years at the court of Henry VIII: selection of despatches written by the Venetian ambassador, Sebastian Giustinian*, 2 vols (London, 1854), i, p. 91; *L. & P. Hen. VIII*, ii, no. 411.
24 Ware, *The antiquities of Ireland*, p. 62; Ellis, 'Sir William Darcy', p. 33.

returned to Ireland in late September, having remained in England for over four months; meanwhile Darcy and the two bishops stayed on: the latter two were present at Westminster for the ceremony marking Wolsey's receipt of the cardinal's hat in November.[25] That which the written material on Ireland could not articulate to the king and his ministers, the several members of the delegation from the lordship surely could.

But probably very little of this information, written or oral, was absorbed at the court of Henry VIII. It is highly unlikely that the king, whose aversion to paperwork is well-known, read these several (lengthy) tracts on Ireland; more likely, he was orally briefed of their contents (Cardinal Wolsey later remarked that O'Donnell's letters in reply to the king 'bee verie humble and pleasaunte … as maye appere to His Highnes, whenne it shall bee his pleasure *to here* the same read').[26] Certain of Darcy's articles and some points made in the 'State of Ireland' could have been understood as an indictment of Kildare-rule. As we know, however, Henry VIII did not understand it that way. He upheld the earl's conduct by strengthening the earl's position: the presence of Kildare, the most powerful figure in Ireland, face-to-face before him at his palace at Greenwich apparently counted for more in the king's mind than the alleged evils arising from the earl's military exactions set out in the written material. Even so, for the first time in the reign, the king and his council had discussed conditions in Ireland in consultation with the king's governor in Ireland and some of the lordship's leading figures. And there were tangible results. Kildare was licensed to assemble the Irish parliament: it was to be the first held in Henry's name and the first convened by the ninth earl. A series of articles for the better government of Ireland were drawn up at court in October to be made law. Among them was the stipulation that merchants travelling from England to Ireland bring over 6s. 8d. worth of long bows and arrows for every £20 of goods, so as to promote archery after the English manner.[27] The waning of English martial prowess in Ireland was a feature in both Darcy's articles and the 'State of Ireland'; and each had drawn special attention to the scarcity of English bows and arrows in the lordship and the tendency, in their absence, for Englishmen to resort to what the article to be put forward in parliament referred to as 'Irish archery'.[28] The new law, coupled with the appointment early the following year of a surveyor and

25 Kildare to Henry VIII, 1 Dec. 1515, TNA, SP 60/1/7, fo. 9; Ellis, 'Sir William Darcy', pp 34–5. Hugh Inge, bishop of Meath, was in his native Somerset in Sept., though it cannot be said with any certaintly whether he was at court: Inge to Wolsey, 12 Sept. 1515, TNA, SP 60/1/6, fo. 8.

26 *SP Hen. VIII*, ii, p. 138 (our italics).

27 *L. & P. Hen. VIII*, ii, no. 996. This is reminiscent of an English statute of 1472 which demanded that all merchant strangers bring into England four bow staves for every tonne of merchandise on account of the scarcity of the weapons in the kingdom: 12 Edw. IV, cap. II.

28 Above, p. 93; *SP Hen., VIII*, ii, pp 12, 19–21.

keeper of the bows within the Tower of London and 'the Tower of Ireland' [Dublin Castle], may indicate that at least one aspect of the information in the written material had found its mark.[29] More remarkably, King Henry intervened personally in 1515 to secure for John Rawson, the English-born prior of Kilmainham, a preceptory in Ireland belonging to the Knights of St John. The order had apparently in their ignorance of the racial divide in Ireland appointed an Irishman to head the chapter. But the king explained in a letter to Fabrizio del Carretto, the order's grand-master based at Rhodes, that Irishmen were regarded as 'sylvestrium' [of the forest] and so were unfit for such preferment: 'ut ips[i] hibernici qui ex syluestriu[m] genere h[ab]ent[r] ab munere et dominio excludantur'.[30] Here, Henry VIII weighed in on a matter that undoubtedly served as the backdrop for the discussion of Ireland that year: the presence in the lordship of Irishmen who were constitutionally non-subjects and officially at war with the king's subjects. The young king probably did not think on this too deeply. Rawson was an Englishman, a loyal subject, who was by all accounts an able administrator and who was then at court, so it was easy for Henry to fall back on the legal separation between Englishmen and Irishmen, which had developed in the lordship in the later Middle Ages. Yet perhaps more should have been expected of Henry VIII. After all, he was the first English king consistently to refer to Irishmen as 'rebels' in his correspondence, with the implication that the king regarded all people living in Ireland, English as well as Irish, to be his subjects.[31] He was also the first Tudor sovereign to have actually interacted with an Irish lord – three years earlier he welcomed to his court Hugh O'Donnell, the distant lord of Tyrconnell in the north-west of Ireland, who was then passing through England en route to Rome. The king, according to the Irish annalists, treated O'Donnell with great honour and respect.[32] But Henry VIII's preferment of Rawson, as with his decision to support Kildare, indicates that he, like his father for most of his reign, was possessed of only a rudimentary understanding of Ireland and had developed no clear plan for its political future; though unlike his father a corpus of literature was now available to disabuse the king of England of his ignorance of that place if only he, or any of his ministers, chose to engage with it.

Four years later Henry VIII decided to do what many in Ireland thought he would do in 1515: take up Ireland's reform. The king would not cross the Irish

---

29 L. & P. Hen. VIII, ii, no. 1828.

30 Henry VIII to Fabrizio del Carretto, c.1515, BL, Cotton MSS, Otho C IX, fo. 32 (L. & P. Hen. VIII, ii, no. 1828).

31 Maginn, 'Civilizing' Gaelic Leinster, p. 74.

32 The Annals of Loch Cé: a chronicle of Irish affairs, 1014–1690, ed. W.M. Hennessy, 2 vols (London, 1871), s.a. 1512; Annála Connacht: the annals of Connacht, 1224–1544, ed. A.M. Freeman (Dublin, 1944), s.a. 1512; AFM, s.a. 1512.

Sea; he sent in his stead Thomas Howard, earl of Surrey, the son of a duke and one of England's best generals – every inch the strong English captain that the Irish parliaments of the last century had asked for in lieu of the king himself. The discussions of Ireland which had taken place in council and at court in 1515 may have reminded the king that he was, as Archbishop Kite had put it in his letter to Wolsey, 'as moche bound to reforme' Ireland 'as to mayntayn the goode ordre & justice off England'; but he appears to have arrived at his decision in 1519 alone and without having engaged in any discernible reflection on conditions in the lordship based either on oral consultation or the reading of documents. The king, as we know, was prone to 'spasmodic fits of reforming energy' and this was one of them.[33] It was brought on in the wake of a remarkable episode in May in which the leading members of Henry's council urged their young king to distance himself from his obstreperous boon companions – the so-called 'minions'. Henry's response was to adopt a more mature attitude towards kingship; he threw himself into the business of government as proof of the newfound royal sobriety and discipline.[34] A paper identified a number of administrative and financial areas which the king 'indendith in his awne p[er]son to debate w^t his counsail and to se reformacon to be don therin'. Ireland was one of these areas of his responsibility that Henry hoped to put right: 'the kyng intendith to devise howe the lande of Irlande may be reduced & broughte to good ordre and obeysaunce' the paper read.[35] By then, criticisms of Kildare rule, emanating from Ireland and sponsored by the Butlers whose relationship with the earl had been strained since 1515, had reached court: Henry had summoned the earl to appear before him to answer allegations of maladministration earlier in the year.[36] But the new royal initiative for Ireland need not be interpreted as royal dissatisfaction with the earl or his style of rule. In fact, the available evidence suggests precisely the opposite. Henry had called the earl to court well before his sudden burst of interest in Ireland. Kildare, moreover, was found innocent of any misconduct and was received into favour. Ware almost certainly had it right when he treated the royal initiative as evolving separately from the criticisms of Kildare rule:

> It was the opinion of wise men, that the king did hitherto neglect too much his Irish affairs: whereupon a serious debate was had in England to rectifie this error, and to send some fit person, of the chief of the nobil-

33 S.G. Ellis, 'Tudor policy and the Kildare ascendancy in the lordship of Ireland', *IHS*, 20 (1977), 239.
34 Scarisbrick, *Henry VIII*, pp 117–19; Greg Walker, 'The expulsions of the minions of 1519 reconsidered', *Historical Journal*, 32 (1989), 1–16.
35 BL, Cotton MSS, Titus B I, fo. 191.
36 Ware, *The antiquities of Ireland*, p. 65; *L. & P. Hen. VIII*, iii, no. 17.

ity, with forces into Ireland, to suppress the rebels, and reduce them to their allegiance.[37]

At no point under the Tudors was it expected that the earls of Kildare reform Ireland; all were agreed that that responsibility lay with the English crown and that only the king could marshal the resources necessary for such an undertaking. In Ireland, the royal honour was at stake and Henry VIII was now suddenly (albeit temporarily, as it transpired) determined to preserve it.

In translating the royal will into action, however, the Tudor regime showed that it lacked the knowledge and experience of Ireland necessary to embark on the lordship's reformation. And nowhere was this more evident than in the preparations and, later, in the course of Surrey's expedition. As argued above in section 1.8, the 'Ordinances and Provisions' for Ireland, later to be included in the Hatfield Compendium, were drafted, probably by Sir William Darcy, in late 1519 (presumably once news reached the lordship that the king was planning a substantial intervention there). Shortly thereafter Darcy travelled to court where he was consulted about the planning of the expedition.[38] Kildare was there too, but there is no record of his role in the preparations. It may be that the quarrel between Kildare and Wolsey, which the Italian historian Polydore Vergil described, occurred at this time: this would explain the earl's marginalization in the months prior to his being bound over in May 1520 not to leave the London area.[39] In any event, the king and Wolsey relied heavily on Darcy for counsel; his unrivalled knowledge of the Irish revenues was of particular interest to the crown. Darcy apparently told them of an eye-watering annual surplus of 2,000 marks in the Irish revenues, a sum that was subsequently built in to the projected overall cost of Surrey's expedition. Darcy probably also offered detailed advice on another area of his expertise: the subject of coign and livery. A thoughtful paper was written up at this time that set out detailed reasons why the immediate abolition of the much-maligned practice of coign and livery and the levy of a double parliamentary subsidy in its place would lead to opposition in the English Pale and so limit the military effectiveness of the planned expedition.[40]

However the information that Darcy furnished Henry VIII and Wolsey with was both inaccurate and contradictory. With regard to the revenues, he overesti-

---

37 Ware, *The antiquities of Ireland*, p. 66.
38 A 'Sir Roger Darcy, of Ireland' (almost certainly a mistake for Sir William) received a reward of £40 from Surrey in Apr. 1520: *L. & P. Hen. VIII*, iii (ii), p. 1540; Ellis, 'Sir William Darcy', p. 35. There is no evidence to suggest that Poynings was consulted, even though he was treasurer of the household in 1519 and attended the king at the Field of Cloth of Gold in June 1520: Ellis, *s.v.* 'Sir Edward Poynings', ODNB .
39 Quinn, 'Henry VIII and Ireland', p. 324; *L. & P. Hen. VIII*, iii (ii), no. 2693.
40 Ellis, 'Sir William Darcy', pp 35–6.

mated the amount of money available for the expedition in Ireland: it was later found that the Irish revenues scarcely amounted to £1,400 per annum. Darcy must surely have known better, but his deliberate inflation of the revenues at this crucial stage in the planning speaks to his desire, and one of the central aspirations of the community from which he came, to see reform begun. The paper on coign and livery, meanwhile, contradicted Darcy's earlier thinking on the subject made known in the articles that he had presented to the council in 1515. More importantly, however, it contradicted those items in the Ordinances and Provisions calling for the abolition of coign and livery, which Darcy himself had brought over and which were presumably drafted to help guide the new governor in Ireland. Indeed upon his arrival Surrey attempted to operate without resort to coign and livery, only to find the wages of his horsemen too expensive to pay. Misleading and contradictory as this information may have been, Darcy did at least provide intimate knowledge of conditions in Ireland, and his Ordinances informed some of the proposals drafted in the various planning papers drawn up in 1520.[41] The contributions to the planning of the expedition made by King Henry and Wolsey, by contrast, showed only ignorance. The king, as is well known, insisted on sending 400 members of the king's guard to accompany Surrey, upon whom he bestowed the more exalted title of lord lieutenant, as opposed to the 400 local troops called for in the Ordinances. Surrey later complained bitterly of the ineffectiveness in Irish warfare of these largely ornamental troops. Other proposals that show signs of royal and ministerial influence were equally unhelpful or unrealistic: it was suggested that Surrey bring 'three Englishmen now dwelling in England' as his councillors in Ireland; royal letters were to be used to prompt distant lords to remember their obedience to the crown and Wolsey's status as papal legate was to be used to reorganize the church in Ireland through which the Irish might be intimidated and controlled.[42]

Not surprisingly, then, given the regime's lack of knowledge of Ireland and the narrow base from which it sought to acquire it, Surrey's expedition was compromised before it began. Instead of heralding the beginning of Ireland's reform the mission quickly became what has been called a 'reconnaissance in

---

41 The third and fifteenth Ordinances, printed above, pp 99–100, read: 'It[e]m that the deputie do his endevoᵣ to see that the churches of the iiii shyres be repayred, also to cause the mynistres of the same to be of goode rule and goode ordre and that no man of Irishe nacyon be p[ro]moted to any dignytie or benefyce'; 'It[e]m that [no] man of the iiiiᵒʳ shyres do make warre or reyse warre eith[er] make preye upo[n] any Irishman but by thadvyse and assent of the deputie and kynges counsayll'. Compare this with two articles in one of the preparatory documents which reads: 'It[e]m that the Churches of Ireland be buylded and repaired and that the ministers of the same be reformed to good ordre …'; 'It[e]m that none of the kinges subiettes do make any pray or araise warre upon any of the Irishe captains or their contreys wᵗout licence of the kinges deputy and his counsaill ther …': TNA, SP 1/30, fo. 90.

42 Quinn, 'Henry VIII and Ireland', p. 324; TNA, SP 60/1/28, fo. 70 (quotation).

force' — in effect a grand information-gathering exercise on behalf of the Henrician regime.[43] It was not long before the king learned of the difficulty which Surrey daily encountered 'for lacke of knoulege of the country, and the variaunt condicions of thinhabitauntes of the same'.[44] The earl was equally unprepared for the widespread sickness that beset him and his men: it was an exasperated Surrey who sought leave to convey his wife and children from Dublin to Wales or Lancashire 'for I know no place in this contre, wherto send them in clene aire'.[45] Surrey was surrounded by a cadre of English officials who had come over with him; it was Darcy and the earl of Ormond, however, who provided him with essential information on Ireland.[46] Yet none could prepare the earl for the day-to-day reality of war and politics there. 'Sethens my coming into this land', Surrey wrote to the king, 'I have been soo troubled with war, in soo many places, that I never yet might have leyser to call the counsaill of the land unto me, to devise with theym, whate ways were best to bee takin, to bring the Irishmen to summe good order'.[47] Surrey quickly came to the view that Kildare, who was continued in England, lay behind many of the difficulties he faced. He, and through his letters Henry VIII and Wolsey, was learning a lesson that had been well-learned decades before by Henry VII: governing Ireland without the support of Kildare presented a host of challenges. Uncooperative Palesmen, untrustworthy clergy, corrupt government officials unlearned in the operation of English law and government, squabbling towns and a galaxy of Irish and English lords — some of whom were aggressive and some of whom were willing to submit to the crown — confronted Surrey in Ireland; Kildare's absence and alleged 'conspiracye' served to exacerbate all of these obstacles to governing the lordship.

Surrey struggled on; but as the cost of keeping the earl there mounted, and the diplomatic situation in Europe again became precarious, so Henry VIII's aims for the mission shifted. By 1521 the reality had set in that the reformation of Ireland would require a much more substantial military and financial commitment than the king could possibly make at this time. Where once the king wrote boldly to Surrey of enlisting support in Ireland for 'our warres for the reduccion of that lande to civilite and due obedience', he now sought to secure 'the suertie of that land, without any farther charges to be sustaynyd and born by the Kynges Hyghnesse'.[48] To that end, he instructed the earl to spread rumours that a great army from England was then bound for the lordship; this, it was

43 Ellis, *Tudor frontiers*, p. 186; idem, *Ireland in the age of the Tudors*, pp 118–19.
44 *SP Hen. VIII*, ii, p. 31.
45 *SP Hen. VIII*, ii, p. 39.
46 TNA, E 101/248/21; Ellis, 'Sir William Darcy', p. 36.
47 *SP Hen. VIII*, ii, p. 37.
48 *SP Hen. VIII*, ii, pp 34, 69.

hoped, would be sufficient to frighten the Irish into seeking peace, which the king intended to keep until such time as he could send over an actual army 'for the totall and finall subduing of that land'. At this point, in what was a subtle move to preserve the royal honour, Surrey self-consciously recast the purpose (and history) of his expedition to bring it into line with what it was actually achieving. He wrote to the king:

> And wher as, at this tyme, all those off Your Graces Counsell here doth advertise Your Highnes off their opinions consernyng the state off this lond, and the meanys for reduccion off the same; consideryng that it is as well expressed in myn instruccions, as in dyvers Your Graces letters sent hither to me, that the principall cause, that Your Grace sent me hither for, was to enforme Your Highnes, by wich meanys and ways Your Grace might reduce this londe to obedience and gode order.[49]

Surrey's mission was, and apparently always had been, intended to furnish the crown with information upon which policy might then be decided. And, indeed, Surrey's time in Ireland gave them a good deal to consider. The earl's presence in the land generated a stream of written correspondence which contained valuable information about the lordship: Surrey wrote at length both to the king and to Wolsey; and through the reports of John Stile, the undertreasurer of Ireland who had come over with the earl, a minister in England like Wolsey was given a much more accurate sense of the yields of the Irish revenues.[50] The written information, however, was always deemed inferior to the power of first-hand accounts. Surrey sent Patrick Finglas, author of the 'Briefe note', to court in late 1520 so that Wolsey might examine him and learn 'of the estate of this land, and the disposicion of the inhabytauntes of the same'.[51] In his famous letter to Henry VIII, Surrey might write that 'this londe shall never be broght to goode order and dew subjeccion, but only by conquest'; but it was his hope that Sir John Peachy, one of Henry's henchmen and a royal councillor whom the king had lately sent to Ireland, would help to impress upon the king the enormity of the undertaking that he had outlined in his letter:

> For, ondowtedly, the countrees here be as strong, or stronger, as Walys, and thenhabitantes off the same can and do lyve more hardly, then any other people, after myn opinien, in Cristendome or Turkey. Wheroff a part Master Peche hath sene, and can enforme Your Grace more largely, as he hath herd by the report of others; who hath not only, sith his commyng

49 *SP Hen. VIII*, ii, p. 73.
50 Quinn (ed.), 'Bills and statutes', p. 115; *SP Hen. VIII*, ii, pp 77–82.
51 *SP Hen. VIII*, ii, p. 63.

hither, takyn contynewall payne in rydyng abowtes with me, but also con-
tynewally serched to attayne to the knowledge off the state and maner of
this londe, and disposicion off the people of the same; and, as I thynk, can
more assewredly asserteyne Your Grace off the same, then any man that
ever came hither, that contynewed no lenger here, then he hath done.[52]

As it happened, Surrey soon had the opportunity to relate his experiences of
Ireland to the king in person: in late 1521 he was recalled to England.

What is remarkable about Surrey's expedition is the fact that it almost
entirely ignored the only known plan for the reformation of Ireland – the 1515
'State of Ireland'.[53] Central to that plan were the suggestions that 'the reude
comyn folke, subgetes to the King' be instructed in the basics of warfare, notably
in the use of guns, and that weapons be made available by the crown and sold to
the lordship's English subjects out of Ireland's cities and port towns. The governor – the author of the 'State of Ireland' almost certainly had the earl of Kildare
in mind – was to oversee this training up and re-arming of the Englishry in conjunction with a military 'captayne' and 500 mounted troops that the king was to
send out of England. The presence of a captain in command of a small army paid
for by the king working in tandem with a resident governor is reminiscent of
Poynings' expedition only with the principal roles reversed: in this scenario
Kildare would continue as governor and the captain would provide added military muscle. However the 1515 plan was predicated on the military reorganization of the Englishry from the bottom up. The process was to begin in Co.
Meath, the largest of the Pale shires, where four noblemen were earmarked to
serve as justices of the peace; the deputy would then select two wardens of the
peace in every barony who would in turn assemble the 'comen folke' in every
parish so that they might choose two constables as their captains. This recom-
mendation is nearly identical to the suggestion, included in the Ordinances
drawn up in preparation for Surrey's expedition, 'that the justyces of peace
shalbe made in everie shyre and they to make wardeynes of the peace in everie
baronye and constables in everie paraiche, and that they kepe mustres ones
everie quarter of the yere', and points strongly to William Darcy's involvement
in the writing of the 'State of Ireland'. Once the process of arming and training
all of the king's subjects in Meath was complete, it was to be replicated in other
counties, and then also among the lordship's urban populations, until the entire
English population of Ireland was placed on a war-footing and capable of seiz-
ing control of neighbouring Irish districts. So ordered, Ireland, a commodious
and fertile land in and of itself, would supposedly attract new English colonists
who would settle in the newly-won Irish districts adjoining English areas in

52   *SP Hen. VIII*, ii, pp 73–4.
53   *SP Hen. VIII*, ii, pp 1–33; BL, Additional MS 4792, fos 107–15v.

south Leinster and Munster. The crown, meanwhile, was then to contribute to the enterprise by ordering the nobility in Ireland and England to re-conquer its inheritance and Ulster and commanding large numbers of Englishmen out of England and Wales both to re-inhabit Ulster and bolster the recent settlements in south Leinster and Munster. With the English counties strong enough to defend themselves from the Irish, the deputy and captain were to compel the English lords in Munster and Connacht – the so-called 'English rebels' – to put in pledges and oversee the same arming and training of the common folk originally begun in Meath. In this way, the English of Ireland were to be transformed into a fighting force, which the author of the 'State of Ireland' reckoned would be 100,000-strong. To complete Ireland's reform, Henry VIII was at this point to come in person at the head of an army numbering 2,000 men. The combined strength of the king's subjects and the royal army would, so the argument ran, put the Irish in such 'dreadde of the swerde' that a final military confrontation would be unnecessary: the great Irish lords were then to be assimilated into a reformed English society.

Thus, apart from the size of the army that Surrey brought over with him, the 'State of Ireland' exerted no discernible influence either on the planning or on the course of the earl's expedition to Ireland.[54] Surrey's expedition highlights the difference between reform in theory, as set out in a written treatise, and reform as it was actually attempted. It is an important distinction that, if not observed, can lead historians to place undue emphasis on the influence that such writings had on policy. It should not be supposed that reform tracts on Ireland – which are now more or less readily available to historians – were read, understood and acted upon by contemporaries in positions of power. Cardinal Wolsey may well have been an avid proponent of Ireland's reform – the council in Ireland referred to his 'graciouse soliciting for the reduccion of this land' – and he may well have read and perhaps even commissioned the 'State of Ireland'.[55] For his part, the king, who ultimately decided policy, almost certainly did not read the political tracts on Ireland available to him, but he supported reform nonetheless, and continued to leave open the possibility of another royal intervention there. In 1522 a clause was included in Henry VIII's treaty, signed at Windsor, with Charles V to that end:

> The contracting princes are to assist one another in case either of them should be engaged in recovering his property from others who withhold it from him as, for instance, if the king of England should undertake to conquer Scotland or to reduce Ireland into his obedience.[56]

54 For a different interpretation of the relationship between the 'State of Ireland' and Surrey's expedition, see Fitzsimons, 'Cardinal Wolsey', pp 96–9.
55 *SP Hen. VIII*, ii, pp 91–2; Fitzsimons, 'Cardinal Wolsey', pp 78–104.
56 *L. & P. Hen. VIII*, iii (ii), no. 2333.

Later, in 1531, O'Donnell's submission to the governor in Ireland included the clause that if the king chose to reform Ireland ['quo dominus rex velit reformare Hiberniam'] O'Donnell would be required to help pay for the king's costs.[57] But without more detailed knowledge of conditions in Ireland at court, any effort to reform Ireland would be as deeply flawed as Surrey's mission. The Tudor regime had no idea, as recent scholarship has revealed for example, that the interconnected web of Irish and English lordships in Ireland was at this time experiencing an acute period of destabilization, brought on both by the sudden passing of a generation of its leaders who had dominated politics in Ireland for decades and by a renewed bout of feuding between the Geraldines and the Butlers.[58] Not in a generation were conditions in Ireland less conducive to a royal reform initiative.

Yet the council in Ireland held out hope that Surrey, with his recent experience of the lordship, would now be in a position to advise the king on Ireland and to oversee its reformation. Surrey had, after all, given the matter a great deal of thought and had come to the conclusion that, in order to reform Ireland, Henry would have to conquer it. This was no wild boast. The earl was an experienced military commander and his belief that the conquest of Ireland would require 6,000 troops sourced and funded from England was precisely the type of force once projected by Henry VII and in fact deployed by Richard II. Pinning their hopes of reform on Surrey, who had supposedly brought the lordship 'in towardnes of reformacion', the council of Ireland noted that 'he hathe the best experience of his lande, and the wayes how the said reformacion may rathest be brought to effect of ony man, that ever came in this lande in our tyme'.[59] The earl saw the obstacles to Ireland's reform primarily in military terms, and as a military man he proposed what was a straightforward military solution. Eighteen months of service in Ireland, however, did not make Surrey an expert on the subject. What he saw as rebellion and Kildare conspiracy was, as we have just observed, actually a deeper problem arising from a systemic fracturing from within of Irish and English lordships across the island. Surrey, moreover, misunderstood the willingness of many Irish lords to cooperate with the crown as evidence of their duplicity and thus put 'smale trust in their promyses'.[60] But, whatever the merits or deficiencies of Surrey's analysis, Henry VIII was not prepared to commit to any reform initiative at this point: the king had what he deemed to be more pressing concerns and Surrey was soon redeployed to another theatre of royal concern,

---

57 *SP Hen. VIII*, ii, p. 152; BL, Additional MS 4792, fo. 117. In accepting the earl of Desmond's submission in Mar. 1494, Henry VII consented to the earl's request that he should not have to present himself to the king's deputy in Ireland 'savynge subsequent reformacone': Conway, *Henry VII's relations*, p. 152.

58 Edwards, 'The escalation of violence in sixteenth-century Ireland', pp 48–53.

59 *SP Hen. VIII*, ii, p. 92.

60 *SP Hen. VIII*, ii, p. 43.

where his experience of Ireland was put to no use. Like his father before him, Henry VIII believed the reform of Ireland could wait.

With any royal reform initiative indefinitely postponed, the king reverted to the policy of governing the lordship through a resident magnate. It was a policy that, at its most basic level, relied on the magnate's knowledge and experience of the land, and so spared the crown and its ministers from having to acquire the information necessary to provide more direct governance. It was also inexpensive and, as had been demonstrated in Henry VII's reign, could be relied upon to provide effective rule until such time as the king was in a position to pursue reform. But Henry VIII's decision to break with recent tradition in 1522, by appointing as governor the earl of Ormond as a counterweight to Kildare, exacerbated what had already developed into a bitter feud between the Geraldines and the Butlers. The king and Cardinal Wolsey, who had emerged as a strident critic of Kildare, failed to appreciate that Ormond would face considerable difficulties governing the lordship when his own power-base lay well outside the counties of the English Pale. They underestimated just how deeply ingrained Kildare power was in Ireland: like his father, the earl could still make the lordship ungovernable if he so chose. Only now, the earl of Ormond was using the same strategy previously employed by the Geraldines to undermine Kildare's ability to govern effectively.[61] The Geraldine–Butler feud dominated the lordship's politics for the next decade and its severity demanded the king's occasional consideration of Ireland as Wolsey and the king's other councillors attempted to sift through allegations and counter-allegations of misgovernment and unprovoked aggression levelled by the leaders, agents and patrons of the two houses.[62] Royal commissioners were hastily despatched from England in summer 1524 in what proved to be a fruitless effort to compose the differences between the two earls. Two years later, Kildare and Ormond (Ossory after 1528) were summoned to appear before the king in England, where they both remained for an extended period. But, as will be discussed below, the earls' long absence from the lordship only intensified the feud. Advised by John Rawson, Wolsey drew up an innovative plan, which would have temporarily established a sort of joint authority in Ireland, with Lord Butler serving as Kildare's vice-deputy. But with Kildare at court before him, the king came to the view that the earl was indeed using his influence to thwart his authority in Ireland and decided to entrust the government wholly to Ossory. Butler fared no better on this occasion. Henry was ultimately forced in 1530 to appoint an English governor, Sir William

---

61 Ellis, 'Tudor policy and the Kildare ascendancy', p. 241; Edwards, *Ormond lordship*, pp 154–6.
62 See, for instance, 'Therle off Ormondis boke agaynste therle off Kyldare', 1525, TNA, SP 1/34, fos 214–18; and Kildare's allegations against Ormond printed in *SP Hen. VIII*, ii, pp 120–4. The latter has been shown to date from Aug. 1526: Fitzsimons, 'Wolsey, the native affinities, and the failure of reform in Henrician Ireland', p. 109.

Skeffington, as deputy to his illegitimate son the duke of Richmond, in an attempt to establish a government that might serve as a bulwark between the feuding noble houses. The unrest soon re-emerged, however, and the king had no alternative but to return to where he had started: Kildare was restored to the highest office in the land in 1532.[63]

Narrowly focused on the actions of the two earls though it was, this royal involvement provided opportunities for some in Ireland to offer the crown information that might be used as the basis for reform. Sir William Darcy, for example, took the opportunity of the arrival of the king's commissioners to present them with a book of the crown revenues that was subsequently entrusted to Patrick Bermingham, the chief justice of the king's bench, to present to the king. The contents of the book, which, as discussed above in section 1.6, was later included in the Hatfield Compendium, contained detailed (and wholly unrealizable) proposals for raising additional revenues, presumably with the view to making the reform of Ireland appear less daunting in financial terms for King Henry. Several years later, a long treatise, entitled 'A discourse on the evil state of Ireland', was written, almost certainly for Wolsey, 'to instruct your mastership' how Ireland might be reformed.[64] The anonymous treatise is not dissimilar to the earlier 'State of Ireland'. It began by showing how the decay of the lordship set in – here the author identified the Wars of the Roses of the later fifteenth century as the 'cause of the desolation of the land' – before proceeding to set out detailed prescriptions for reform. The 'discourse', however, was of its time. On one level, it was overtly critical of Kildare and can be read as a deliberate effort on the part of the Butler faction to employ the familiar rhetoric of reform as a means of undermining the earl's position.[65] Yet, on another level, the author introduced a new distinction within the concept of reform: what he referred to as a 'particular reformation' was to serve as a prelude to 'general reformation'.[66] The king's reluctance to commit the resources necessary to see Ireland reformed was well known – Surrey's expedition and the subsequent reversion to aristocratic delegation had confirmed as much. However, by presenting plans for a 'particular reformation', whereby 'a discreet mean gentleman of England', in conjunction with the earls of Kildare and Ormond, was to oversee the piecemeal expansion of the borders of the Pale in south Leinster, the treatise offered an inexpensive plan which, so its argument ran, would pave the way for the 'general reformation', which entailed the sending over of a 4,000 man army led by a nobleman 'with experience of the land, like the duke of

---

63 Ellis, *Tudor frontiers*, pp 184–9.
64 *L. & P. Hen. VIII*, iv (ii), no. 2405.
65 Fitzsimons, 'Cardinal Wolsey', pp 85, 110 where it is plausibly argued that Robert Cowley – Ossory's agent at court – was the author of the treatise.
66 Bradshaw, *The Irish constitutional revolution*, pp 44–56.

Norfolk'. That army was to begin its advance south of Dublin, where the Irish would be expelled and their lands re-inhabited with Englishmen living in England but who were born in Ireland. In this way, the army was to proceed, Irish lordship by Irish lordship, until it reached the banks of the Shannon.[67]

In any event, reform – particular, general or otherwise – was not forthcoming; Darcy's book and the anonymous treatise exerted no discernible effect on royal policy. Ironically, it was Henry's disastrous decision to call both the earl of Ormond and Kildare out of Ireland, in an effort to end their feud once and for all, that created the circumstances in which a royal reform initiative again seemed possible. O'Connor Faly's capture in May 1528 of the baron of Delvin – acting as vice-deputy in Kildare's absence – thrust the lordship's government into crisis.[68] Days later, the duke of Norfolk received a letter from Ireland describing the situation:

> Allmightie God grante that our Sovereigne Lorde may provide breve remedye; or elles this poor Englishrie is lyke to have suche ruyne, that will nat be repaired in eny mans daies lyving: for the Hiresheman (being never so strong as nowe) have spied their tyme, and our debilitie never more then at this houre. The Holy Trinitie defend us, for here is none othir hope of socoure.[69]

Such grave words would not have been out of place in the lordship's darkest days of the mid-fifteenth century; and not since the days of the duke of York had an English nobleman of sufficient power and experience of Ireland been sought out as a potential saviour. Norfolk duly wrote to Wolsey that unless immediate action was taken Henry VIII would be forced 'to begyn a new conquest, as King Henry the IIth dyd'.[70] The following month the duke received Thomas Bathe, a Drogheda merchant, whom he had encountered during his service in Ireland. Bathe related to the duke some particulars of the state of the lordship, notably the proclivity of English marchers to allow Irishmen through their territories to attack the Pale. Norfolk deemed Bathe knowledgeable enough about Ireland to send him to attend on Wolsey: 'ye shall know many

---

67 In his discussion of the English shires of Ireland beyond the Pale, the author makes reference to a 'platt' – 'as by the platt may appear': *L. & P. Hen. VIII*, iv (ii), no. 2405. This has been taken to mean that a map, or a visual representation of some kind, accompanied the treatise: J.H. Andrews, 'Colonial cartography in a European setting: the case of Tudor Ireland' in David Woodward (ed.), *Cartography in the European Renaissance: part 1* (Chicago, 2007), p. 1673. In this context, however, 'platt' could equally refer to the treatise itself.
68 Ellis, *Tudor frontiers*, pp 182–3; Power, *A European frontier elite*, p. 70.
69 *SP Hen. VIII*, ii. p. 130.
70 *SP Hen. VIII*, ii. p. 134.

thynges by hym', the duke wrote to the cardinal.[71] Bathe, for his part, had reput-
edly prepared a book of information on Ireland especially for Wolsey. Yet news
of the book's existence was greeted with alarm among Butler supporters. Robert
Cowley, the earl of Ossory's attorney and man at court, wrote to Wolsey, warn-
ing him that Bathe's book, 'feigning it to be for the reformation of Ireland', was
in fact intended 'to dryve the kynge to the extremytie to sende home my Lord
of Kildare with auctoritie'.[72] There is no known record of Bathe's book – indeed
it cannot be said definitely that this book was not the anonymous treatise 'A discourse on the evil state of Ireland' that we already had cause to discuss above.[73]
Nevertheless, Cowley's comments show how written material calling for reform
might be used (or, at least, perceived to be used) for a less lofty political purpose:
in this case to manipulate councillors, ignorant of Ireland, into despairing of
reform and so urging the king to reappoint Kildare. And, as demonstrated above
in section 1.1, Finglas was at court in 1529 where he wrote 'An abbreviatt' of his
'Brief note' of 1515. Finglas now sought, through an augmented version of his
history of the lordship, to show Henry VIII that, despite the recent unrest and
O'Connor's affront to royal authority, Ireland in 1529 was more easily reformed
'than it was to be conquered at the fyrste conquest'.

As we have seen, convincing an English king to commit to Ireland's reform
was at all times difficult. But in the circumstances of the late 1520s and early
1530s, when Henry VIII's 'great matter' was consuming king and court and the
crown was finding itself short of money, the reform of Ireland simply could not
be countenanced – it would take a major rebellion in the heart of the English
Pale to force the crown to intervene in Ireland, and even that great show of
royal power fell well short of reform as it had been typically conceived since the
fifteenth century. Cardinal Wolsey's dramatic fall from power, moreover,
robbed the regime both of the minister to whom most of the information on
Ireland had been directed in the first two decades of Henry's reign and an insti-
tutional memory that stretched back nearly two decades. Historians sifting
through the primary evidence often accept that the royal government steadily
accumulated knowledge about Ireland. But Wolsey's papers were confiscated
and 'disappeared into the royal archives in the Tower'.[74] Thus, any minister
wishing to absorb and then employ the information contained in Wolsey's correspondence, which included the 'State of Ireland' and probably 'A discourse on
the evil state of Ireland', would have to go searching for it.[75] The duke of

71 *SP Hen. VIII*, ii. pp 135–6.
72 *SP Hen. VIII*, ii. p. 142.
73 Bradshaw, *The Irish constitutional revolution*, pp 56–7.
74 G.R. Elton, 'Review of Muriel St Clare Byrne (ed.), *The Lisle letters* (Chicago, 1980)', *London Review of Books*, 3:13 (1981), 3–5.
75 Listed among the 'repertory of letters, instructions and other matters of state, as were in the

Norfolk, who now assumed an even more pronounced role in any discussions of Ireland at court, was not so inclined. Nor was Thomas Cromwell – Wolsey's former servant who began his meteoric rise to prominence in the king's counsels in the wake of his master's fall – who appeared, initially at least, to have sought out the existing information on Ireland, but ultimately preferred to acquire and compile it anew through his own correspondence and agents.[76] After more than two decades in power, Henry VIII and the men who served him had attained precious little knowledge of the state and manner of Ireland. The historian Polydore Vergil, who had spent the better part of the previous three decades at the Tudor court, included Ireland in his landmark work *Anglica Historia* (1534). But his knowledge of Ireland, and the Irish in particular, was stale, derived as it was almost entirely from ancient sources, notably Gerald of Wales and the medieval French chronicler Jean Froissart.[77] Against this, however, a new medium of communication had developed in these years. It came in the form of the written treatise, which at once imparted to the reader information on Ireland and called for the lordship's reform, and there were no signs of the new medium diminishing so long as the king and his ministers remained disinterested in and ignorant of Ireland. And the written treatise was evolving in the face of royal indifference. The basic reform-by-conquest formulation typical of the fifteenth century had become not only more elaborate, but also more nuanced to include the so-called 'particular reformation', either as a prelude to the traditional formulation of reform, or as a means of securing immediate factional advantage.

Paper-house in the time of Queen Elizabeth', was a 'bundle' that contained 'certayne discourses and devyses for reformacon of Ireland': BL, Cotton MSS, Vitellius C XVII, fo. 79v.

76 Brendan Bradshaw, 'Cromwellian reform and the origins of the Kildare rebellion, 1533–4', *TRHS*, 5th series, 27 (1977), 75–7. In January 1532 Ossory wrote to Cromwell: 'This acqueyntaunce is but newe betwixt us, but I trust soo to use me unto you, as the contynuaunce shalbe olde and long': *SP Hen. VIII*, ii. p. 155. See also below, p. 159.

77 Eric Haywood, 'Humanism's priorities and empire's prerogatives: Polydore Vergil's description of Ireland', *PRIA*, sect. c, 109 (2009), 195–237, esp. 200.

2.3

The reformation of the country taken in hand

An Elizabethan official in England investigating the state of the royal revenues in Ireland wrote that, 'in anno 8', of the reign of Henry VIII, 'the said king tooke in hande the generall reformacon of the country'.[1] Another Elizabethan looking back on the old king's reign, in this case as part of an effort to ascertain the military strength of Irishmen bordering English areas, dated and glossed a copy of 'A description of the power of Irishmen': 'an° H.8. when the reformacon of the countrie was taken in hand'.[2] In this latter example the dating was wrong: the 'A description of the power of Irishmen' and the information in it, as we know, belonged to the reign of the first Tudor, Henry VII. And in the former example, though the writer specifically identified 8th Henry VIII – that is, 1516–17 – as the year in which 'the generall reformacon' of Ireland had commenced, as we have seen no such undertaking was launched (or even considered) at that time. The same writer went on to observe that the reformation coincided with 'the submission of the Irisherie', when, he remarked, 'divers principall lordshippes and especially suche as laye co[m]modious for service, wer by them surrendred into the kinges hand, wth an annuall rent ... and war beside bound to holde their landes of the king onely ...' It is clear from this allusion to the submissions of Irishmen that the writer ought to have dated 'the generall reformacon' to the early 1540s, when in fact dozens of Irish and some English lords submitted to the crown – the central feature of what modern historians refer to as the policy of 'surrender and regrant'. Still, what these Elizabethan recollections show is that Henry VIII's reign, his final decade-and-a-half on the throne in particular, was remembered by near contemporaries, however imprecisely, as the point at which the crown began the reformation of Ireland. Modern historians have also understood that the final years of Henry's reign were pivotal, even revolutionary, in Ireland and in the Tudor state more generally.[3] Within the span of ten years, the Kildare rebellion and the destruction of the Fitzgerald power base had eliminated the tried and tested policy of aristocratic delegation as a viable means of governing Ireland for the Tudors; and Henry VIII had broken with Rome, established the Church of Ireland, assumed

---

1 'Towching the revenues both auncient and present', BL, Cotton MSS, Titus B XII, fo. 324v.
2 LPL, Carew MS 635, fo. 62v (*Cal. Carew MSS*, iv, no. 398).
3 See, for example, Ellis, *Tudor frontiers*, p. 269; Bradshaw, *The Irish constitutional revolution*; G.R. Elton, *The Tudor revolution in government* (Cambridge, 1953).

the kingship of Ireland and had lent his support to a far-reaching new political initiative whereby English noble titles were extended to some of the leaders of the Irish polity who agreed to hold their lands of the king by feudal tenure. Not since the days of Henry II had the crown of England undertaken and maintained such sustained engagement with Ireland; and not since the late-thirteenth century had English royal power been stronger in the neighbouring island. An important result of the crown's sustained, though directionless, commitment to Ireland was the sharp increase of written accounts of the country and suggestions for its reform, and so also the rapid accumulation of knowledge available in England about Ireland. The Hatfield Compendium was borne of this necessity for information at a time when politics had broken free of its late medieval inertia and when information was becoming more readily available. Reform, it appeared, was indeed at hand.

But royal engagement must not be mistaken for reform: at no point did Henry VIII ever formally commit to Ireland's reform. Indeed, as will be discussed in the section below, it took a crisis as sudden and as serious as the Kildare rebellion of 1534 to jolt the crown into action, and it was only the consequences of that action that forced the regime in the years immediately thereafter to cast about for a means of governing Ireland which would not commit the crown to reform. Thus, what the Elizabethans understood as the beginning of reform and what historians often refer to as the beginning of the Tudor conquest of Ireland, was, in actual fact, the advent of a rather different but a very tangible process: the sustained engagement of the Tudor regime with Ireland. Ireland's reform remained the ultimate aspiration, but faced with the new reality of greater Anglo-Irish interaction the concept of reform was employed increasingly to refer to the steady extension of Tudor rule in Ireland as opposed to the short, sharp reform-as-conquest strategy that earlier generations of Englishmen had envisaged.

The show of royal might, which destroyed Kildare power in 1535, altered the prospects of Ireland's reform. With the lordship's most powerful magnate gone, and with a royal minister in England actively pursuing the reorganization of royal government throughout the Tudor territories, the possibilities for a royal possession like Ireland must have seemed endless. In mid-1533, however, such an eventuality was inconceivable. Kildare was governor and with Henry VIII presiding over a revolution in church-state relations in England, the likelihood of the crown taking up Ireland's reform was slim. It was not reform but the instability arising from hostility between the earls of Kildare and Ossory that continued to dominate discussions of Ireland at court.[4] Still, for Kildare's enemies, recent experience had shown that while the king might be unwilling to

<hr>

4   *L. & P. Hen. VIII*, vi, nos. 551, 1056.

commit to 'general reformation', the rhetoric of reform might be employed to undermine the earl in the near term. And they had, by then, an especially receptive outlet for their complaints in Thomas Cromwell, now the chancellor of the exchequer and the king's most influential councillor. Cromwell had been accumulating information on Ireland by establishing contacts there and, crucially, by procuring written materials.[5] Among the mass of variegated papers that came into Cromwell's possession between late 1532 and 1534 was diverse material on Ireland. It included, as might be expected, allegations against Kildare, Kildare's complaints about Skeffington's government and several reports on the state of the army and the revenues made by the latter. But more eclectic information had come to Cromwell as well: a paper made by an intermediary with 'the Great O'Neill', a 'devise for matters of Ireland' drawn up by John Alen and 'two books of the description of Ireland'.[6] So informed, Cromwell was coming to the view that some new political initiative was necessary for Ireland; in autumn 1533 the king summoned Kildare and Ossory to court for discussions. Sensing the weakness of the earl's position, Kildare's enemies penned five papers that sought to convince Cromwell, and ultimately the king, to replace the earl as governor and to begin Ireland's reform.

By the time Kildare reached court – in February 1534 – these papers were informing royal policy for Ireland. One paper, seemingly the work of Robert Cowley, offered a comprehensive geo-political description of Ireland (it was, perhaps, one of the 'books of the description of Ireland' that had come into Cromwell's possession).[7] In a preamble it took the reader through the country's 'fyve notable portions', interweaving geographical descriptions with descriptions of the most important families, whose loyalties to the crown Cowley was careful to set out. The body of the paper, however, was used as a means to show how decades of Kildare-rule had weakened royal authority in Ireland; the earl of Ossory, by contrast, was held up as a loyal English subject whose power and wisdom could prove a key aid to the crown. Cowley was clearly alive to the fact

5 Bradshaw, 'Cromwellian reform', p. 77.

6 *L. & P. Hen. VIII*, vi, no. 299; ibid., vii, no. 923; Bradshaw, 'Cromwellian reform', p. 76.

7 Robert Cowley's book on the state of Ireland, *c*.1533, TNA, SP 60/6/53, fos 117–22. This paper, which survives only in a later sixteenth-century copy originally preserved among the Hanmer papers, was placed under the year 1538 by the editor of the *CSPI* who noted that it was likely in the hand of the Irish antiquarian Thady Dowling (1544–1628). On a separate slip of paper a heading ascribed the work to Cowley and claimed that it had been delivered to the king 'after the execution of the Geraldines': *L. & P. Hen. VIII*, xiii (i), no. 83. While some of the comments in the margins suggest such a dating, the body of the text was clearly written prior to the Kildare rebellion. References – at fo. 119 – to the occupation of the manor of Rathwire, Co. Meath, by Kildare's son, Thomas, and the uncertainty over whether Kildare would continue as deputy – at fo. 121v – suggests a date of late 1533 (custody of Rathwire was granted to Thomas in Nov.) or early 1534 when Kildare went to court to defend his conduct as deputy.

that the crown was then seriously considering replacing Kildare as deputy and intended for his paper to show the possible consequences of such an action: who could be counted upon in Ireland 'if the kinge should have need', and who could not.

The second paper was a series of 'Articles for Reformation' drawn up by a majority of the king's council in Ireland. It was an explicitly collective effort, as the signatures attached to the 'Articles' bear testimony, and so was more akin to the parliamentary declarations of the fifteenth century than the individualistic (and often anonymous) work exhibited earlier, and at other times, in Henry's reign. The articles were entrusted to John Alen, one of Cromwell's clients, lately appointed master of the rolls; he was instructed by the signatories to report on the state of the lordship and to present the articles to the king.[8] What Henry VIII probably heard, and what Cromwell undoubtedly read, cannot have come as a surprise: the lordship, Alen was instructed to declare, was in a decayed state, principally on account of the 'immoderate takeng' of coign and livery by Englishmen and the malice of the Irish; the English Pale was in danger of becoming like the rest. Nor did the articles articulate any detailed plan to rectify the situation. However, the council in Ireland had reached two important conclusions. First, was that no man born in the lordship should have the government of Ireland; they suggested instead that an Englishman 'as hathe experience of the lande, and the knowledge of the peple' should be appointed deputy. Second, was that 'the negligente keeping of the Kingis recordes' and the appointment of 'onlerned' men to the courts had combined to create a situation in which the 'Kingis Courtes and revenues be gretelie decaied, and his recordes imbecilde, and his inheritaunce and right therbie onknowen'.[9] The former conclusion owed much to the instability wrought by the Fitzgerald–Butler feud. Yet it is also reflective of the belief, by then shared by Cromwell and King Henry, that an Englishman, of the social degree of a Skeffington (as opposed to a Norfolk), could be made deputy in Ireland, without incurring great costs, until such time as a thoroughgoing reformation could be begun. There remained only the matter of making Kildare accept his dismissal and support the new political arrangement.[10] The latter conclusion, meanwhile, represented a rare admission from within Tudor government in Ireland that its own manifest inability to master present and historical knowledge was limiting the yields of the royal revenues and thus also retarding the crown's efforts to initiate reform. We have already witnessed, in the preparation for Surrey's expedition, how a poor grasp of the revenues in Ireland could undermine the carrying out of political policy;

8   SP Hen. VIII, ii, pp 162–6; Bradshaw, 'Cromwellian reform', p. 82. See also Power, A European frontier elite, pp 71–2.

9   SP Hen. VIII, ii, pp 163, 165.   10 Ellis, Tudor frontiers, pp 195–6.

here, the king's government of Ireland was for the first time admitting to its ignorance of its own revenues – the effect of this was to move Cromwell to address the 'iudges of Irelonde and other offices there' as part of a shake-up of some of the personnel in the Irish government.[11]

Around this time, another paper, endorsed 'a reputacon for misorder in Irelond to be reformed', was drawn up specifically for Cromwell, so that the minister might present the information it contained to King Henry. As argued above, this anonymous paper was almost certainly written in England by Walter Cowley, another of Cromwell's clients and the son of Robert Cowley, the earl of Ossory's agent at court.[12] It began with prefatory remarks to the king noting the 'ardent deasire, that Your Grace hath always had, to have a reformacion in your lande of Irlande', before setting out the causes of the 'mysordre and debate' in Ireland; it then offered remedies for the same.[13] The paper was decidedly present-centred, laying most of the lordship's ills at the feet of Kildare, portraying him as a power-hungry and bloody-minded nobleman who had abused the authority that the king had vested in him. Like the material drawn up by the council, the paper placed great emphasis on having an Englishman as governor: Norfolk and Skeffington were held up as the leading candidates on account of their experience of the place. That appointment was to serve as the first step toward reforming the lordship's English population, for only then, so it was argued, could a 'generall reformacion' have any hope of success. It was suggested that 'to encrease thEnglish ordre, habyte and maner, and to expel and put awaye the Irishe rule, habite, and maner' the new governor should begin by reforming the English of Munster, notably the many noblemen of the province, whom the paper listed by name and who, it was claimed, were 'furthest from good ordre or obedyencie, soo that noo difference is betwixt theym and the mere Irishmen, but oonly the veray surname'. This done, though it did not spell out how exactly this feat was to be accomplished, the governor, through the newly-reconciled English of Munster, was to strike a conciliatory tone with several Irishmen, each of whom was identified as 'denizen' – that is, who had been granted English liberty – and so was assumed to be more amenable to English government and society. With the Englishry and some Irishmen behind him, the governor was then to use force against O'Neill and put the Burkes of Connacht 'to a better ordre'. At this point, according to the author, 'a generall reformacion may ensue', by which he presumably meant the sending over from England an

11 Bradshaw, 'Cromwellian reform', pp 77–8.
12 A report to Cromwell, 1533, TNA, SP 60/2/3, fos 4v–9v (*SP Hen. VIII*, ii, pp 166–79). Above, p. 63. The editor of the *CSPI* reckoned that the document dated from July 1533, but it is clear from its references to Ossory 'now here' (p. 170) that it was drawn up in England in late 1533 or in early 1534.
13 *SP Hen. VIII*, ii, p. 167.

army of conquest. O'Brien's bridge across the Shannon, the infiltration into east Ulster of Scots and the necessity of establishing a regional council in Munster headed by a president to minister the king's laws to the English population there were further identified as areas which would then demand the king's attention.[14]

A fourth paper was also written in England by John Alen around this time, though it has been conflated with Cowley's paper just discussed.[15] It was endorsed 'a discruption of Irelonde', and so was most likely one of the two descriptions of Ireland alluded to above that had come into Cromwell's possession by September 1534; in its margins several manicules highlighting key passages are evident, though it is impossible to say with any certainty to whom these marks belonged. The paper offered a damning criticism of Kildare rule. It was the actions of the Geraldines, Alen argued, which more than anything else had thwarted previous Tudor efforts to reform Ireland undertaken by Norfolk, by Poynings and by Skeffington. 'What subjectis', Alen asked rhetorically, 'under any prince in the worlde, wold love, obey, or defende the right of that prince, which (notwithstanding ther true hertis and service towarde him) wold afterwarde putt them under the governaunce of soche, as shuld daylie practise to prosecute and destroy them for the same?'.[16] The paper recommended that the king's records from the reigns of Henry VI and Edward IV should be searched to show 'what revenues the Kinge had than in Ireland; also what landis, castels, and townes he had in possession; what suertie of strength; what Inglishe inhabitacion and ordere' – these findings were then to be considered against how things now stood after decades of Kildare rule. Like the previous two papers, Alen's conclusion was impossible to misconstrue: 'that no man of that lande shall from hensfurth be his [the king's] Deputie ther, but always an Inglishman'.[17] And like in the previous papers, the appointment of an Englishman was to be a cure-all for the decayed state of Ireland, only here Alen did not offer any specific guidelines for the new governor to follow beyond the belief that his presence alone would, within a short time, increase the revenues; a carefully drawn manicule pointed to the line that read: 'that within iii yeres ther shall growe to his grace and his heires 3 or 4000 markis yerely more than he hathe at this day'.[18]

A fifth paper on Ireland drawn up at this time, an anonymous series of articles and instructions prepared for the king, blamed the decay of English govern-

14 Ibid., ii, pp 170–3.
15 Though the editors of the printed State Papers, Henry VIII recognized (at fo. 10) that the handwriting shifts to the distinctive style of John Alen, the master of the rolls, they failed to appreciate that this was an entirely separate paper: TNA, SP 60/2/3, fos 10–12v (*SP Hen. VIII*, ii, pp 173–9).
16 *SP Hen. VIII*, ii, pp 173–4.
17 Ibid., ii, pp 174–6.
18 TNA, SP 60/2/3, fo. 12 (*SP Hen. VIII*, ii, p. 178).

ment and society on the lordship's three resident earls.[19] Any reformation of
Ireland, the paper maintained, would have to begin with Kildare, Ossory and
Desmond whose domination of Irish lords, and their alliances with Irishmen,
had allegedly created a situation 'that if any of thes Erls be at ware with the
othyr, such Irish capteins, as is bandyt with ethyr of them, tak ther part, and if
aney of thes Erles be Kinges Deputie, and that is awn streinthe do not extend to
mayntein his Irish friend, then will he proclayme an hosting or jorney within
your English pall, which will, at the lest, cost your subjectes 2000 markes'.[20]
Thus it was recommended that the earls be forever deprived of the lordship's
government in favour of 'a born man of this noble Realm of England' and,
through a proposed sweeping act of resumption, they were to be stripped of any
revenues accruing to them (the yields of fee farms and customs, as well as profits from castles and manors) which could be shown to have belonged to the
crown. 'When thes Erldes be reformyd, all thes Irish captains, which undyr ther
trubut, and at ther comaundment, must at all tymys yeld Your Grace trubut and
service'; and the king's revenues, once possessed by the three earls contrary to
right, would be diverted to the new governor, who could then begin the reform
of the king's English subjects. As was typical of these Henrician treatises, the
reform of Ireland was treated separately (and secondarily) from the reform of the
king's subjects. In this paper, however, there was no discussion of a second
phase, that is, a general reform or a conquest of Ireland. Rather, the Irish of
south Leinster were themselves earmarked for reform:

> The leinth and qwantite of soille or land, that the forsaid Irish captains
> and their kinsmen occupy and have dominion of, is at the lest 40 mylys
> long, and 16 mylis brod, wherin ther is a plesaunt land, forest, and rever,
> adyoynyng to the see, on the est syd; your countes of Vexford and
> Kilkenny, of the south syd of them; and wher the Erle of Kildar, within
> the countie of Kildar, haiv dominion un the west syd of them; and your
> English pale of the countie of Dublin on the north syd of them; so that
> ware may be made by your English subjectes on every quarter.

This greatly limited version of reform by conquest was to be emulated in the
Irish midlands and 'by this meane', the paper concluded, 'Your Grace shall
reforme all your land within short tyme'.[21] Though these recommendations for
the king were almost entirely lacking in specificity, and were, in many ways, similar in their thrust to the other papers written at around this time, the paper broke

19 TNA, SP 60/2/11, fos 31–6 (*SP Hen. VIII*, ii, pp 182–92). The paper is endorsed, in a later
     hand, 'Articles & instructions to the king concerning Ireland'.
20 *SP Hen. VIII*, ii, pp 186–7.
21 Ibid., ii, p. 190.

new ground in two respects. It presented the king with a plan for incremental, or particular, reforms that could be accomplished in stages, thereby sparing the crown any immediate commitment and the expense of sending over an army of conquest. More importantly, however, this was the first paper to apply the well-established rhetoric of reform to the Irish. The belief among Englishmen in both Ireland and England had always been that the king's subjects, and by extension the king's land of Ireland, could be brought back, restored or recovered, to the glories of their previous condition. To what formerly civil and perfect state were the Irish to be restored to? That the Irish were to be reformed in a manner different from the king's English subjects is clear – Englishmen were to make war on them from 'every quarter'. Even so, this paper offers evidence of a shift in the Tudor understanding of the concept of reform. It may be that the rhetoric of reform was catching up with that other subtle shift in Tudor terminology that had occurred in Henry VIII's reign: the reference in official correspondence to Irish lords as 'rebels', as opposed to 'enemies', with the implication that Irishmen, though they were not quite subjects, owed the king of England their allegiance nonetheless. Seen in this way, Irishmen could also be reformed.[22]

Informed by these papers, whose contents were doubtless amplified both by the presence at court of a number of figures from the Irish government, including John Alen and the Cowleys, and amid disturbing reports that Kildare had transferred ordnance out of Dublin Castle into his own stores, Henry VIII decided to reappoint Sir William Skeffington as deputy.[23] That decision, urged on it would seem by Cromwell, had been made by May 1534, when we learn that 'manyfold enormyties' had been proved against Kildare; but the king had made up his mind to dismiss Kildare many months earlier.[24] On the face of it, Skeffington would seem a poor choice: he was 70 years of age, unpopular at court and had openly clashed with Kildare less than two years before. But, as the papers directed to the king had made clear, Skeffington had experience of Ireland, a distinction to which no other English-born official at court, apart from the duke of Norfolk, could lay claim. Cromwell, moreover, worked to prepare the ground so that Skeffington might succeed this time around. He managed, for example, to convince Ossory to sign an indenture binding him to support the new deputy and seems to have attempted to do likewise with Kildare.[25] Cromwell also took part in drafting a detailed set of *Ordinances for the government of Ireland*, which was intended to regu-

---

22 It is perhaps significant, in light of Spain's interaction with native peoples in the New World, that in Spanish, 'to be reduced' [*reducir*] would, by the beginning of the seventeenth century, be defined as 'to be convinced', with the implication that people could be converted to a way of thinking or a mode of behaviour through persuasion and/or force: Elliott, *Empires of the Atlantic world*, p. 66.

23 Ellis, *Tudor frontiers*, p. 196.

24 *SP Hen. VIII*, ii, pp 194–5; *Cal. Carew MSS*, i, no. 41.

25 Bradshaw, 'Cromwellian reform', pp 83–4.

late the conduct of the king's deputy and also the king's subjects there.[26] The *Ordinances*, which became the first document in Ireland's history to be printed, has been viewed as the physical manifestation of a 'programme of Cromwellian reform'.[27] This may be so, but as we have seen above in section 1.8, they were in many respects identical to the 'Ordinances and Provisions for Ireland' drawn up for Surrey in 1519 and so were, in the main, a printed edition of standard articles of indenture agreed to by incoming governors of Ireland.[28] When, the previous year, the council of Ireland sent over the 'Articles for Reformation' they requested that a new deputy be appointed; but for the time being the earl of Kildare was the king's governor and the council had to make do with him: they made reference to 'the Kingis boke of instructions sente hither by my Lord Chauncelour' in the hope that the king would ensure that this 'boke', probably Kildare's articles of indenture, 'may be observed from hensforthe by the Deputie'.[29] For an Irish government, whose record-keeping was less than fastidious and which regularly exhibited complaints about the actions of the king's deputy and the dysfunction of royal government in the lordship, an easily circulated version of the duties and responsibilities of the governor of Ireland and the obligations of the king's subjects was a tangible announcement of the crown's intentions to see its will and its laws observed.[30]

In autumn 1535, Cromwell pored over a number of his remembrances for Ireland. He corrected one remembrance that questioned: 'whether it shalbe expedient to begynne a conquest or a reformation'.[31] By then, Gerald, the ninth earl of Kildare, was dead and his son, Thomas, had taken his father's place in the Tower, under attainder and awaiting sentence for having led a major rebellion against the king. Skeffington was governor, but the great challenge to royal authority, which began in summer 1534, had transformed his deputyship into a purely military operation. Skeffington had arrived in late 1534 at the head of an English army of just over 2,500 men, which he used to devastating effect, suppressing the rebellion and restoring order.[32] Cromwell's remembrance clearly speaks to the dilemma facing the Tudor regime in the aftermath of the Kildare rebellion. But, if it is considered within the context of the contemporary understanding of 'reformation', Cromwell makes a false distinction. The reformation of

26 Ordinances for the government of Ireland, TNA, SP 60/2/26, fos 64–71v (*SP Hen. VIII*, ii, pp 207–16).

27 Bradshaw, 'Cromwellian reform', pp 84–6.

28 S.G. Ellis, 'Thomas Cromwell and Ireland, 1532–1540', *Historical Journal*, 23 (1980), 502–3; above, pp 57–62.

29 *SP Hen. VIII*, ii, p. 166.

30 D.B. Quinn, 'Government printing and the publication of the Irish statutes', *PRIA*, sect. c, 49 (1943), 48–9.

31 Remembrances for Ireland, 1535, TNA, SP 60/2/31, fo. 83 (quotation); Bradshaw, *The Irish constitutional revolution*, pp 106–7.

32 Ellis, *Tudor frontiers*, pp 210–13.

Ireland, as we have seen, almost invariably meant the conquest of Ireland. That was the understanding of the concept offered by Skeffington and the Irish council as recently as June of that year. Within months of Skeffington's capture of Kildare's castle of Maynooth, they wrote to the King, and to Cromwell, seeking direction on a number of matters but none more important than 'yoᵣ finall pleasure concerning thordering of all other yoᵣ affaires for the reformacon of this land'.³³ Around this time, the earl of Ossory through his agent at court urged the king to instruct Skeffington to 'make sore warre in Mounster for the bringing of them there to obedience wherin consistith moche of the reformacon of this lande'.³⁴ Though Skeffington, in what was a remarkable misrepresentation of the situation on the ground, could also write to King Henry at this time of his belief that 'this land is nowe in like case to Your Highness, than yt was in at the firste conqueste', Norfolk knew better: months later he cautioned Cromwell that Kildare's execution would provoke a war by the Irish, forcing the king to commit 'incontinently' to what he called 'the generall conquest of the land'.³⁵ Cromwell, for his part, seems to have employed the term reformation to denote a policy that was more limited than conquest (in correcting his remembrance he was careful to insert 'a' before reformation). There is no evidence to suggest that Cromwell had read the documents prepared earlier in the reign, which had elaborated on the traditional meaning of reformation in an Irish context. But men regularly about him, like Robert Cowley, who were experts on Ireland, certainly had read (and had written) such material, and so would have acquainted him with the antiquity and meaning of the concept in an Irish context. Still, his usage of the term was similar to that expressed in the paper prepared in England in winter 1533–4, which in effect called for a series of particular reforms, including the reform of the Irish. This understanding of reform was more in line with its application in an English context – that is, the correction of a particular thing (an endeavour with which Cromwell was closely associated by contemporaries and historians alike): in early 1536 John Barlow, dean of Westbury, wrote to him, 'knowyng the good zele that your maistershippe beryth to the comyn welth as by the reformation of meny thinges lately by your high pollyce & wysdome'.³⁶ Its usage may also reflect Cromwell's belief that Henry VIII would not commit the necessary resources for reform in a traditional sense. For Cromwell, and for others in the Irish government, the reform of Ireland had come to be understood as a limited forward policy that was an alternative to general conquest.

33 Deputy and council to Henry VIII, 16 June 1535, TNA, SP 60/2/47, fo. 116; Deputy and council to Cromwell, 16 June 1535, TNA, SP 60//2/49, fo. 119.
34 Ossory to Cowley, June 1535, TNA, SP 60/2/53, fo. 132v.
35 *SP Hen. VIII*, ii, p. 248; Norfolk to Cromwell, 9 Sept. 1535, TNA, SP 60/2/61, fo. 154.
36 John Barlow to Cromwell, 3 Jan. 1536, TNA, SP 1/101, fo. 11 (quotation); G.R. Elton, *Reform and renewal: Thomas Cromwell and the common weal* (Cambridge, 1973).

Henry VIII's decision in late 1535 to reduce the English army in Ireland ruled out the possibility of conquest. The king was bent on recouping the costs he had incurred in putting down the rebellion (reckoned by Cromwell to have been £40,000) and making his government in Ireland self-sustaining; any forward policy for the lordship would have to be pursued within these fiscal parameters imposed by the king.[37] But, as Cromwell surely appreciated, the English crown was now poised to assume a greater stake in Ireland than it had known at any time in the Anglo-Irish relationship: the royal supremacy and its attendant legislation had to be introduced; a stable government had to be established; the traitors had to be disposed of; and, above all, the lordship had to be made secure against the king's Catholic enemies on the Continent. There could be no going back to the system of rule that had allowed the king's government in Ireland so much freedom of operation: royal control had to be strengthened. For the next five years Cromwell sought to reconcile the need to strengthen the king's position in Ireland with the imperative of reducing royal expenditure. This does not, however, mean that Cromwell was possessed of a clear plan for how to go about this, beyond a desire to recover royal revenues and establish new ones, and to subject the Irish executive to his closer supervision. We have precious few of Cromwell's own writings concerning Ireland and so few clues to his thinking on the subject, but it is clear from the growing stream of information which was directed to him in the later 1530s that the lordship was an important area of his ministerial responsibilities, if not an area of his especial interest.[38] Not for nothing did the deputy and council of Ireland recall, in a letter to Cromwell, 'the good mynde ye bere to the releve of this poure lande, and that ye have been, under the Kinges Highnes, a singular patrone and preferrer of the causes of the same'.[39]

The Irish political establishment, shorn of Kildare adherents and now augmented by a number of English-born clerks and military officers who had come over with the royal army, was determined not to allow the opportunities created by Kildare's destruction to be squandered. The new deputy, Leonard Grey, and the Irish council conveyed the expectant mood in a letter to King Henry in summer 1536:

> After this enterprise, so well and so breflie achived ... (wherby such oportunytie, meanes, and waies for coquesting, subduying, and reformyng of your hole domynion, or any place within the same, be opened unto Your Grace, as the like hath nat ben seen theise hunderith yeres past, and God knowith whether the like shall ever be seen agayne in our daies ...).[40]

---

37 Ellis, 'Cromwell and Ireland', p. 510.

38 It is clear that Cromwell dispatched more letters into Ireland than have survived: Memorandum of letters, 3 June 1536, TNA, SP 60/3/36, fo. 71.

39 *SP Hen. VIII*, ii, p. 318.

40 Ibid., ii, p. 337.

When victory over Kildare seemed assured, its members, together and individually, began writing to Cromwell in the hope that the minister would use his influence to convince the king to launch a reform initiative. The reform of the Irish of south Leinster – the lordships of the O'Tooles, O'Byrnes and Kavanaghs which were situated between Dublin and Wexford – was the focus of their entreaties, which came in the form of official and personal letters reporting on the state of Ireland and in the reform treatise more typical of Henry's reign. This region, as we have seen, had already been identified prior to the rebellion as the logical starting point for reform, but now the government of Ireland pressed more stridently for royal action there as a prelude to a general reformation. In January 1536, Ossory, Grey, Lord Butler, the treasurer, Gerald Aylmer, the chief justice, and John Alen, the master of the rolls, described these lordships in a letter to Cromwell as 'requiren (of all others first and principall reformation)', noting that unless they were reformed 'the kingis maiestie shall never be at any stay or likeliode of reformacon of this lande'.[41] More than half a dozen times over the next two years Cromwell was asked to read some variation on the necessity of expelling the Irish of south Leinster and re-inhabiting the region with Englishmen; and it was in early 1537, as we have shown above, that Patrick Finglas' 'Breviate' reached the court.[42] Apart from the Breviate, two of the more considered reform statements came from Robert Cowley and John Alen.[43]

The elder Cowley offered (as might be expected from an observer of his long experience) a traditional means for, as he put it, 'the readopting of the Kinges dominion in Irland and to attain the further possessions hitherto never had'. He highlighted the need, 'a commen opinion alwey', to reform the king's English subjects before a war of conquest was begun against the Irish. It was, he claimed, the interrelated evils of coign and livery and the failure to observe or enforce the king's laws that most afflicted the Englishry. The re-establishment of royal title to lands in Ireland – written proof of the king's claims was to 'be sought up in the Treasoury' in England – was to signal the government's enforcement of English law in English areas; once the law was put in execution, so Cowley's argument ran, the resort of Englishmen to coign and livery would cease. The deputy and council, with the support of an army, were then 'to joyne and lynke togithers' the English subjects 'in one trayne ordre, and conformitie' and march against the Irish. O'Connor, on

41 Ossory et al. to Cromwell, 2 Jan. 1536, TNA, SP 60/3/1, fo. 1. On the strategic importance of these lordships and this region in Tudor thinking about Ireland in these years, see Maginn, 'Civilizing' Gaelic Leinster, pp 46–9.

42 See, for example, Deputy and council to Cromwell, 29 Oct. 1536, TNA, SP 60/3/79, fo. 165v; Deputy and council to Cromwell, 23 Nov. 1536, TNA, SP 60/3/83, fos 175–75v. See also above, p. 33.

43 Robert Cowley to Cromwell, June 1536, TNA, SP 60/3/35, fos 63–70 (SP Hen. VIII, ii, pp 323–30); Alen to Henry VIII, 6 Oct. 1536, TNA, SP 60/3/75, fos 155–7 (SP Hen. VIII, ii, pp 373–7).

the Pale's western borders, was to be attacked first; the English force was then to turn its attention south where it would seize, one-by-one, a series of castles stretching from the O'Byrnes' country into north Wexford. These castles and their hinterlands were to be inhabited by Palesmen, the Irish population (presumably) would be banished: 'Then shall all Leynyster be clier Englissh, without any of the Irisshery amongst them'. Cowley also envisaged another three armies proceeding in a similar way through east Ulster, into the midlands to Athlone and from Limerick across the Shannon into O'Brien's country. Cowley's plans were pure fantasy, and he of all people should have known as much; but such was the uncertainty of the lordship's future after the Kildare rebellion that he shared his ideas, however far-fetched, with Cromwell. Cowley concluded his treatise by setting out a timeline that culminated with the arrival in Ireland of Henry VIII and perhaps Cromwell himself: 'These devises to be begon this next Marche, and so to be throughout continued all that yere next following; and then the Kinges Highnes, with certain of his Counceill, to comme next somer therafter'.

Alen's treatise was, by contrast, a more realistic document. Addressed to the king several months after Cowley's work, Alen expressed his desire to see the king 'banishe all the wilde Irishe out of their landis'; but he understood that such a policy would be costly and impractical – it would pose 'not a little difficultie to inhabite the lande agayne'. He argued, moreover, that the crown should not attempt to reform 'all Irlande'. Such a grand aspiration, he claimed with a directness unseen in the writings of his contemporaries, had thwarted all previous efforts to strengthen royal authority in Ireland:

> For as I suppose that deasire in your noble progenitors to reforme all Irlande at oon instante hath bene thoccasion that it is soo ferre out of order and frame as it is; for, as I have lerned, these 250 yeres together the same hath decaied, from tyme to tyme, alwaais differing [=deferring], and expecting tyme to reforme all, wherby the lande hath soo decaide, from oon tyme to another, that ever, either for other outwarde busuines of your Realme of Englande, for lak of preparacion, or sume other thing, tyme never served.[44]

Alen, as his allusion to his own acquisition of knowledge on the subject shows, had given the history of reform in Ireland some consideration, and in so doing exposed an uncomfortable truth that lay at the heart of the Anglo-Irish relationship. It is a remarkable distillation by a contemporary of the problem facing the Tudors in Ireland. Working from that premise, Alen outlined three policy options for the king to consider. The first reflected the consensus that had emerged within the Irish government by this time: the Irish of south Leinster should be 'conquest,

---

44 Alen to Henry VIII, 6 Oct. 1536, TNA, SP 60/3/75, fo. 155v.

reformed, or subdued' to the king's obedience. Alen reckoned that this could be accomplished with a small English army of 700 men. In this way, he concluded, 'ye may accompte that ye have the better parte of the lande to reform the residewe, what tyme so ever ye shall please'. This was Alen's preferred option, but he appreciated that the king might shrink from any further expense. So, he next outlined a policy that would see the king's deputy concentrate on defending the shires of Kilkenny, Tipperary, Waterford and Wexford where, he believed, English law and customs could be quickly re-established. The third and least expensive option, and also the least palatable in Alen's view, was to entrust the government of Ireland to 'sume man of this land' for a specific number of years.

It is now impossible to know how much consideration these proposals for Ireland's reform received at court, or whether Henry VIII or Cromwell supported them in principle. What is clear, however, is that the crown did not act on the suggestions advanced in these writings. Cromwell, probably under pressure from the king, was already taking a decidedly more narrow view of reform, one which was concerned with restoring law and order in English areas and ascertaining the extent of the royal revenues and, where possible, finding ways to increase them.[45] With this in mind, Ossory and other leading members of the Irish government had received a commission to travel through the south-eastern shires to hear and determine the grievances of the king's subjects there, to enquire into the king's landed revenues and profits and to oversee elections for the forthcoming parliament.[46] But King Henry's overriding concern was 'to knowe certainly' his revenues. Early in 1536 a paper came before Cromwell which reckoned that were an inquisition to be made into the 'kynges castells maners and honours and of religious houses ... that then his highness shulde knowe more now then hath bene knowne this xl yeres afore'.[47] In June Cromwell's servant William Body was sent to Ireland to assess what progress had been made with regard to ascertaining crown revenues.[48] Body was no exchequer official, but he had handled money for Cromwell in the past.[49] After several delays, owing apparently to his own clashes with several members of the Irish government, Body reported to Cromwell in August that he was preparing to survey the accounts.[50] His findings, however, some of which he set down in writing for Cromwell, were vague and failed to provide anything approaching a detailed statement of the king's revenues.[51] Of course the old exchequer system in Ireland was difficult to penetrate and, in any

45 Ellis, *Ireland in the age of the Tudors*, p. 145.
46 Ossory et al. to Cromwell, 2 Jan. 1536, TNA, SP 60/3/1, fo. 1.
47 Proposals before Cromwell, Jan. 1536, TNA, SP 60/3/3, fo. 5.
48 Cromwell to Deputy and council, 3 June 1536, TNA, SP 60/3/37, fo. 74.
49 He had been suspected of embezzling plate: *L. & P. Hen. VIII*, ix (ii), nos. 235, 478.
50 Body to Cromwell, 9 Aug. 1536, TNA, SP 60/3/59, fo. 121.
51 Body to Cromwell, 1536, TNA, SP 60/3/94, fos 201–4v.

case, its accounts provided little sense of the crown's profits in real terms (even when a copy of the undertreasurer William Brabazon's accounts for the three-and-half-year period from 1534 made its way to court in 1538, it did little to explain to Henry's satisfaction why the royal revenues were not greater).[52] Henry VIII wrote angrily to his deputy and council in February 1537: 'A greate sorte of you (We must be plain) desire nothing ells, but to reign in estimacion, and to fleece, from tyme to time, all that you may catche from Us'. The king, by then facing another major rebellion, this time in the north of England, expected the vast accessions of monastic wealth and the forfeited Fitzgerald estates to have increased crown revenues substantially. An extent of monastic lands in the English Pale was prepared, but obtaining further information on the Kildare lands was frustrated by the disappearance of the old earl's 'leger booke'.[53] Dissatisfied with the information he was getting from Ireland, the king decided 'to sende thither a personage of reputacion, whom we specially trust, both to see the perfite extent of our revenues there, to way, and consider with you our charges growing upon the same, and aswell to receyve due and perfite informacion touching all thinges concerning the state of our said lande'.[54]

Yet, amid the efforts to ascertain the crown revenues and the advancement of the various proposals for the reform of Ireland – both largely theoretical exercises – something very tangible was happening on the ground: royal power in Ireland was reaching beyond those areas where it was normally felt. It was carried deep into the south and west by English soldiers and officials who ranged widely through the country after the Kildare rebellion. They were strangers to Ireland, but some were cognizant of the fact that they were passing through parts of the lordship that had not known royal authority in some time. Certainly, the comparisons and contrasts to English society that they witnessed in these areas moved several of them to describe their experiences, and often in a way that highlighted more fundamental details, such as geography and culture, which were omitted in the descriptions of Ireland then being offered in the correspondence of Englishmen more intimately familiar with the country. Captain Steven Ap Parry, for example, who travelled with James Butler on an expedition through Munster, reported to Cromwell in October 1535 'that all thys jurney, frome Dungarvyn forthe, ther ys none alive, that ever cane remember that ever Ynglysche mene of war was ever in that partys'.[55] Ap Parry was careful to name all the places he went, often giving a sense of the distances between them, and described in great detail the abilities of the local figures he met, commenting in particular on their facility in the English language. The following year another

52 Brabazon's accounts, TNA, SP 65/1, fo. 2; Ellis, *Reform and revival*, pp 86–105.
53 Extent of the abbeys, 1536, TNA, SP 60/3/87, fo. 191; Body to Cromwell, 1536, TNA, SP 60/3/94, fo. 203v.
54 *SP Hen. VIII*, ii. pp 422–3.   55 Ibid., ii, p. 286.

English captain, Francis Herbert, accompanied Lord Deputy Grey to a meeting with a number of Irishmen whose lordships bordered the English Pale. Herbert reported to Cromwell some of what he learned there: most notably that O'Brien 'es the chyf capten of all Eyrresmen. Yef he were soubdueyt, and hes pryd betten down, and he to be mad know hes pryns es power, het would cawxe all the Eyrres men of Irland to quaylle, and enclyn to ther prynses plessur'.[56] However it was Grey who, more than any figure in the Irish government, was responsible for ignoring the accustomed boundaries of English Ireland. He too wrote frequently to Cromwell. Grey, who began his career in Ireland as marshal of the army, had a gift for battle and, as deputy, led the king's forces along the coast through south Leinster, prompting Alen to remark to Cromwell that 'no Inglishe deputie cam theis 100 yeres, nor non like enterprise attemtated, ne atchived, theis 100 yeres'.[57] Grey then met with O'Neill on the borders of Ulster before leading the royal army toward O'Brien's country in Munster where, after capturing a number of strategic castles, he destroyed O'Brien's bridge over the Shannon. William Body accompanied the deputy, and he provided Cromwell with another detailed account of these districts outside the regular control of the crown.[58] Grey had pushed into Munster only after he was disappointed in his request to be furnished with ships, sailors and additional wages so that he might strike into north-east Ulster against invading Scots.[59] It seemed that under Grey's leadership nowhere in Ireland was beyond the reach of royal power.

Grey's campaigning also broadened the geographical horizons of English administration in the lordship. One of the keys to his success lay in his willingness to bring the fight into Irish districts, in effect turning on its head the strategy pursued by the king's government in Ireland for the past century. In the absence of maps or charts of the terrain, he relied on local guides to show him the way. Later, in 1538, he arrived in Galway having travelled through the wilds of O'Brien's country guided by a galloglass, much to the astonishment of the Irish government and Ulick Burke whose lordship suddenly was host to the king's governor; and in 1540, while campaigning in central Ulster – the heart of what was in the Middle Ages known as 'the Great Irishry' – Grey complained that he would have taken O'Neill by surprise 'yf my gydys had gyded right'.[60] Grey also regularly cut passes through the woodlands and undergrowth of sufficient breadth to allow him (and the field artillery that he employed to such great effect) access to Irish lordships once shrouded in wilderness.[61] And where Grey went parlia-

---

56 Ibid., ii, pp 306–7.   57 Ibid., ii, pp 347–8.
58 Body to Cromwell, 9 Aug. 1536, TNA, SP 60/3/59, fos 120–1.
59 *SP Hen. VIII*, ii, p. 314.
60 Gerald Power, 'The viceroy and his critics: Leonard Grey's journey through the west of Ireland, June–July 1538', *Journal of the Galway Archaeological Society*, 60 (2008), 80; *SP Hen. VIII*, iii, p. 183.
61 See, for example, *SP Hen. VIII*, iii, p. 7.

ment, a potent symbol of English administration in Ireland, followed, moving between May and September 1536 beyond the English Pale to Kilkenny and then on as far west as Cashel and Limerick. In Leinster, meanwhile, Grey re-built bridges and manors on the borders of the Pale; he rebuilt castles in Munster as well, though he struggled to ward these newly captured castles so that districts once beyond royal control might be held for the king.[62] Men like Francis Herbert recognized the need for more Englishmen in Ireland to hold and inhabit parts of the lordship (many of the castles won by Grey were handed back to Irishmen); William Body, too, called for the colonization of Ireland by Englishmen, and recognized the opportunities for his family and friends presented by the relative dearth of English clerks in the country: he requested permission from Cromwell to have his kinsman sent over with two or three clerks 'at the leest'.[63] Such sharp campaigning against Irishmen also moved many a lord to submit so as to avoid further hostilities. In 1536 alone Grey accepted the submission of at least half-a-dozen Irish lords, including O'Neill.[64] Each of these submissions required a written indenture between the deputy, acting on the king's behalf, and the submitting lord as proof of the covenant entered into. Indentures of this kind held Irish lords to a set of political and military expectations unknown in Tudor times; at the same time, however, they demanded more of the king's government: this kind of engagement generated paper-work, necessitating additional clerks to make copies of these records and some procedure to file and store them. For Grey, this kind of engagement with Irishmen was to be temporary – it was to last until such time as the king began the reform of Ireland. In practice, however, the indentures he concluded with Irish lords served further to blur the distinction between 'Irish enemies' and loyal English subjects.

Thus, by mid-1537, Henry VIII was receiving, through Thomas Cromwell, a steady stream of information about Ireland. It came mainly in three interrelated forms: proposals for reform; material pertaining to the revenues; and the information generated through the sudden extension of royal government into regions outside the normal control of government. The information reflected the concerns and aspirations of the political establishment in Ireland and the crown on the one side and the new reality of conditions in the lordship on the ground on the other. All of this was to be declared orally by a delegation of councillors who travelled to court in the spring.[65] The king, however, was evidently unhappy with the substance of the information he was receiving. In what was, in effect, a vote of no confidence in the ability of his government to appraise him to his satisfaction of the state of his lordship, Henry appointed four high commissioners, none with any

62 *SP Hen. VIII*, ii, pp 335, 350–1.
63 Ibid., ii, p. 308; Body to Cromwell, 1536, TNA, SP 60/3/94, fo. 203v.
64 See, for example, *Cal. Carew MSS*, i, nos 71–2, 76–7, 80, 82, 90.
65 Brabazon to Wriothesley, 29 Apr. 1537, TNA, SP 60/4/21, fo. 70.

experience of Ireland, to take 'an order and establishment ... of our lande of Irelande ... for the reduccion of the sayd lande to a due civilitie and obedience and thadvauncement of the publique weal of the same'.[66] The commissioners' instructions reflected the king's narrow view of reform. They were to 'make a perfyt booke' of the royal revenues, to further reduce the army, to reform the courts, to introduce further legislation in parliament (which then stood prorogued), to investigate the payment of 'black rents' to Irishmen and to 'enserche, who hath served His Magestie best, and who hathe moste earnestly and trewly, from the begynnyng, persevered his faythfull subjects'.[67] This last direction was a reflection of the king's belief that members of his government in Ireland had been negligent in the execution of their duties. In this case the king was referring specifically to their alleged failure to prevent the reedification of O'Brien's bridge, but the sentiment was symptomatic of the king's deeper mistrust of his servants in Ireland. We have already seen that he thought that they were defrauding him of money. And there were also reports of discord within the Irish government and allegations that Grey had prevented information from being sent back to England – Walter Cowley reported to Cromwell that the deputy had intercepted his letters to England and opened them.[68] The despatch of the royal commissioners to Ireland was thus Henry's attempt to ascertain, even in the face of an unprecedentedly large amount of information about Ireland coming into his court, a more accurate picture of the situation in Ireland through four trusted courtiers.

However the king's view of reform, the viability of which was soon to be tested by the commissioners, was out of step with the view of at least some in the Irish political establishment on the subject. Robert Cowley, for one, hoped against experience that the commissioners would spearhead a reform initiative that would unify the Englishry and expel all Irishmen across the Shannon. He wrote to Cromwell how the Irish were 'never in suche feare to be clerely exiled, as at this day'; they were, he claimed, 'nowe in extreme drede, in that they see that little armye so well prosper'. The moment to implement his plan to reform the Englishry was at hand: 'in the tracting of tyme, and with litle charges, this is, in my moste symple mynde, the nerist way, oonles the generall reformacion shulde followe immedietly'.[69] There was nothing new in Cowley's plan for reform, but his opinion that the military balance with the Irish had been tipped in the crown's favour by 'that litle armye' would appear to have had some substance. Officials in Ireland had reported that the Irish were impressed with the crown's display of power in destroying the earls of Kildare and their adherents,

---

66 Minute of Commission, 31 July 1537, TNA, SP 60/4/33, fo. 99; *Calendar of the patent and close rolls of chancery in Ireland, Henry VIII to 18th Elizabeth*, ed. James Morrin (Dublin, 1861), p. 35.
67 *SP Hen. VIII*, ii pp 452–63 (quotation, p. 462).
68 Ibid., ii, p. 322; Cowley to Cromwell, 1 June 1536, TNA, SP 60/3/34, fo. 80.
69 *SP Hen. VIII*, ii, p. 452.

and that was before Grey had begun striking deep into Irish areas at will. By August 1537, a month prior to the arrival of the royal commissioners, Grey and the council could write to Cromwell:

> We begynne to come to soche knowledge of Irishmen, and ther countries, that we consider no soche difficultie to subdue or exile them ... so as, to be playne ... the Kinges Highnes may have his plesur upon them, if he wold ernestly set to them.[70]

Grey had just finished a hosting in which he trampled through the Irish lordships south of Dublin and in the midlands. The governor had discovered that the use of sharp military force in Irish areas – complemented by the seizure of strategic castles, the taking of pledges and the conclusion of indentures – rendered most Irish lords powerless against him.

But there was a sudden shift in expectations by the time the commissioners reached Ireland in September. We have noticed above, in section 1.9, how the commissioners came armed with a tranche of various written material on Ireland (which may well have included a copy of the Hatfield Compendium); and how, following their arrival, they received written proposals from within the Irish government that sought to frame how they should proceed. The chief concern of these proposals was to offer suggestions for the defence of the Englishry and the strengthening of English law and government there. Word must have filtered to Ireland that the commissioners' mission was conservative, chiefly to enquire into the state of English areas (the south-eastern shires outside the Pale in particular) and to report back to the king – a general reformation, in other words, was not in the offing. Grey, whose campaigning had over the previous eighteen months demonstrated what moving beyond the traditional borders of the Englishry might achieve, now outlined for the commissioners in a 'book' the importance of fortifying the borders of the Pale and the dangers that coign and livery, and Irish culture more generally, posed to Englishmen.[71] In two long papers prepared for the commissioners by John Alen, a similar shift of emphasis to the reform of the Englishry is evident. In his first paper, Alen, who once prioritized the reform of the Irish of south Leinster, now reverted to more traditional arguments, which spoke of the need to appoint two captains in every English barony and two constables in every parish so as to strengthen the defences of each shire.[72] He also drew attention to the 'neglygent keeping of the Kinges recordes' and the great losses that, he claimed, the

---

70 Ibid., ii, p. 469.
71 Grey to Commissioners, Sept. 1537, TNA, SP 60/5/14, fos 25–6v (TNA, SP 60/5/24, fos 55–9 contains extracts from Grey's 'book'). There is another contemporary copy of this in BL, Additional MS, Yelverton 48017, fos 164–5v.
72 *SP Hen. VIII*, ii, pp 480–6. A portion of a contemporary copy of Alen's 'book' may be found in BL, Additional MS, Yelverton 48017, fos 161–3v.

king had incurred as a result. It was necessary, he continued, to order and then place 'all the rolles and mynymentes' in Bermingham's Tower at Dublin Castle behind a door with two locks and to entrust the keys only to the constable and the undertreasurer, who he suggested should be born in England.[73] When it came to the Irish, Alen adopted an ambivalent stance. He referred to Irishmen as 'our nat-urall enymyes', and was keen to impress upon the commissioners the importance of keeping the Irish out of the English Pale; and yet he also made the striking sug-gestion that Henry VIII should assume 'the name of King of Ireland' as a means of disabusing the Irish of their belief that the king of England governed Ireland only by right of the papacy. As king of Ireland, Alen reasoned, Henry VIII could bring hitherto recalcitrant Irish lords 'to dew obeydence'. Alen's second paper was also concerned primarily with the Englishry.[74] But in this paper he placed special emphasis on the importance of the governor to any future policy of reform. He used this argument to criticize Grey's behaviour as governor, although he also devoted space to reiterating his argument about the necessity of expelling the Irish from south Leinster and re-establishing the king's laws in the south-eastern shires. A fourth paper, written by Thomas Luttrell, the chief justice and a Palesman, echoed many of the ideas advanced by Grey and Alen, but offered a much more detailed insight into conditions in the English Pale and especially along its borders.[75]

It is difficult to know how well prepared the commissioners were to receive all of this information. It was observed around this time that it typically took an English governor one or two years to become acquainted with conditions in the lordship.[76] The commissioners were accompanied into Ireland by the soldier, Thomas Agard, who had served the king in Ireland since 1534, and they were briefed on the state of things there by Grey and others of the council soon after their arrival.[77] Also in attendance upon the commissioners was Robert Cowley, who later recalled bringing Anthony St Leger, one of the commissioners, 'regys-ters of all the kinges rightes and inherydetamentes in Irland sethens the first con-quest ... And divers bokes ... expressing the enormyties and remedyes'.[78] The commissioners communicated regularly with Cromwell, but their writings exhibit a reticence uncommon for Tudor officials experiencing Ireland for the first time: they offered little personal insight into that which they were witnessing. Two of the commissioners, St Leger and George Paulet, had recently served on a com-mission to survey the defences at Calais and seem to have understood and to have approached the English areas of Ireland as a similar border region.[79] A month after their arrival they had surveyed the king's lands in six shires in the south-east,

73 *SP Hen. VIII*, ii, p. 486.   74 Ibid., ii, pp 486–501.
75 Ibid., ii, pp 502–10.   76 *Cal. Carew MSS*, i, no. 91.
77 *SP Hen. VIII*, ii, p. 510.   78 Ibid., iii, p. 50.
79 David Grummitt, *The Calais garrison: war and military service in England, 1436–1558* (London, 2008), p. 51; Ellis, *Ireland in the age of the Tudors*, p. 146.

remarking that there were 'diverse goodly mannors and castelles, the more parte of theym ruinous, and in great decaye, the townes and lands aboughtes theym depopulate, wasted, and not maynured'. When, in a letter, the commissioners failed to expound upon the 'diverse thinges' which they deemed 'worthie reformacion', and expressed their preference to communicate their findings orally to Cromwell and King Henry upon (what they clearly hoped would be their speedy) return, the king reprimanded them: he insisted that they should write 'amplely and largely' of conditions in Ireland and, seeing as they were his representatives there, that they should reform that which needed reforming.[80]

For the next two months the commissioners journeyed through the English shires in the south-east, holding inquests that heard grand juries present on oath the manifold grievances of the region; they also received the submissions of several Irish lords bordering the Englishry and travelled the Pale shires of Dublin, Meath and Louth.[81] This kind of mission gave the commissioners a unique view of the intersection and intermingling of English law and culture with Irish law and culture; there can be little doubt that it proved a formative experience for St Leger, who emerged as the most influential of the commissioners. But they were still reluctant to put in writing their own ideas and impressions of what they were seeing. All that the commissioners were willing to offer, and only in direct response to the king's demand for information, was their opinion that a 'lacke of mynystracion of justice' in Cos Kilkenny, Tipperary and Waterford was the most glaring area in need of reform. They recommended that the king send over two justices from England to oversee the re-introduction of the king's laws in these counties (Alen had suggested a similar course of action in his letter to the commissioners).[82] Beyond this, the commissioners reported in early 1538 that they had finished their survey of the king's lands and had leased some of them; they had also issued the king's pardon in return for fines totalling 2,000 marks and had dissolved, at long last, what became known as the Irish Reformation Parliament. All that was left to do, they wrote, was to complete their examination of the vicetreasurer's accounts. The commissioners completed their audit of the accounts in February, a task that they described as 'a tedious werk' and an 'intrycat busyness', which was made worse by the 'lack of good recordes, as well concerning the kyngis olde inherytaunce, as also other landes and possessions, commen to His Gracys handes by atteynder, or otherwyse; for none in effect ben here, but suche as hath ben lately made by the said Vicethesaurer'.[83]

The commissioners left Ireland in April. As a reconnaissance mission, carried out on behalf of a distant king and his minister, the commissioners' mission must

80 *SP Hen. VIII*, ii, pp 519, 521.
81 The jury presentments are printed in *The social state of the southern and eastern counties of Ireland in the sixteenth century*, ed. H.F. Hore and J. Graves (Dublin, 1870).
82 *SP Hen. VIII*, ii, pp 498, 538.   83 Ibid., ii, p. 547.

be accounted a success: Patrick Barnewall, the king's serjeant-at-law, remarked in a letter to Cromwell, 'Y recken they knowe moche of the mysdemenurs here, and the redresse of the same, so that hit shall be nessesary that they be well harde, and ther devysses followit'.[84] Indeed, they returned to court with first-hand knowledge of Ireland, and what must have been an intimate view of the king's lands and revenues, the state of English law and government and an insight, at least, into the Irish polity across the borders. But the king had expected his commissioners to address administrative and legal deficiencies in Ireland: beyond reducing the army and overseeing several final pieces of legislation pass through parliament, the commissioners stopped short of implementing any reforms. No more than Skeffington, Surrey or Edgecombe before them, the commissioners, though they carried the king's authority, were not the king, and were thus reluctant to assume the responsibility for making policy decisions about a country they hardly knew.[85] And like these earlier Englishmen who had travelled to Ireland in the service of a Tudor king, their mission shone light on only a part of the island – Ulster and Connacht, for example, where much of the king's inheritance lay, remained beyond their comprehension. The real achievement of the commissioners would be measured by whether the knowledge they acquired about Ireland, which included the copies of the jury presentments from the towns and shires of the south-east and other written material they carried back to England with them, could be digested at court and then put to use in creating and pursuing a policy for Ireland.

We can assume that the commissioners, who were accompanied to England by the master of the rolls and the chief justice, were debriefed upon their return to court. But there is no indication that their homecoming occasioned any sustained discussion of Ireland. It may be that the information that they now possessed was initially overshadowed by the diplomatic negotiations surrounding the arrival in May of a delegation from the Schmalkaldic League; or that the arrest that month of one of the commissioners, George Paulet, for having allegedly spoken slanderous words against Cromwell while in Ireland cast a pall over the commissioners' return.[86] Certainly in June, with the king on his summer progress, Cromwell's chaplain John Deythyke reported from London to the archbishop of Dublin that he had spoken to Cromwell, but that the minister and the council were by then so occupied with ambassadors from France and Spain that 'ther ys nothing doune as consernyng Ireland matters'.[87] Lacking any direc-

---

84 Ibid., ii, p. 571.
85 Following his decision to appoint the commissioners Henry VIII instructed Grey: 'We wolde have there woordes and doinges ... no lesse esteemed, thenne yf the lyke shuld be doon by Us': ibid., ii, p. 464.
86 Rory McEntegart, *Henry VIII, the League of Schmalkalden, and the English Reformation* (Rochester, 2002), p. 116; *L. & P. Hen. VIII*, xiii (i), no. 1538.
87 John Deythyke to archbishop of Dublin, 8 June, 1538, TNA, SP 1/133, fo. 6.

tion for a forward policy from England, Lord Deputy Grey continued where he had left off prior to the commissioners' arrival. Over six months, from April to October, Grey campaigned against the Irish in south Ulster and in the midlands; he then struck out all the way to Galway by way of Munster and through Thomond (O'Brien's country) before returning to Dublin whence, after a brief respite, he invaded the Kavanaghs' lordship in south Leinster; he subsequently reversed course and attacked the Scots along the coast in east Ulster.[88] What Grey accomplished with so few troops was, in military terms, an extraordinary feat. The king's governor had not been to Galway in over thirty years and no Tudor governor had ever ventured through Thomond. In October, Grey wrote to the king that Ireland 'is at soche staie and peas at this season, as it hath not been theis many yeres; noither was there any King of Englande theis hundredth yeres past so esteemed, knowen, obeid, and feared, as Your Grace is'.[89] Neither Grey nor the Irish council, however, were under any illusion that the peace that the deputy had won was permanent. When Grey wrote to Henry he had the Kavanaghs at his mercy and asked the king whether he should accept their submission, or if he should procede 'clerely to exile them', a course that he favoured and which had been suggested countless times before. In November the council acknowledged the return from court of Aylmer and Alen but indicated to Cromwell their continued ignorance of the king's plans for Ireland.[90]

Meanwhile, Grey's relentless campaigning in 1538 had brought to the surface two long-simmering tensions in Ireland. The first was dissension within the king's government. Grey's abrasiveness and his wilful disregard of the Irish council had alienated so many in the Irish government that he increasingly turned for support and counsel to his own servants and what remained of the Geraldine affinity. This, and the fact that Grey was married to the ninth earl of Kildare's sister, gave rise to the view expressed by James, Lord Butler that Grey was 'the Erle of Kildare newly borne againe'.[91] Butler wrote these words to Robert Cowley, his father's agent at court, and it was not long before the latter penned a 'devise' for the reformation of Ireland which was implicitly critical of the deputy's conduct.[92] Cowley took particular issue with the deputy's efforts to 'subdue or yet refo'me mere Irishmen which never were under obeysa[u]nce' while 'the wilde conterfeatid Englishmen' were ignored. This, according to Cowley, was akin to 'a man that seeth his awne house on ffyre, suffreth his house to burne and rynneth out to rescue a straungiers house'. This is a revealing metaphor. It reflects Cowley's long-held conviction, as set out again here, that the English population of Ireland must be reformed before any attempt was made to address the Irish. His suggestions for how this was to be

---

88 Power, 'The viceroy and his critics', 78–87.
89 *SP Hen. VIII*, iii, p. 100.   90 Ibid., iii, p. 105.
91 Ibid., iii, p. 32.
92 Cowley's devise, Aug. 1538, TNA, SP 60/7/44, fos 132–6v.

achieved were vague: the appointment of a new deputy (who was to operate 'not wᵗ hedy rage') and captains to defend outlying English areas along with the provision of justice in the shires. But Cowley broke new ground by outlining a plan for the 'reformacion of the mere Irishmen', which relied on persuasion rather than pure military force, or the threat of military force. He called for the appointment of 'discrete p[er]sonages having an earnest mynde to see the lande brought to the kinges obeysaunce and good ordre' to express to 'the capitaynes of Yrishmen' the king's intention to reform Ireland. Crucially, the Irishmen were to be made to understand that the king did not seek their destruction or the confiscation of their goods. Rather, it was to be made plain that the king wanted 'to reduce theme to a civile ordre as all other regions be', and to wean them away from 'their detestable warres murders spoiles burnynges and other enormyites'. If they agreed to hold their lands of the crown and put away Irish law and culture and adopt English law and custom, then the king would accept them as 'his true subiectes but also at all tymes defende theme as any other his subiectes of thEnglish pale'. This was a marked departure from Cowley's earlier insistence on waging war against the Irish and speaks, at one level, to his realization that the king was unlikely to commit to an army of conquest and 'general reformation'. At another level, however, Cowley's devise alluded to the fact that such frenetic campaigning risked provoking a combination of Irish and rebel English lords against the king. 'If they all did confederate in oon', he warned, 'it were no smale power that wolde be hable to resiste theme'.[93]

Cowley's fear was realized when, in 1539, the long-swirling rumours that an accord had been reached between O'Donnell, O'Neill and other powerful lords, like the Fitzgerald earl of Desmond, was confirmed: Grey's harrying of individual Irish lordships had indeed given rise to a confederacy whose aims included not only the restoration of the fugitive Fitzgerald heir, who was then in O'Donnell's care, but also, with the support of the Pope and the backing of the king of Scots, the restoration of the old religion.[94] The sudden seriousness of the situation must have come as a shock at King Henry's court. Irish affairs, as we have seen, had been receiving scant attention in England. Reports from and about Ireland continued to flow to Cromwell, but it was late in 1538 before he got round to addressing the Irish government. He sent out letters to the council (now lost) which, *inter alia*, instructed them to put aside their divisions and to move Grey 'to have recoʳse to a boke', evidently given to the deputy by the lord chancellor and council when the commissioners were in Ireland, 'of divers thingis to be refoʳmed: which been not all as yet redressed'.[95] The contents of the book are unknown; but

93 Ibid., fo. 133v.
94 *SP Hen. VIII*, iii, pp 136–42; Maginn, *'Civilizing' Gaelic Leinster*, pp 56–7; Power, *A European frontier elite*, pp 83–92.
95 Memorial, 10 Dec. 1538, TNA, SP 60/7/58, fo. 165.

Grey certainly ignored whatever proposals for reform it contained: before long he launched a campaign in the north against O'Neill. The Irish council, meanwhile, seems to have understood the crown's interest in providing law and good government in English areas outside the Pale. This narrow view of reform was as close to a forward policy as Cromwell had to offer. In early 1539 the councillors followed the trail blazed by the commissioners, moving widely through the south-east administering justice, setting forth the new religion and collecting fines which they duly lodged in the exchequer 'the like precedent whereof have not been seen thies 200 yeres'. By May, Brabazon was suggesting that a permanent council be established to administer the law in the south-east.[96]

The emergence of the confederacy in summer 1539 (the so-called Geraldine League) fundamentally altered this decidedly conservative approach to reform. Though Grey routed the combined forces of O'Neill and O'Donnell in August, the confederacy held together and continued to pose an existential threat to Tudor rule in Ireland. Robert Cowley now called for a great army to be sent from England to destroy the confederates; 'it shalbe necessary to plante Englishmen here', he continued: 'sethens the traictours have made their avaunce, that they woll have all, or lose all, that they maybe soo handelid, that they may lose all'.[97] James Butler, having succeeded his father to the newly restored earldom of Ormond, and who was then engaged in fighting the combined forces of O'Brien and Desmond in the south, appealed to Cromwell as 'the oonly procurer and setterforth of reformacion for this pore lande', urging him to 'let nothing let you now to take paynes for the generall reformacion of the hole lande'. Like Cowley, Ormond hoped that the king would despatch into Ireland 'a mayne armye with reasonable victaile, as also artificers and craftysmen to remayne and inhabite' for, he pointed out,

> though it be somewhat laborious and costly to goo forward to this generall reformacion ... it shalbe moche better, than yerelie to exburse great somes of money, and noo good successe to ensue the same, but as fer from all good ordre and civilitie, as when it was begon first of all, saving oonly the preservacion and defence of us, a fewe of His Highnes subjects, whiche lyveth in a maner as wretchedly as the rest.[98]

William Wise, the sheriff of Waterford and once one of Henry VIII's grooms-men, reported to Cromwell on the situation in Munster, and in particular on whether the government-backed claimant to the earldom of Desmond, James Fitzmaurice, would remain loyal to the crown once Grey's army departed the region. Fitzmaurice had been in England for four years prior to his return to

---

96 *SP Hen. VIII*, iii, pp 111–18, 134 (quotation, p. 118).
97 Ibid., iii, pp 147–8.   98 Ibid., iii, pp 166–7.

Munster and was well thought of at court, where he may have served as one of the king's pages.[99] Wise echoed Ormond's call for a general reformation as well as some of the earl's despair of his own country and community:

> it co[m]myth ofte to pass that men wele estemyd in Ingland change here ther honest condicons so that they ar soner ov[er]com with our vices than we made honest through ther good ensample. I wish that yo[r] lordship moght ons in person se this poor land so as then trouth shold be avaunissid and falsed receive condigne ponyshime[n]t and sith by dyv[er]s argume[n]tes y[e] ar fully enstructed of o[r] defawtes and mysorder which by manyfold devices could not hith[er]to be remedyed. My singular good lorde the pynyon of them that be taken for wisemen here is that w[th]out a gen[er]all reformacon the Kinges Ma[tie] shall vaynly consume his treasure in this land ....[100]

Much as Wise would have liked to have Cromwell experience and 'see' Ireland for himself, this was not the time. What was now needed, the information out of Ireland made clear, was an English army, and only the king could provide that.

Henry VIII's reaction to this sudden challenge to his sovereignty over Ireland is largely obscure because the letter (or letters) that he sent to the Irish council has not survived. But we know from the official response of the lord deputy and council of Ireland in early 1540 that the king had 'determyned to susteyn' a 'great charge ... to advaunce hither a mayne army for the reducing of this Your Graces lande to a civile ordre and reformacion'.[101] The Irish government recognized the opportunity and presented the king with an audacious plan for general reformation. 'To enterprise the hole extirpation and total destruccion of all the Irishmen of the lande' was impractical, they claimed. Such a course would be expensive and would necessitate the large-scale repopulation of Ireland with Englishmen – 'there is noo prince cristened', they reasoned, 'that commodiously might spare soo many subjectes to departe out of his region'. Rather they sought to follow the example of the English Conquest of Ireland: the king of England should come in person and at the head of a powerful army which, they believed, would induce a rash of submissions and allow his army to punish rebels and oversee the disarmament and subjection of the Irish. They reckoned that an English army of 6,000 men (including tradesmen), backed by an additional 1,000 men which were to be put in wages from Ireland, plus Grey's army (of approximately 350 soldiers) and the support of the king's subjects, would be sufficient for this purpose. The army from England was to be divided into six contingents and deployed in O'Donnell's country in the north-west, at the English outpost

99 Anthony McCormack, s.v. 'James fitzMaurice Fitzgerald', *ODNB*.
100 William Wise to Thomas Cromwell, 23 Dec. 1539, LPL, Carew MS 602, fo. 109 (*Cal. Carew MSS*, i, no. 138).
101 *SP Hen. VIII*, iii, p. 176.

of Knockfergus in the north-east, at Galway in the west and, in the south, at the cities of Limerick and Cork; the remaining contingent was to be placed (in three garrisons) in south Leinster. The belief that an army numbering 6,000 men was necessary to reform Ireland was familiar, but the island-wide reform strategy that the deputy and council proposed was not. Until that army arrived and the reformation began, the government in Ireland had no choice other than to play for time, by turns negotiating and skirmishing with members of the confederacy.[102]

Money and some reinforcements had been sent over in November 1539, but no large army was forthcoming.[103] It was not until April that the king wrote to Grey to call him back to England so that he might be in a position to return to Ireland with troops at the end of May. It is difficult to say how the threat in Ireland was perceived at court. At the time of the Kildare rebellion, a relief army arrived in Ireland three months after the king declared his intention to raise it. Nine months had now elapsed since John Alen informed Cromwell of the confederacy; it had been five months since the king had promised an army. The delay may be explained, in part, by the distraction caused by the marriage and subsequent annulment of Henry's marriage to his fourth wife, Anne of Cleves. But the king doubtless also recalled his prior expenditure and knew all too well the difficulty of seeking recompense from the Irish revenues. The confederacy, moreover, had as yet failed to penetrate English areas. So while the deputy and council might write that 'withowt a great ayde of the Kinges Majestie ... the lande might be destroyed and lost, before her arryvall', Henry was prepared to wait at least until he heard what Grey had to say. As it transpired, Henry was rewarded for his patience. In June, Manus O'Donnell, one of the leaders of the confederacy, broke ranks and offered his submission to the crown. It was the first sign that the confederacy, which had failed to make good on its efforts to internationalize its campaign, would gradually come undone under its own weight, and without any confrontation with a large English army.[104]

Yet potentially more disruptive in the longer term for England's relationship with Ireland was the fall of Thomas Cromwell. Cromwell's arrest in June and execution a month later paved the way for the arrest and ultimately the execution of his client, Leonard Grey, as well. But Cromwell's removal from the political scene also meant that the man at court to whom the overwhelming majority of information about Ireland had been directed for the previous decade and who was the principal author of Henry VIII's policy for Ireland (such as it was) was gone; his papers, like Wolsey's, were confiscated and, rather than being put to use, disappeared into the Tower. Unlike on the fall of the cardinal, however, Cromwell's fall signalled the end of kingly-rule by minister and the beginning of a period of conciliar government: there would be no ministerial

102 Ibid., iii, pp 179–82.   103 Bradshaw, *The Irish constitutional revolution*, pp 179–85.
104 O'Donnell's submission, 20 June 1540, TNA, SP 60/9/34, fo. 71.

successor to take up Irish affairs under Henry VIII. The first surviving letter out of Ireland to the king's council exhorted the councillors to remind the king 'that reformation may be had in this land' and alerted them to the fact that 'here is diverse urgente causes to be loked apon to be refourmed'.[105] Of the nearly twenty councillors whose names appear on the first council register of August 1540, only Norfolk had any first-hand experience of Ireland, and only Thomas Wriothesley, Cromwell's former secretary and now one of the king's secretaries, can be said definitively to have handled paperwork concerning Ireland before.[106] There was still King Henry of course. At nearly 50 years of age, his own memories of Irish affairs stretched back longer than many of his councillors, and for the first time the king was taking an active (and sustained) role in the government of Ireland: where once the correspondence from Ireland had gone to Wolsey or Cromwell, now it came directly to him. The king, however, lacked the detailed knowledge of Ireland that Cromwell had come to possess from working through the written material on Ireland, which for years had passed through him. And the king, for all his new-found maturity in middle age, was not prepared to assume such an intricate bureaucratic burden himself.

But just when it looked, in summer 1540, like the government of Henry VIII was at risk of losing some of the understanding of Ireland that it had gained over the previous two decades, the appointment of Anthony St Leger as governor rescued the situation. While St Leger did not have access to the papers on Ireland amassed by Cromwell, the former commissioner had a brief but intensive personal experience of Ireland that included the handling of a wide range of written material which, quite possibly, included the Hatfield Compendium. A well-educated and discreet gentleman courtier, St Leger was the antithesis of Grey. This immediately won for him broad support in the Irish political establishment and so also access to their ideas and writings on the subject of Ireland's reform. At court, meanwhile, St Leger had the backing of the king and had adroitly aligned himself with Norfolk, now the most influential figure in England after Henry, as his erstwhile patron fell from power. Most importantly of all, however, St Leger would seem to have actually sought his appointment, identifying Ireland as a theatre of Tudor operation within which he might advance his career.[107]

In addition to fulfilling the standard duties as governor, St Leger was faced with a still formidable confederacy whose supporters included O'Toole in the south-east, Desmond and now O'Brien in the south-west, O'Neill in the north and many more Irish lords in between. The confederacy had indeed taken on the look of a national movement. St Leger was also appointed as commissioner,

---

105 SP Hen. VIII, iii, p. 219.
106 TNA, PC 2/1, fo. 1; Memoranda in Wriothesley's hand, 1 Apr. 1540, TNA, SP 60/9/17, fo. 34.
107 Bryson, s.v. 'Anthony St Leger', ODNB .

along with three others, to survey crown possessions in Ireland, to investigate the accusations Grey was levelling against members of the Irish government and to reduce the number of soldiers in garrisons.[108] These were formidable challenges; but within months it was evident that St Leger's administration had struck a new tone with the Irish and in Ireland. After a devastating campaign in south Leinster, St Leger informed the king that he had accepted the submission of MacMurrough and that he would handle him 'very gentilly' henceforth.[109] Before long Irish lords were submitting to St Leger in large numbers. Each entered into a detailed written indenture as proof of their willingness to acknowledge Henry VIII as their sovereign lord; they swore to abjure papal authority, to hold their land of the crown by knight's service and to abandon Irish customs. Initially, the king clung to the notion that the Irish of south Leinster had to be banished or placed under military subjugation. Henry was apparently working from what he described as 'the platt of the lande', which evidently revealed to him the centrality of the earl of Ormond in any strategy to reform the Irish of that region.[110] It is difficult to say which 'platt' [a tract, treatise or paper] Henry was referring to – many tracts and letters had sought over the previous decade to demonstrate the strength of the earls of Ormond vis-à-vis the earls of Kildare and their importance to any particular reformation in Leinster. The plat backfired however: Ormond's power had aroused the suspicions of a king who desperately wanted to avoid another Kildare at this juncture. Remarkable as it was that Henry VIII was taking such a close interest in Ireland, St Leger's selective use of force and his success in inducing the Irish to submit had caused the confederacy to disintegrate and was fast rendering obsolete the reform of Leinster as it was traditionally presented. At the end of the year Turlough O'Toole, the leader of the confederacy in Leinster, who had lately submitted to St Leger, was sent to court to present himself before the king. O'Toole was the first Irish lord with whom Henry VIII had come face-to-face in nearly thirty years. It was an important moment: following his experience with O'Toole the king declared his convinction that all Irish lords should submit before him in like manner.[111]

Here, then, in what historians refer to as 'surrender and regrant', was what some Elizabethans remembered as Henry VIII having taken 'in hande the generall reformacon of the country'. The new political direction owed much to what had come before. The intellectual and political impulse for St Leger's conciliatory engagement with the Irish polity, for example, may be traced to Henry VIII's communications with the earl of Surrey two decades earlier. At that time, the king, unintentionally as we have seen, was already bridging the constitutional gap that existed between 'English subjects' and 'Irish enemies' by referring to the

108 SP Hen. VIII, iii, pp 227–31.   109 Ibid., iii, p. 236.
110 Henry VIII to Ormond, 26 Sept. 1540, TNA, SP 60/9/57, fo. 146v; SP Hen. VIII, iii, p. 247.
111 Maginn, 'Civilizing' Gaelic Leinster, pp 65–76.

majority of the latter as 'our ... Irische rebelles' – it was not long before the king's taxonomy rubbed off on Tudor officials.[112] Still, formidable legal, social and cultural differences separated the Irish from the English. Grey's efforts in the 1530s to conclude written indentures with Irishmen and to have them hold their land of the king by feudal tenure may be seen as a temporary means of accommodating Irish lords within English law, custom and culture. St Leger witnessed much of this as a commissioner and adopted a similar strategy after 1540. Raising Irishmen to the peerage, meanwhile, was suggested as far back as 1515 in the 'State of Ireland and Plan for its Reformation'; later, in 1520, Surrey found himself confronted with Irish lords seeking English noble titles in return for their loyalty. Even the famous act that erected Ireland into a kingdom, enacted by the Irish parliament in June 1541, which was to become the centrepiece of St Leger's strategy in Ireland, was first suggested to him by John Alen, the lord chancellor, during his stint as a royal commissioner.

Yet it was St Leger, in the unique circumstances of the early 1540s, who gathered all of these disparate ideas together and fashioned them into a new political policy for Ireland. Ironically, St Leger's engagement with the Irish eliminated the need, in the short term at least, for reformation as it had typically been formulated in Henry's reign and before. Instead, the developments of the early 1540s in Ireland offered the possibility that reform could be achieved through the agreed extension of English government, law, culture and now religion throughout the island; the problems which beset the Englishry, which had featured so prominently in the written material from Henry's reign, were, initially at least, overshadowed by the new governor's other successes among the Irish. The sheer number of submissions by Irish and some wayward English lords, most notably MacWilliam Burke, the erection in June 1541 of Ireland into a kingdom and the distribution of new peerages, all in such a short span of time, gave the real impression that the general reformation of Ireland had well and truly begun.[113] Certainly, Henry VIII had, by the end of his reign, begun an engagement with all of Ireland and all of its inhabitants from which his children could not draw back.

---

112 *SP Hen. VIII*, ii, pp 60 (quotation), 69, 93, 188–9.

113 On the importance of the events of the 1540s, see Bradshaw, *The Irish constitutional revolution*, pp 187–257; Christopher Maginn, '"Surrender and regrant" in the historiography of sixteenth-century Ireland', *Sixteenth Century Journal: Journal for Early Modern Studies*, 38 (2007), 955–74; idem, 'The limitations of Tudor reform: the policy of "Surrender and regrant" and the O'Rourkes', *Breifne*, 43 (2007), 429–60; idem, 'The Gaelic peers, the Tudor sovereigns and English multiple monarchy', *Journal of British Studies*, 50 (2011), 566–86.

Conclusion

The events of the early 1540s did not mark the end of the Tudor discovery of Ireland. The gradual acquisition of knowledge about Ireland was to continue under the later Tudors because, like their father and grandfather before them, they were unwilling (or unable as they may have seen it) to discover the country for themselves, either by going there or by taking the time to develop a deep understanding of the place, people and conditions in Ireland by other means, notably the careful study of documents. Still, the final decade and a half of the reign of Henry VIII did witness a quickening and an intensification of the process that had begun half a century earlier. The assembly of the Hatfield Compendium in these years attests to the discovery that had taken place. The Tudor regime in England had by the time of Henry VIII's death attained an understanding of Ireland that the later Tudors took for granted but which Henry VII and his government could scarcely have imagined. Ireland was no longer the obscure and unfamiliar remnant of a once-proud medieval English inheritance where the name of York counted for more than Lancaster and the name of Tudor counted for nothing at all. Henry VIII died the king of a second Tudor kingdom and the supreme head of a church that unambiguously encompassed the entire island of Ireland and all of its inhabitants. Where once Henry VII struggled to identify and to control his government in Ireland and questioned the loyalty of its leaders, now that administration was abjectly beholden to their king and his council in England; its head, the lord deputy, was a minor English-born official who presided over an administration whose members included a sizeable and growing number of his countrymen. Greater control of the Irish government, in turn, meant that information about Ireland, which had once trickled into England infrequently and idiosyncratically, now came more regularly, in greater quantities and from a wider variety of sources. Henry VIII, unlike his father, who died accepting the late medieval notion that a state of war existed between Englishmen and Irishmen, was of the view that there was no war in Ireland, only rebellion against the crown. His support for the policy of surrender and regrant in his last years offers the most striking evidence of that royal conviction. Henry VIII came face-to-face with some of the shadowy enemies of his father, but did so at the centre of Tudor power in a carefully staged display of his own majesty: there he accepted their submissions and pledges of loyalty; there he ennobled the greatest of them; and there he even permitted the son and heir of a newly-created Irish peer to be educated alongside his own son and heir, Edward, prince of Wales. For all the emphasis placed on the flashes of modernity that are evident in Henry's reign, the king employed a personal, and recognizably feudal, approach to achieve Ireland's reform: the leaders of the Irish polity accepted the king of Ireland as their sovereign lord and spiritual leader, agreed to hold their lands of the crown by feudal tenure and cast aside their own, and any native, kingly or noble pretensions.

Quite how he arrived at this point, how he had in effect discovered Ireland, probably did not much trouble the royal mind. Henry VIII was always equally certain of two things: the absoluteness of his power within the territories over which he ruled and the obligations that his subjects owed him. Had he not destroyed the Geraldines for challenging his authority? Had he not suggested an engagement with Irishmen akin to surrender and regrant two decades before the likes of O'Neill and O'Brien came to his court to kneel before him? Was he not able in the mid-1540s to harness the same Irish military power that had threatened his father's lordship for use in his own wars against Scotland and France?[1] A lack of knowledge about Ireland had not hindered him in any of these things. Ireland's reform was not yet complete, all would agree, but King Henry was pursuing from the early 1540s a means to reform his new kingdom that, so far as he was concerned, would redound to his royal honour and majesty. He had, so far as he was concerned, taken the general reformation of Ireland in hand and probably died safe in the knowledge that he had at the very least set his kingdom on the right trajectory.

But, as an examination of the development of the concept of reform has shown, there was more behind the emergence of surrender and regrant as a policy than Henry VIII's decision, in the end, to make good on his absolutist claims. Reform was a concept borne of the English belief that Ireland had been conquered in the twelfth century and that, therefore, only a restoration of what had already been was necessary. Surrender and regrant marked an implicit acceptance that reform would not (and perhaps could not) be pursued as it had been traditionally framed: either as a general reformation – reform by the use of overwhelming military force – which had for more than a century been the central aspiration of both the English of Ireland and the crown of England; or even as the more recently evolved particular reformation – reform by the use of limited military force – which had grown out of Henry VIII's consistent failure to commit to a general reform. At the same time, surrender and regrant contained elements of a reform agenda that had over the previous decade or so been moving toward a rationalization of the crown's relationship with Irishmen: some kind of accommodation was necessary to go along with the use of force. St Leger was exposed to many of these ideas through both his personal experience in Ireland, first as a royal commissioner and then as governor, and the written materials made available to him – as an Englishman with no prior knowledge of

---

1   D.G. White, 'Henry VIII's Irish kerne in France and Scotland, 1544–1545', *Irish Sword*, 3 (1957–8), 213–25.

Ireland – to acquaint him with the state of the lordship. Thus what St Leger presented to the king in the early 1540s, and what the king came so stridently to support, was a variation of reform whose emphasis on a conciliatory engagement with Irish and English lords promised to obviate the need for a show of overwhelming military force. In surrender and regrant, reform had entered on a radically different phase in its evolution.

That surrender and regrant proved in political terms to be an evolutionary dead-end is well known: the policy lost its greatest proponent when the old king died in 1547 and was, in effect, radically modified thereafter, having failed to achieve Ireland's reform.[2] Yet the very fact that surrender and regrant, such a clear departure from traditional reform strategies, was attempted at all underscores the continued superficiality of the royal government's understanding of Ireland. It is true that the English of Ireland, and English officials in the Irish government, had long sought the greater involvement of the crown in the affairs of Ireland, but there is no evidence of their wide-spread support for an engagement with Irishmen that placed conciliation before coercion and ignored the alleged decay of the Englishry. Military force, or the threat of military force, had always been central to reform, even if it had lost much of its earlier, more purely military connotations over the course of Henry's reign. The submissions of dozens of lords, and the act for the kingly title which underpinned them, were not enough to sweep away the deeply-ingrained antagonisms and cultural differences that had existed between Irishmen and Englishmen for centuries. Beyond the submissions themselves, there was no apparatus of conciliation in place (and none planned) to assist and oversee the peaceful extension of Tudor rule throughout Ireland – nothing to match the powerful royal army that had almost always been intended to provide the backbone of reform in the countless written proposals advanced over the course of the early Tudor period. Had Henry VIII mastered the information contained in these proposals then, perhaps, he would have better appreciated the sheer ambitiousness of the policy that he had come to support and the demands that it would make on his government. But as we have seen, the king did not subject these proposals to close scrutiny. Rather he acted on the knowledge that he was sure derived from his royal station. It is a telling example of Tudor absolutism and indicative of the limited influence which written political discourse exerted on royal policy.

It is not surprising, then, that the discourse of reform reverted before long to the twin strategies of coercion and conciliation that had come to characterize the concept in the years prior to the emergence of the policy of surrender and regrant. Writing some thirty years later, during the reign of Elizabeth I, William

2   Ellis, *Ireland in the age of the Tudors*, pp 149–57. See also Christopher Maginn, 'Surrender and regrant, mark II: the indenture between Brian O'Rourke, chief of west Breifne, and Sir Nicholas Malby, 1577', *Breifne*, 42 (2006), 227–34.

Cecil determined that the 'best' way to achieve the reformation of Ireland was to proceed by force as well as 'ordre', in other words through a mixture of the two. Cecil was by then, through his immersion in written material on Ireland, as well acquainted with the kingdom as anyone in England who had not been there and had been working to frame Tudor policy for Ireland for two decades. He still aspired to 'ye generall reformation of Irland', but Elizabeth, like her father, would not commit to such an exercise of force: Cecil was forced to plan for a series of piecemeal reforms – particular reformations in Henrician parlance.[3] For the rest of the century, Tudor policy for Ireland was pursued within a conceptual framework that had evolved in the reign of Henry VIII, until the rebellion by the earl of Tyrone and the prospect of a Spanish invasion gave the queen no choice but to despatch a massive royal army to the kingdom.

Even in the face of the steady extension of Tudor rule throughout the island, the concept of reform remained the prism through which the Tudors – and most of the political establishment in England – viewed the kingdom of Ireland. In Ireland, more than anywhere else, the Tudors took the future into account by looking to the past. Reform was the nearest approximation to a grand political idea or strategy pursued by the Tudors in Ireland and as such needs to be considered alongside conquest in the narratives of the relationship between Ireland and England in these years. Ironically, in striving to restore the country to a previous perfect condition allegedly created by the English Conquest in the twelfth century the Tudors were forced to discover Ireland and in the process created something entirely new there.

3   Maginn, *William Cecil, Ireland, and the Tudor state*, pp 93–4,

Bibliography

MANUSCRIPT SOURCES

British Library, London
Additional MSS: 4791, 4792, 15891, 19865, 48015, 48017, 62540
Cotton MSS: Caligula C III, Caligula D VI, Domitian A XVIII, Lansdowne 159, Otho
 C IX, Titus B I, Titus B XI, Titus B XII, Titus B XIII, Vitellius C XVII
Royal MS 18 C XIV

Hatfield House Archives, Hertfordshire
Cecil Papers: MSS 144, 201

Lambeth Palace Library, London
MSS 600–35: Letters and Papers Relating to the Government of Ireland

The National Archives, Dublin
Ferguson collections from memoranda rolls
Ferguson repertory to memoranda rolls
Lodge MSS

The National Archives, London
E 101 King's Remembrancer: Accounts Various
MPF 1/68: Hibernia, 1567
PC 1 Privy Council Registers
SC 1 Ancient Correspondence
SP 1 State Papers, Henry VIII
SP 12 State Papers, Elizabeth I
SP 60 State Papers, Ireland, Henry VIII
SP 61 State Papers, Ireland, Edward VI
SP 63 State Papers, Ireland, Elizabeth I
SP 65 Exchequer Records, Ireland, Henry VIII

National Library of Ireland, Dublin
MS 16 Harris Collectanea de Rebus Hibernicis
MS 669

Trinity College, Dublin
MSS 581, 594, 595, 664, 786, 842

PRINTED SOURCES

The Anglica Historia of Polydore Vergil, AD1485–1537, ed. Denys Hay (London, 1950).

Annála Connacht: the annals of Connacht, AD1224–1544, ed. A.M. Freeman (Dublin, 1944).

Annála ríoghachta Éireann: annals of the kingdom of Ireland by the Four Masters from the earliest period to the year 1616, ed. John O'Donovan, 7 vols (Dublin, 1851).

Annála Uladh, Annals of Ulster ... a chronicle of Irish affairs ... 431 to 1541, ed. W.M. Hennessy and Bartholomew MacCarthy, 4 vols (Dublin, 1887–1901).

The Annals of Loch Cé: a chronicle of Irish affairs, 1014–1690, ed. W.M. Hennessy, 2 vols (London, 1871).

Bacon, Francis, *The history of the reign of King Henry the Seventh*, ed. F.J. Levy (Indianapolis, 1972).

Bayne, C.G. and W.H. Dunham (eds), *Select cases in the council of Henry VII* (London, 1958).

Bradshaw, Brendan (ed.), 'A treatise for the reformation of Ireland', *Irish Jurist*, 16:2 (1981), 299–315.

Calendar of letters and state papers relating to English affairs preserved principally in the archives of Simancas, ed. Martin Hume, 4 vols (London, 1892–9).

Calendar of letters, despatches, and state papers, relating to the negotiations between England and Spain, Henry VIII, 1542–1543. Preserved in the Archives at Simancas, Vienna, Brussels, and elsewhere, ed. Pascual de Gayangos (London, 1895).

Calendar of the manuscripts of the ... marquis of Salisbury ..., preserved at Hatfield House, 24 vols (London, 1883–1973).

Calendar of Ormond deeds, ed. Edmund Curtis, 6 vols (1932–43).

Calendar of the patent and close rolls of chancery in Ireland, Henry VIII to 18th Elizabeth, ed. James Morrin (Dublin, 1861).

Calendar of the patent rolls, Henry VII, 1494–1509 (London, 1916).

Calendar of state papers and manuscripts relating to English affairs, existing in the archives and collections of Venice and in other libraries of northern Italy, ed. Rawdon Brown, 6 vols (London, 1864–86).

Calendar of state papers relating to Ireland, 1509–1670, 24 vols (London, 1860–1912).

Calendar of the Carew manuscripts preserved in the archiepiscopal library at Lambeth, ed. J.S. Brewer and William Bullen, 6 vols (London, 1867–73).

Catalogue of the manuscripts preserved in the British Museum, ed. Samuel Ayscough (London, 1782).

Chartularies of St Mary's abbey, Dublin; with the register of its house at Dunbrody, and annals of Ireland, ed. J.T. Gilbert, 2 vols (London, 1884).

Chronicles of London, ed. C.L. Kingsford (Oxford, 1905).

Davies, John, *A discovery of the true causes why Ireland was never entirely subdued ... until the beginning of his majesty's happy reign* (London, 1612).

Davies, John, *Historical tracts: by Sir John Davies* (London, 1786).

Fourth report of the royal commission on historical manuscripts (London, 1874).

Four years at the court of Henry VIII: selection of despatches written by the Venetian ambassador, Sebastian Giustinian, ed. R.L. Brown, 2 vols (London, 1854).

Harris, Walter (ed.), *Hibernica, or, some ancient pieces relating to the history of Ireland*, 2 vols (Dublin, 1747, 1750).

Hickscorner, c.1497–1512, ed. John Farmer (London, 1908).

Holinshed, Raphael, *The … chronicles of England, Scotlande and Irelande …* (London, 1577) ed. Henry Ellis, 6 vols (London, 1807–8).

The Irish fiants of the Tudor sovereigns, 1521–1603, 4 vols (Dublin, 1994).

The knights of England, ed. William Arthur Shaw, 2 vols (London, 1906).

Lancashire, Ian (ed.), *Two Tudor interludes: Youth and Hick Scorner* (Manchester, 1980).

Leabhar mór na ngenealach: the great book of genealogies. Compiled, 1645–66, by Dubhaltach Mac Fhirbhisigh, ed. Nollaig Ó Muraíle, 5 vols (Dublin, 2004).

Letters and papers, foreign and domestic, Henry VIII, 21 vols (London, 1862–1932).

Letters and papers illustrative of the reigns of Richard III and Henry VII, ed. James Gairdner, 2 vols (London, 1861–3).

The Libelle of Englyshe Polycye: a poem on the use of sea-power, 1436, ed. George Warner (Oxford, 1926).

Liber munerum publicorum Hiberniae, ed. Rowley Lascelles, 2 vols (London, 1852).

Maley, Willy (ed.), 'A supplication of the blood of the English most lamentably murdered in Ireland, cryeng out of the yearth for revenge (1598)', *Analecta Hibernica*, 36 (1994), 1–90.

McNeill, Charles (ed.), 'Lord Chancellor Gerrard's notes of his report on Ireland, 1577–8', *Analecta Hibernica*, 2 (1931), 93–291.

O'Flaherty, Roderic, *A chorographical description of west or h-Iar Connaught*, ed. James Hardiman (Dublin, 1846).

Quinn, D.B. (ed.), 'Guide to English financial records for Irish history, 1461–1558, with illustrative extracts, 1461–1509', *Analecta Hibernica*, 10 (1941), 1–69.

— (ed.), 'The bills and statutes of the Irish parliaments of Henry VII and Henry VIII', *Analecta Hibernica*, 10 (1941), 71–169.

Rotulorum patentium et clausorum cancellariae Hiberniae calendarium, ed. Edward Tresham (Dublin, 1828).

The social state of the southern and eastern counties of Ireland in the sixteenth century, ed. H.F. Hore and J. Graves (Dublin, 1870).

State papers, Henry VIII, 11 vols (London, 1830–52).

The statutes at large passed in the Irish parliaments held in Ireland, 1310–1800, 20 vols (Dublin, 1786–1801).

Statutes and ordinances, and acts of the parliament of Ireland, King John to Henry V, ed. H.F. Berry (Dublin, 1907).

Statute rolls of the Irish parliament, Richard III–Henry VIII, ed. Philomena Connolly (Dublin, 2002).

Statute rolls of the parliament of Ireland, reign of King Henry VI, ed. H.F. Berry (Dublin, 1910).

Statute rolls of the parliament of Ireland, twelfth and thirteenth to twenty-first and twenty-second years of the reign of Edward IV, ed. James Morrissey (Dublin, 1939).

Ware, James, *The antiquities and history of Ireland* (Dublin, 1705).

SECONDARY SOURCES

Andrews, J.H., 'Colonial cartography in a European setting: the case of Tudor Ireland' in Woodward (ed.), *Cartography in the European Renaissance*, pp 1670–83.

Ball, F.E., *The judges in Ireland, 1221–1921* (London, 1926).

Bouwsma, William, *The waning of the Renaissance, 1550–1640* (New Haven, 2002).

Brackmann, Rebecca, *The Elizabethan invention of Anglo-Saxon England: Laurence Nowell, William Lambarde and the study of Old English* (London, 2012).

Bradshaw, Brendan, *The dissolution of the religious orders in Ireland under Henry VIII* (Cambridge, 1974).

— 'Cromwellian reform and the origins of the Kildare rebellion, 1533–4', *Transactions of the Royal Historical Society*, 5th series 27 (1977), 69–93.

— *The Irish constitutional revolution of the sixteenth century* (Cambridge, 1979).

Brady, Ciaran, *The chief governors: the rise and fall of reform government in Tudor Ireland, 1536–1588* (Cambridge, 1994).

— 'Comparable histories? Tudor reform in Wales and Ireland' in Ellis and Barber (eds), *Conquest and union*, pp 64–86.

— 'From policy to power: the evolution of Tudor reform strategies in sixteenth-century Ireland' in Mac Cuarta (ed.), *Reshaping Ireland, 1550–1700*, pp 21–42.

Bryan, Donough, *The great earl of Kildare, Gerald FitzGerald, 1456–1513* (Dublin, 1933).

Bryson, Alan, 'Anthony St Leger', *ODNB* (Oxford, 2004).

Burke, M.J., 'Notes on the persons named in the obituary book of the Franciscan Abbey at Galway', *Journal of the Galway Archaeological and Historical Society*, 7 (1911), 1–28.

Cameron, Euan, 'The power of the word: Renaissance and Reformation' in Cameron (ed.), *Early modern Europe*, pp 63–101.

— (ed.), *Early modern Europe: an Oxford history* (Oxford, 2001).

Campbell, L.B., *Tudor conceptions of history and tragedy in 'A Mirror for Magistrates'* (Berkeley, 1936).

Canny, Nicholas, *Making Ireland British, 1580–1650* (Oxford, 2001).

Carey, Vincent and Ute Lotz-Heumann (eds), *Taking sides? Colonial and confessional mentalités in early modern Ireland* (Dublin, 2003).

Cavill, P.R., *Henry VII and his English parliaments, 1485–1504* (Oxford, 2009).

Chrimes, S.B., *Lancastrians, Yorkists and Henry VII* (London, 1966).

— *Henry VII* (Berkeley, 1972).

Clavin, Terry, 'Walter Cowley' in *Dictionary of Irish biography* (Cambridge, 2010).

Collinson, Patrick (ed.), *The short Oxford history of the British Isles: the sixteenth century, 1485–1603* (Oxford, 2002).

Conway, Agnes, *Henry VII's relations with Scotland and Ireland, 1485–1498* (Cambridge, 1932).

Cosgrove, Art (ed.), *A new history of Ireland*; ii, *Medieval Ireland, 1169–1534* (Oxford, 1987).

Crawford, Jon, *Anglicising the government of Ireland: the Irish privy council and the expansion of Tudor rule, 1556–1578* (Dublin, 1993).

Crooks, Peter, 'Factions, feuds and noble power in late medieval Ireland', *IHS*, 35 (2007), 425–54.

Cunningham, Sean, *Henry VII* (London, 2007).

Curtis, Edmund, 'Richard duke of York as viceroy of Ireland, 1447–60', *JRSAI*, 62 (1932), 158–86.

Davies, R.R., 'The peoples of Britain and Ireland, 1100–1400. 1: Identities', *Transactions of the Royal Historical Society*, 6th series iv (1994), 1–20.

Dictionary of Irish biography (eds), James McGuire and James Quinn (Cambridge, 2010).

Dovey, Zillah, *An Elizabethan progress: the queen's journey to East Anglia, 1578* (Frome, 1996).

Duffy, P.J., David Edwards and Elizabeth FitzPatrick (eds), *Gaelic Ireland, c.1250–c.1650: land, lordship and settlement* (Dublin, 2001).

Edwards, David, 'Beyond reform: martial law and the Tudor reconquest of Ireland', *History Ireland*, 5 (1997), 16–21.

— 'Collaboration without Anglicization: the MacGiollapadraig lordship and Tudor reform' in Duffy et al. (eds), *Gaelic Ireland*, 77–97.

— *The Ormond lordship in county Kilkenny, 1515–1642: the rise and fall of Butler feudal power* (Dublin, 2003).

— (ed.), *Regions and rulers in Ireland, 1100–1650: essays for Kenneth Nicholls* (Dublin, 2004).

— 'The escalation of violence in sixteenth-century Ireland' in Edwards et al. (eds), *Age of atrocity*, pp 34–78.

— Pádraig Lenihan and Clodagh Tait (eds), *Age of atrocity: violence and political conflict in early modern Ireland* (Dublin, 2007).

Elliott, J.H., *The old world and the new, 1492–1650* (Cambridge, 1970).

— *Empires of the Atlantic world: Britain and Spain in America, 1492–1830* (New Haven and London, 2006).

Ellis, Steven, 'Tudor policy and the Kildare ascendancy in the lordship of Ireland', *IHS*, 20 (1977), 235–71.

— 'Taxation and defence in late medieval Ireland: the survival of scutage', *JRSAI*, 107 (1977), 5–28.

— 'Thomas Cromwell and Ireland, 1532–40', *Historical Journal*, 23 (1980), 497–519.

— 'Henry VII and Ireland, 1491–1496' in Lydon (ed.), *England and Ireland in the later Middle Ages*, pp 237–54.

— *Reform and revival: English government in Ireland, 1470–1536* (London, 1986).

— and Sarah Barber (eds), *Conquest and union: fashioning a British state, 1485–1725* (London, 1995).

— *Tudor frontiers and noble power: the making of the British state* (Oxford, 1995).

— 'The Tudor borderlands, 1485–1603' in Morrill (ed.), *The Oxford illustrated history of Tudor and Stuart Britain*, pp 53–73.

— *Ireland in the age of the Tudors, 1447–1603: English expansion and the end of Gaelic rule* (London, 1998).

— 'More Irish than the Irish themselves? The "Anglo-Irish" in Tudor Ireland', *History Ireland*, 7:1 (1999), 22–6.

— 'The collapse of the Gaelic world, 1450–1650', *IHS*, 31 (1999), 449–69.

— 'The limits of power: the English crown and the British Isles' in Collinson (ed.), *The short Oxford history of the British Isles*, pp 46–80.

— 'An English gentleman and his community: Sir William Darcy of Platten' in Carey and Lotz-Heumann (eds), *Taking sides?*, pp 19–41.

— 'Sir Edward Poynings', *ODNB* (Oxford, 2004).

— 'Gerald Fitzgerald, eighth earl of Kildare', *ODNB* (Oxford, 2004).

— *Defending English ground: war and peace in Meath and Northumberland, 1460–1542* (Oxford, 2015).

Elton, G.R., *The Tudor revolution in government* (Cambridge, 1953).

— *Reform and renewal: Thomas Cromwell and the common weal* (Cambridge, 1973).

— 'Review of Muriel St Clare Byrne (ed.), *The Lisle letters* (Chicago, 1980)', *London Review of Books*, 3:13 (1981), 3–5.

Falkiner, C.L., *Illustrations of Irish history, topography, mainly in the seventeenth century* (London, 1904).

FitzGerald, Charles William, *The earls of Kildare, and their ancestors from 1057 to 1773* (Dublin, 1858).

Fitzsimons, Fiona, 'Cardinal Wolsey, the native affinities and the failure of reform in Henrician Ireland' in Edwards (ed.), *Regions and rulers in Ireland*, pp 78–121.

Fletcher, A.J., *Drama and the performing arts in pre-Cromwellian Ireland: sources and documents from the earliest times until c.1642* (Cambridge, 2001).

Flower, Robin, 'Laurence Nowell and the discovery of England in Tudor times' in *Proceedings of the British Academy*, 21 (1935), 47–73.

Grummitt, David, *The Calais garrison: war and military service in England, 1436–1558* (London, 2008).

Gunn, Steve, 'Henry VII', *ODNB* (Oxford, 2004).

Haywood, Eric, 'Humanism's priorities and empire's prerogatives: Polydore Vergil's description of Ireland', *Proceedings of the Royal Irish Academy*, 109, section C (2009), 195–237.

Hore, H.F., 'Woods and fastnesses in ancient Ireland', *Ulster Journal of Archaeology*, 6 (1858), 145–61.

Jones, E.T., 'Alwyn Ruddock: "John Cabot and the discovery of America"', *Historical Research*, 81 (2012), 224–54.

Kelly, Stephen and J.J. Thompson (eds), *Imagining the book: medieval texts and cultures of Northern Europe* (Turnhout, 2005).

Kirby, J.L., 'Sir Richard Edgcumbe [Edgecombe]', *ODNB* (2004).

Lennon, Colm, *Sixteenth-century Ireland: the incomplete conquest* (Dublin, 2nd ed., 2005).

Levy, F.J., *Tudor historical thought* (San Marino, 1967).

Lubimenko, Inna, 'England's part in the discovery of Russia' in *Slavonic Review*, 4 (1927), 104–18.

Lydon, J.F., 'Richard II's expeditions to Ireland', *JRSAI*, 93 (1963), 135–49.

— (ed.), *England and Ireland in the later middle ages: essays in honour of Jocelyn Otway-Ruthvan* (Dublin, 1981).

Lyons, Mary Ann, 'Patrick Finglas', *ODNB* (Oxford, 2004).

Mac Cuarta, Brian (ed.), *Reshaping Ireland, 1550–1700: colonization and its consequences* (Dublin, 2011).

Maginn, Christopher, *'Civilizing' Gaelic Leinster: the extension of Tudor rule in the O'Byrne and O'Toole lordships* (Dublin, 2005).

— 'Surrender and regrant, mark II: the indenture between Brian O'Rourke, chief of west Breifne, and Sir Nicholas Malby (1577)', *Breifne: Journal of Cumann Seanchais Bhréifne*, 42 (2006), 227–34.

— 'The limitations of Tudor reform: the policy of 'Surrender and regrant' and the O'Rourkes', *Breifne: Journal of Cumann Seanchais Bhréifne*, 43 (2007), 429–60.

— 'The Tudor policy of "surrender and regrant" in the historiography of sixteenth-century Ireland', *Sixteenth Century Journal: Journal for Early Modern Studies*, 38:4 (2007), 955–74.

— 'Gaelic Ireland's English frontiers in the late middle ages', *PRIA*, 110, section C (2010), 191–215.

— 'The Gaelic peers, the Tudor sovereigns and English multiple monarchy', *Journal of British Studies*, 50 (2011), 566–86.

— *William Cecil, Ireland, and the Tudor state* (Oxford, 2012).

Matthew, Elizabeth, 'Henry V and the proposal for an Irish crusade' in Smith (ed.), *Ireland and the English world in the late Middle Ages*, pp 161–75.

McCormack, Anthony, 'James fitzMaurice Fitzgerald', *ODNB* (Oxford, 2004).

— *The earldom of Desmond, 1463–1583: the decline and crisis of a feudal lordship* (Dublin, 2005).

McEntegart, Rory, *Henry VIII, the League of Schmalkalden, and the English Reformation* (Rochester, 2002).

McGowan-Doyle, Valerie, *The Book of Howth: the Elizabethan re-conquest of Ireland and the Old English* (Cork, 2011).

Montaño, John, *The roots of English colonization in Ireland* (Cambridge, 2011).

Moody, T.W., F.X. Martin and F.J. Byrne (eds), *A new history of Ireland; iii, Early Modern Ireland, 1534–1691* (Oxford, 1976).

Morgan, Hiram, (ed.), *Political ideology in Ireland, 1541–1641* (Dublin, 1999).

— 'Giraldus Cambrensis and the Tudor conquest of Ireland' in Morgan (ed.), *Political ideology in Ireland*, pp 22–44.

Morrill, John (ed.), *The Oxford illustrated history of Tudor and Stuart Britain* (Oxford, 1996).

Mund, Stéphane, 'The discovery of Muscovite Russia in Tudor England' in *Revue Belge de Philology et d'Histoire*, 86 (2008), 351–73.

Newcombe, D.G., 'William Rokeby', *ODNB* (Oxford, 2004).

Nicholls, K.W., 'Gaelic society and economy in the high middle ages' in Cosgrove (ed.), *A new history of Ireland; ii, Medieval Ireland*, pp 397–438.

— 'Crioch Branach: the O'Byrnes and their country', *Feagh McHugh O'Byrne*, 7–39.

— 'Worlds apart? The Ellis two-nation theory of late medieval Ireland', *History Ireland*, 7:2 (1999), 22–6.

— 'Woodland cover in pre-modern Ireland' in Duffy et al. (eds), *Gaelic Ireland*, pp 181–206.

— *Gaelic and Gaelicized Ireland in the Middle Ages* (Dublin, 2nd ed., 2003).

Noble, T.A., 'Scripture and experience' in Satterthwaite and Wright (eds), *A pathway into the Holy Scripture*, pp 277–96.

O'Brien, Conor (ed.), *Feagh McHugh O'Byrne, the Wicklow firebrand* (Rathdrum, 1998).

Otway-Ruthven, A.J., *A history of medieval Ireland* (London, 1980).

Oxford dictionary of national biography, eds H.C.G. Matthew and Brian Harrison (Oxford, 2004).

Oxford English dictionary, ed. John Simpson and Edmund Weiner (2nd ed., Oxford, 1989).

Palmer, William, *The problem of Ireland in Tudor foreign policy, 1485–1603* (Woodbridge, 1994).

Parker, Geoffrey, *The grand strategy of Philip II* (New Haven and London, 2000).

— *Empire, war and faith in early modern Europe* (London, 2002).

Pearsall, Derek, 'The whole book: late medieval English miscellanies and their modern interpreters' in Kelly and Thompson (eds), *Imagining the book*, pp 17–29.

Polwhele, Richard, *The history of Cornwall, civil, military, religious, architectural, agricultural, commercial, biographical, and miscellaneous*, 7 vols (London, 1816).

Power, Gerald, 'The viceroy and his critics: Leonard Grey's journey through the west of Ireland, June–July 1538', *Journal of the Galway Archaeological Society*, 60 (2008), 78–87.

— *A European frontier elite: the nobility of the English Pale in Tudor Ireland, 1496–1566* (Hannover, 2012).

Price, Liam, 'Armed forces of the Irish chiefs in the early 16th century', *JRSAI*, 62 (1932), 201–7.

Quinn, D.B., 'Government printing and the publication of the Irish statutes', *PRIA*, 49 section C (1943), 45–130.

— 'Henry VIII and Ireland, 1509–34', *IHS*, 12 (1960–1), 323–4.

— *The Elizabethans and the Irish* (Ithaca, 1966).

— and K.W. Nicholls, 'Ireland in 1534' in Moody et al. (eds), *A new history of Ireland*; iii (1976), pp 1–18.

Richardson, H.G. and G.O. Sayles, *The Irish parliament in the middle ages* (Philadelphia, 1952).

Satterthwaite, P.E. and D.F. Wright (eds), *A pathway into the Holy Scripture* (Grand Rapids, 1994).

Sayles, G.O., 'The vindication of the earl of Kildare from treason, 1496', *IHS*, 7 (1950–1), 39–47.

Scarisbrick, J.J., *Henry VIII* (London, 1968).

Shaw, Barry, 'Thomas Norton's "Devices" for a Godly realm: an Elizabethan vision of the future', *Sixteenth Century Journal: Journal for Early Modern Studies*, 22:3 (1991), 495–509.

Smith, Brendan (ed.), *Ireland and the English world in the late Middle Ages: essays in honour of Robin Frame* (London, 2009).

Smyth, William, *Map-making, landscapes and memory: a geography of colonial and early modern Ireland, c.1530–1750* (Cork, 2006).

Thorton, Tim, 'Henry VIII's progress through Yorkshire in 1541 and its implications for northern identities', *Northern History*, 46 (2009), 231–44.

Walker, Greg, 'The expulsions of the minions of 1519, reconsidered', *Historical Journal*, 32 (1989), 1–16.

Warnicke, R.M., 'The Laurence Nowell manuscripts in the British Library', *British Library Journal*, 5 (1979), 201–2.

White, D.G., 'Henry VIII's Irish kerne in France and Scotland, 1544–5', *Irish Sword*, 3 (1957–8), 213–25.

— 'The reign of Edward VI in Ireland: some political, social and economic aspects', *IHS*, 14 (1965), 197–211.

Williams, R.H., 'The Cecil Papers: four centuries of custodial history', www.cecilpapers.chadwyck.co.uk/info/essay.do. Accessed on 17 Feb. 2014

Woodward, David (ed.), *Cartography in the European Renaissance: part 1* (Chicago, 2007).

UNPUBLISHED THESES

David, S.J., 'Looking east and west: the reception and dissemination of the Topographia Hibernica and the Itinerarium ad partes orientales in England, 1185–c.1500' (PhD, St Andrews, 2009).

Elton, G.R., 'Thomas Cromwell: aspects of his administrative work' (PhD, University of London, 1948).

White, D.G., 'Tudor plantations in Ireland to 1571' (PhD, University of Dublin, 1968).

Index

Absentees, act of, 30, 33
Agard, Thomas, 176
Alen, John, master of the rolls, 64–5, 111, 159–60, 162, 164, 168–70, 172, 175–7, 179, 183, 186
Anne of Cleves, queen, 183
Antrim, county of, 92
Ap Parry, Steven, 171
Ards, the, 38
Arklow, 30, 78
'Articles for the reformation of Ireland', 19, 49, 94–6
Athlone, 137, 169
Athy, 30, 78
Atlantic Ocean, 14
Aylmer, Gerald, chief justice of the king's bench, 168, 179

Balliehony (Ballyshannon), 54
Ballymascanlan, 54, 98
Ballymergy, manor of, 127
Baltinglass, abbey of, 77–8
Bann, 42, 106
Barlow, John, dean of Westbury, 166
Barnewall, Patrick, king's serjeant-at-law, 34, 178
Barry, family, 72
Bathe, Thomas, 154–5
Beacon, Richard, 22
Belacke, county of, 45
Bermingham, family/lord of Conmaicne of Dunmore, 86
Bermingham, Patrick, chief justice of the king's bench, 96, 153
Bigod, Hugh, 3rd earl of Norfolk, 70
Blagg, Hugh, chief chamberlain, 127
Body, William, 170, 172–3
Boleyn, George, viscount Rochford, 30
Boleyn, Thomas, 9th earl of Ormond and earl of Wiltshire, 30

Book of Howth, 120
Bosworth Field, battle of, 13
Bowring, Thomas, chief justice of the common pleas, 126–7
Brabazon, William, undertreasurer, 171, 181
Bradshaw, Brendan, historian, 21, 137–8
Brady, Ciaran, historian, 22
de Braose, William, lord of Abergavenny, 70
Bray, manor of, 127
Brefny (O'Reilly), 94
Brefny (O'Rourke), 94
Brendan, St, 77
Bristol, 13
British Library, 38–40, 43, 129
British Museum, 38–9
Browne, George, archbishop of Dublin, 178
Burke (de Burgh), family, 41, 55, 75, 161
    Edmund 'Albunaghe', 54, 97–8
        his son, Thomas, 97–8
            his sons:
                Edmund, 97–8
                Richard, 54, 97–8
                Thomas, 97–8
                Walter, 97–8
    Elizabeth, 72, 75, 92, 97
    Historia et genealogia familiae de Burgo (Senchas Búrcach), 54
    John, 74, 97
    MacWilliam Burke (Lower), 38, 53–4, 76, 86, 97–8
    MacWilliam Burke (Upper), lord of Clanrickard, 53, 76, 85–6, 97–8, 186
    Richard, 97–8
    Richard, 2nd earl of Ulster, 53–4, 75, 97–8
    'Pedigrees of the Burkes', 19, 53–5, 97–8
    Ulick, 172
    Ulick, 'an fhíona', 54, 98
    Ulick, 'fionn', 54, 98

Ulick, 'ruadh', 54, 98
Walter, 1st earl of Ulster, 53, 75, 97–8
William FitzAdelm, lord of Connacht, 53, 97–8
his sons: Hubert, Richard, William, 97–8
William, 97–8
William 'Liath', 53, 97–8
William, 3rd earl of Ulster, 53, 74–5, 92, 97
Burke, family (of Tipperary and Limerick), 83
Butler, family, 39, 47, 72–3, 81, 83, 92, 122, 125, 131–2, 144, 151, 153, 155, 160, 185
earls of Ormond:
James, 1st earl, 72
James, 5th earl, 118
James, (lord Butler) 9th earl, 152, 168, 171, 179, 181–2, 185
Piers, 8th earl and 1st earl of Ossory, 32, 96, 147, 152–4, 158–9, 161, 163–4, 166, 168, 170
Thomas, 7th earl, 14, 41, 116, 122, 125, 130–3, 135
Thomas 10th earl, 14
James Ormond, governor, 53, 122–3, 125–6, 131–2
Thomas, master of the rolls, 124–5

Calais, 126, 176
Calendar of State Papers relating to Ireland, 28, 159, 161
Calendar of the Carew Manuscripts, 29–30
Calendar of the Salisbury (Cecil) manuscripts, 17
Calverstown, 40
Carew, George, 27
Carew Papers, Lambeth Palace (London), 27, 29, 45
Carlingford, manor of, 76
Carlow
castle of, 30, 78, 126
county of, 40, 57, 60, 69–71, 77, 81, 101
del Carretto, Fabrizio, grand-master of the Knights of St John, 143
Carrickfergus, county of, 92
Carrick-on-Suir, 132
Cashel, 173
Castlekevin, 78
Cavan, county of, 94
Cecil House (London), 65

Cecil Papers, Hatfield House Archives, Hertfordshire, 17–18, 49, 67
Cecil, Robert, principal secretary, 15, 94
Cecil, Sir William, lord Burghley, 15, 18, 38, 65, 189–90
Charles V, Holy Roman Emperor, 37, 150
Charles VIII, king of France, 40, 122, 125, 131
Christ Church Cathedral, 118
Church of Ireland, 157
de Clare, Elizabeth, 74, 97
Gilbert, 5th earl of Hertford, 70–1, 74
Gilbert, earl of Gloucester and Hertford, 74
Richard FitzGilbert (Strongbow), earl of Pembroke, 69
Isabel, 69
Clonmore, manor of, 78
Cogan, family, 72
coign and livery, 45–7, 72–3, 90, 92–3, 99, 103, 145–6, 160, 168, 175
colonization:
projected settlement of Englishmen in Ireland, 32, 50, 79, 128, 138, 150, 154, 168–9, 173, 181–2
Columba, St, 77
Connacht, lordship of, 47, 53, 74–6, 127–9, 138, 141
province of, 35–7, 51, 53–4, 69, 71, 75–6, 80, 84, 94, 150, 178
conquest (of Ireland):
12th century, *see* Henry II
Conway, Hugh, treasurer, 126–7
Cork, city of, 61, 108, 127, 183
county of, 69, 71, 92, 128
region of, 71
Cornwall, 32
Cotton, Roger, royal commissioner, 123, 133
de Courcy, John, 74–5
Cowley, Robert, 63, 155, 159, 164, 166, 168–9, 174, 176, 179–81
Walter, 63–4, 161–2, 164, 174
Croft, James, governor, 15
Cromwell, Thomas, lord privy seal, 15, 29, 60, 63, 65–6, 156, 159–62, 164–71, 173, 175–84
his *Ordinances for the government of Ireland*, 29, 57–60, 164–5

Cusack, Christopher, sheriff of Meath, 42, 137–8
 his commonplace book, 42, 50–1, 137

Darcy, William, undertreasurer, 19, 46–7, 52, 62, 90, 137, 139, 141–2, 145–7, 149, 153
 his 'articles', 19, 28, 30–1, 45–9, 62, 90–3, 137, 139, 141–2
Davies, John, attorney-general for Ireland, 15, 34, 94
 his *A discovery of the true causes why Ireland was never entirely subdued*, 34
Dean, Henry, bishop of Banger, 127
Denton, James, royal commissioner, 95
'A description of the power of Irishmen', 18–19, 35–41, 56, 63, 80–9, 132, 157
Desmond, earls of, *see* Fitzgerald (south Munster), 35–6, 80–1, 94
Deythyke, John, 178
Donegal, 43
Dowdall, Christopher, archdeacon of Meath, 125
Dowling, Thady, antiquarian, 159
Down, 75
Drogheda, town of, 51, 95, 100–1, 103–4, 107
Dublin:
 castle of, 118, 126, 143, 164, 176
 city of, 43, 51, 79, 95, 100, 103–4, 107, 124, 130–1, 147, 154, 175, 179
 county of, 60, 69, 73, 77, 80, 93, 101, 104, 116, 127–8, 163, 168, 177
Dudley, John, duke of Northumberland, 15
 Robert, earl of Leicester, 15
Duiske, abbey of, 77–8
Dumfries (Scotland), 42
Dunamase, manor of, 70
Dunbrothy, abbey of, 77–8
Dundalk, 54, 98, 100, 107
Dungarvan, 106, 171

Edgecombe, Richard, royal commissioner, 14, 118–20, 122, 126, 130, 133–4, 178
Edward I, king of England and lord of Ireland, 70
Edward II, king of England and lord of Ireland, 70, 127
Edward III, king of England and lord of Ireland, 51, 71–2, 74–5, 95, 97, 117

Edward IV, king of England and lord of Ireland, 32, 51, 53, 55, 76, 97, 113, 116, 121, 128, 138, 141, 162
Edward VI, king of England and Ireland, 14, 187
Egerton, Ralph, royal commissioner, 95
Ellis, Steven, historian, 40
Elizabeth I, queen of England and Ireland, 13–16, 18, 22, 34, 43, 56, 189–90
Elizabeth of York, 53
English Conquest of Ireland, *see* Henry II
English government (in Ireland):
 its records and record-keeping, 22, 51–2, 65, 114, 127–9, 153, 160, 162, 165, 170, 173, 175–7
English of Ireland, 13, 17–21, 27, 31, 34, 36–40, 48–9, 59, 66, 89, 100–2, 106, 108, 113, 121, 126, 130–1, 138, 140–1, 143, 149–50, 154, 160–5, 168, 170, 173–6, 179, 185–7, 189
Estrete, John, 116–17, 122, 133

Fassaghbantry, abbey of, 78
Ferns, castle of, 78
 diocese of, 127
de Ferrers, William, 5th earl of Derby, 70
Finglas, Co. Dublin, 27
Finglas, Patrick, chief baron of the exchequer, 17, 27–8, 30–4, 79, 137, 139, 141, 148, 155
 his 'Breviate', 17–19, 27–35, 56–7, 63, 69–80, 155, 168
 Thomas, 28
Fitzgerald, family (of Desmond), 39, 47, 73, 81, 83
 earls of Desmond:
  James, 6th earl, 46, 92–3
  James, 8th earl, 139
  James, 10th earl, 37
  James, 13th earl, 180–1, 184
  James Fitzmaurice, 181–2
  Maurice, 1st earl, 72
  Maurice, 9th earl, 37, 92, 151
  Thomas, 7th earl, 46, 93, 118
  Thomas, 11th earl, 163
Fitzgerald, family (of Kildare), 30, 66, 72–3, 122, 125, 135, 145, 151, 157, 160, 162, 167, 171, 174, 179, 185, 188

earls of Kildare:
  Gerald, 8th earl, 31, 36, 40, 81, 116–18,
    120–3, 125–6, 129–33, 135, 139
  Gerald, 9th earl, 30–2, 46–8, 57, 60, 96,
    131, 135, 141–5, 147, 149, 152–5,
    158–65, 179
  John, 1st earl, 72
  Thomas, 7th earl, 117
  Thomas, 10th earl, 30, 157–9, 165–9,
    171, 174, 183
Fitzherbert, Anthony, royal commissioner, 95
Fitzroy, Henry, duke of Richmond, 153
Fitzsimons, Fiona, historian, 137
Fitzsimons, Walter, archbishop of Dublin,
  122–5, 132–3
Fleming, Christopher, baron of Slane, 47, 125
  Thomas, second baron of Slane, 74, 132–3
Forster, John, clerk of the hanaper, 127
Foucault, Michel, 20
Fox (Sionnach), clan/lord of Monthycagan,
  87
Foxe, Richard, bishop of Winchester, 15
France, 32, 135, 140, 178, 188
Francis I, king of France, 140
Froissart, Jean, historian, 156
de Furnival, Thomas, 74

Galway, town of, 53, 61, 108, 132, 172, 179
Garth, Thomas, royal commissioner, 122–6,
  133
de Geneville, Geoffrey, 73
Gerald of Wales, 34, 113, 156
Geraldine League, 180–1, 183–4
Geraldines, see Fitzgerald (of Kildare)
Gerrard, William, lord chancellor, 47
Goghe, John, cartographer, 43
Grane, abbey of, 77–8
Greenwich, palace of, 45, 90, 120, 141–2
Grey, Leonard, governor, 33, 167–8, 172–6,
  179–86

Hanmer, Meredith, historian, 44, 159
Harris, Walter, historian, 28–9, 45, 56, 74
Hatfield Compendium, 16–20, 23, 28, 31,
  33–5, 39, 41–4, 49–50, 54, 56, 63–6, 137–
  8, 145, 153, 158, 175, 184, 187
Hattecliffe, William, undertreasurer, 127–9
'Havens of Ireland', 18–19, 42–5, 90
Henri IV, king of France, 15

Henry II (FitzEmpress), king of England,
  15, 34, 53, 69, 71–4, 158
  his conquest of Ireland, 15, 27, 32–4, 51,
    53, 71, 76, 78–9, 103, 113, 154–5, 182,
    188, 190
Henry V, Holy Roman Emperor, 69, 114,
  116
Henry VI, king of England and lord of
  Ireland, 73, 131, 162
Henry VII, king of England and lord of
  Ireland, 13–15, 21, 40–1, 53–4, 57, 113–
  26, 128–34, 138–40, 147, 151–2, 157, 187
  his planned expedition to Ireland, 14,
    132–5, 151
Henry VIII, king of England and Ireland,
  13–18, 20–1, 23, 27, 30–3, 42, 47, 51, 63,
  65–6, 90, 96, 111, 126, 135–48, 150–8,
  160–1, 164–71, 173, 176–80, 182–90
  rumours of/suggestions for his coming to
    Ireland, 14, 48, 140–1, 143–4, 150, 169
Herbert, Francis, 172–3
Herbert, William, 22
Hickscorner, 31–2
Hogan, Edmund, historian, 38
Holland, Eleanor, daughter of Thomas, earl
  of Kent, 97
Holywoode, Robert, 74
Howard, Thomas, earl of Surrey and 3rd
  duke of Norfolk, governor, 14, 29–30,
  32–3, 46, 52, 60–1, 76, 129, 144–51, 153–
  6, 160–2, 164–6, 178, 184–6

Idrone, barony of, 70
Inge, Hugh, bishop of Meath, 142
Irish Sea, 14, 32, 131, 133, 143–4
Italy, 140

James IV, king of Scotland, 126
James V, king of Scotland, 180
James VI and I, king of England, Ireland
  and Scotland, 15
John, king of England and lord of Ireland, 74–
  5

Kenilworth, castle of, 124
Kerry, county of, 69, 71, 92
Kildare:
  county of, 57, 60, 69–70, 77–8, 80, 93,
    101, 104, 163

earls of, *see* Fitzgerald
rebellion, *see* Fitzgerald, Thomas, 10th
    earl
Kilkenny, town of, 72–3, 173
  county of, 39, 54, 69–70, 77, 81, 92, 98,
    128, 131–2, 163, 170, 177
  statutes of, 72
Kinsale, 61
Kite, John, archbishop of Armagh, 31, 137,
  140–1, 144
Knockdoe, battle of, 132
Knockfergus (Carrickfergus), 183

de Lacy, Hugh, 73
  Hugh, earl of Ulster, 73, 75
  Margaret, 73
  Matilda, 73
  Walter, 73
Lambay, island of, 130
Lancashire, 147
Lancaster, house of, 116–17, 187
Lane, Edmund, bishop of Kildare, 125
Lecale, county of, 45, 92
Leicester, 128
Leighlin, castle of, 78
Leighlinbridge, 40
Leinster, province of, 30, 33, 35–7, 39–40,
  51, 56, 66, 69–72, 76–7, 80–1, 94, 138,
  150, 153, 172–3, 179, 183, 185
  Mountains of, 40
  reform of, *see* reform
Leitrim, county of, 94
The Libel of English Policy, 113, 116, 123
Limerick, city of, 61, 71, 108, 125, 127, 132,
  169, 173, 183
  county of, 54, 69, 71, 92, 98, 128
Lismore, diocese of, 127
London, 65, 120, 128, 145, 178
  Tower of, 143, 165, 183
Loughfoyle, 42
Loughsewdy, manor of, 73
Louth (Uriel), county of, 60, 73, 80, 93,
  101, 104, 177
Low Countries, the, 15
Luttrell, Thomas, chief justice of the
  common bench, 176

MacAveely (Staunton), family/lord of
  Carra, 86

MacBrien, clan/lord of Coonagh, 84
MacCartan, clan/lord of Kinelarty, 87
MacCarthy More, clan/lord of Desmond,
  37, 71
MacCarthy, Donough Oge, lord of
  Duhallow, 40, 82
MacCarthy, MacTeige MacCormac, lord of
  Muskerry, 82
MacCarthy Reagh, clan/lord of Carbery, 82
MacCawell, clan/lord of Kinel-Farry, 87
MacCoughlin, clan/lord of Delvin, 87
MacDavy (Burke), family/lord of
  Clanconway, 86
MacDermot, clan/lord of Moylurg, 85
MacDonagh, clan/lord of Tiraghrill, 85
MacDonough, clan/lord of Hy Kinsellagh,
  40, 80
  Art, 40, 80
  Donough, 40
MacEoin, clan/lord of the Glens, 86
Mac Firbisigh, Dualtagh, historian, 54
  his *Book of Genealogies*, 54
MacGillapatrick, clan/lord of Ossory, 81
MacGillycuddy, clan/lord, 82
Mac-I-Brien, clan/lord of Arra, 84
MacJordan (de Exeter), family/lord of
  Gallen, 86
MacKenna, clan/lord of Truagh, 87
MacKiernan, clan/lord of Tullyhunco, 85
MacMahon, clan/lord of Corca Baiscinn, 83
MacMahon, clan/lord of Farney, 87, 126
MacManus (O'Connor Sligo), clan/lord of
  Carbury, 85
MacMorish (O'Connor), clan/lord of Irry,
  81
MacMurrough-Kavanagh, clan/lord of
  Leinster, 69–71, 77–9, 168, 179, 185
  Art More, 71
  Dermot, king of Leinster, 69
    his daughter, Eva, 69–70
MacNamara, clan/lord of Clancullen, 83
MacPhilbin (Burke), family/lord of Oyell,
  86
MacQuillan, clan/lord of the Route, 86
MacRannell, clan/lord of Munterolis, 85
MacTeige, clan/lord of Ormond, 84
Magauran, clan/lord of Tullyhaw, 85
Magawly, clan/lord of Calrige, 87
Magennis, clan/lord of Iveagh, 87

Mageoghegan, clan/lord of Kineleagh, 87
Maguire, clan/lord of Fermanagh, 87
Mandeville, family, 97
Mantua, marquis of, 45
maps of Ireland, 43, 154, 172
March, earl of, *see* Edward IV
Marches and Maghery, act of, 59
Marshal, family:
    Anselm, 70
    Eva, 70
    Gilbert, 7th earl of Pembroke, 70
    Isabel, 70, 74
    Joan, 70
    Matilda (Maud), 70
    Richard, 6th earl of Pembroke, 70
    Sibyl, 70
    Walter, 8th earl of Pembroke, 70
    William, 4th earl of Pembroke, 69–70
    William, 5th earl of Pembroke, 70
Mary I, queen of England and Ireland, 14,
    18
Matilda, empress, 69
Maximilian I, Holy Roman Emperor, 125
Maynooth, castle of, 166
Meath, county of, 19, 46, 60, 62, 73–4, 80,
    87, 93, 101, 104, 128, 149–50, 177
    liberty of, 128, 138
    province of, 35, 51, 53, 69, 71, 76, 94
'A memorial for the winning of Leinster',
    33–4
Moling, St, 77
Montano, John, historian, 138
More, Barry, 40
Mortimer, Anne, 97
    Edmund, 74
        his daughter, Matilda, 74
    Edmund (III), 3rd earl of March, 92, 97
    Edmund (V), 5th earl of March, 97, 128
    Roger, 4th earl of March, 97
Morton, John, archbishop of Canterbury,
    15
Munster, province of, 37, 41, 51, 69, 71–3,
    76, 83, 94, 108, 116, 131, 138–9, 150,
    161–2, 166, 171–3, 179, 181–2
Muscovy, 14

Nangle, family/lord of Clan Costello, 86
New Ross, town of, 127
New World, the, 21, 164

Newfoundland, the, 14
Newtown, county of, 92
Nicholls, Kenneth, historian, 40
Nine Years War (Tyrone's rebellion), 15–
    16, 190
Nowell, Laurence, antiquary/cartographer,
    38, 43, 65
Nugent, Richard, baron of Delvin, 32, 154

O'Breen, clan/lord of Brawney, 87
O'Brennan, clan/lord of Odogh, 80
O'Brien, clan/lord of Thomond, 41, 71, 76,
    83, 122, 131–4, 172, 181, 184, 188
    O'Brien's bridge, 162, 172, 174
    O'Brien's country, *see* Thomond
O'Brien, clan (of Carrigogunnell), 82
O'Brien, clan (of Aherlow), 82
O'Brien, clan (of the Comeragh
    Mountains), 82
O'Byrne, clan/lord of Crebranagh, 40, 71,
    77–9, 80, 168–9
O'Byrne, Redmund MacShane, lord of
    Culraynell, 40, 80
O'Cahan, clan/lord of Irraght Ichan, 86
O'Carroll, clan/lord of Ely, 84
O'Connor, clan/lord of Connacht, 71, 84
O'Connor, clan/lord of Corcomroe, 83
O'Connor-Faly, clan/lord of Offaly, 32, 78,
    81, 154–5, 168
O'Connor Kerry, 82
O'Connor Sligo, *see* MacManus
O'Crowley, clan/lord, 82
O'Dea, clan/lord of Ifearmaic, 83
O'Dempsey, clan/lord of Clanmaliere, 81
O'Donnell, clan/lord of Tyrconnell, 37, 87,
    142, 151, 180–2
    Hugh, 143
    Manus, 183
O'Donoghue Glenflesk, clan/lord, 82
O'Donoghue More, clan/lord of Lough
    Lene, 82
O'Donovan, clan/lord, 82
O'Dowd, clan/lord of Tireragh, 85
O'Driscoll, clan/lord of Baltimore, 35, 82
O'Dunne, clan/lord of Iregan, 81
O'Dwyer, clan/lord of Kilnamanagh, 84
O'Farrell, clan/lord of Annaly, 85
O'Flaherty, clan/lord of Iar-Connacht, 84
O'Gara, clan/lord of Coolavin, 85

O'Hanlon, clan/lord of Oriel, 87, 126
O'Hara Boy, clan/lord of Leyny, 85
O'Keefe, clan/lord, 82
O'Kelly, clan/lord, 71, 84
O'Kennedy, clan/lord of (Lower) Ormond, 84
Old Ross, abbey of, 78
O'Loghlen, clan/lord of Burren, 83
O'Madden, clan/lord of Silanchia, 85
O'Mahony, clan/lord of Fonn Iartharach, 82
O'Malley, clan/lord of Owles, 35, 84
O'Meagher, lord of Ikerrin, 84
O'Melaghlin, clan/lord of Clonlonan, 71, 87
O'Molmoy, clan/lord of Fircal, 87
O'More, clan/lord of Leix, 70, 78
O'Morrough, clan/lord of Ifelymye, 40
O'Mulryan, clan/lord of Owney, 84
O'Neill, clan/lord of Ulster, 37, 71, 86, 159, 161, 172–3, 180–1, 188
O'Neill, Conn MacHugh Boy, lord of Clandeboy, 40, 86
O'Nolan, clan/lord of Forth, 80
'Ordinances and provisions for Ireland', 19, 28–9, 51–2, 56–62, 99–109, 145–6, 149, 165
Ormond, earls of, see Butler
O'Reilly, clan/lord of (east) Brefny, 85, 126
O'Rourke, clan/lord of (west) Brefny, 85
O'Ryan, clan/lord of Idrone, 81
O'Shaughnessy, clan/lord of Kinelea, 85
O'Sullivan, clan/lord of Kenmare and Bantry, 82
O'Toole, clan/lord of Fercullen, 71, 77, 79, 168, 184
 Turlough, 185

del Palagio, Octavian, archbishop of Armagh, 125
Pale, the English, 17–19, 29, 32–3, 45–7, 51–2, 54, 56–9, 62, 66, 73–4, 96, 100–1, 105–6, 108, 126–9, 139–40, 145, 147, 149, 152–5, 160, 163, 169, 171–3, 175–7, 181
'Pander', historian, 137, 139
Parker, Geoffrey, historian, 20
passes (to be cut), 56–7, 108–9, 172

Patrick, St, 77
Paulet, George, royal commissioner, 176, 178
Peachey, John, 148
Philip II, king of Spain, 15, 20–1
Plantagenet, Lionel, duke of Clarence, 72, 75, 92, 97
 his daughter, Phillippa, 97
 Edward, earl of Warwick, 113, 118
 George, duke of Clarence, 118
 Richard of Conisbrough, 4th earl of Cambridge, 97
 Richard, duke of York, 37, 97, 131, 154
 Richard, duke of York (son of Edward IV), 121
Plunkett, Alexander, lord chancellor, 124
Pole, Reginald, cardinal and archbishop of Canterbury, 15
pope, 114, 176, 180
Powerscourt, manor of, 78
Poynings, Edward, governor, 14, 40, 54, 126–9, 131, 133–5, 145, 149. 162
Preston, Robert, viscount Gormanston, governor, 123, 125
Price, Liam, historian, 38–40
Pympe, John, treasurer of the wars, 127

Radcliffe, Thomas, 3rd earl of Sussex, governor, 14–15
Rathangan, manor of, 30, 78
Rathdown, manor, 78
Rathvilly, manor of, 78
Rathwire, manor of, 159
Rawson, John, prior of Kilmainham, 141, 143, 152
de Ré, Sebastiano, printer, 43
reform:
 Elizabethan 'reform literature', 22, 28
 general reformation, 16, 33, 64, 153–4, 157, 159, 161, 163, 166, 168, 174–5, 180–2, 186, 188, 190
 Henrician 'reform literature', 17, 19, 21–2, 27, 29–30, 34, 49, 63–4, 137–8, 140–3, 150, 163
 of Leinster, 77–9, 163, 168–70, 175, 185
 particular reformation, 153–4, 156, 163–4, 166, 185, 188, 190
 Tudor concept of, 16–17, 19–23, 29–30, 33, 47, 76, 111, 121, 130–1,135, 137–

71, 173–5, 177, 179–80, 182, 184–5, 188–90

Reformation Parliament (Irish), 177

Renaissance humanism, 21, 114, 138–40

'Revenues of Ireland', 19, 50–2, 138

Rhodes, 143

Rich, Barnaby, 22

Richard II, king of England and lord of Ireland, 71, 74–5, 133, 151

Richard III, king of England and lord of Ireland, 114, 117–18, 139

Roche, family, 72

Rokeby, William, archbishop of Dublin, 137, 141

Rome, 39–40, 89, 143, 157

St John's priory, Kilmainham, 143

St Lawrence, Nicholas, lord of Howth, 125

St Leger, Anthony, governor, 42, 64, 176–7, 184–6, 189

St Michael's Mount (Cornwall), 42

priory of (at Holmpatrick), 130

Savage, family/lord, 38, 87

Scotland, 35, 50, 119, 150, 188

Scots, 162, 172, 179

Seymour, Edward, duke of Somerset, 15

Shannon, river, 69, 71, 132, 154, 162, 169, 172, 174

Shmalkaldic League, 178

Sidney, Henry, governor, 15

Simnel, Lambert, 113, 118, 122–3

Skeffington, William, governor, 57, 152–3, 159–62, 164–6, 178

Sligo, 42–3, 74

Spain, 15, 20, 164, 178, 190

Spenser, Edmund, 22

Stafford, Henry, 2nd duke of Buckingham, 126

Staffordshire, 13

Stanihurst, Richard, chronicler, 124

Star Chamber, court of, 15

'State of Ireland and plan for its reformation', 30, 32, 35, 135, 137, 139–42, 149–50, 153, 155, 186

Stile, John, undertreasurer, 46, 148

Stoke, battle of, 118

surrender and regrant, policy of, 157, 185–9

Talbot, earls of Shrewsbury and Waterford, 30

Thames Valley, 13

Thomond (north Munster), 35, 69, 71, 74, 80, 83, 94, 169, 172, 179

Tintern, abbey of, 77–8

Tipperary, county of, 54, 69, 71, 83, 92, 98, 128, 131–2, 170, 177

Toppcliffe, John, chief justice of the king's bench, 127

Trim, lordship of, 127–8

manor of, 73

Trinity College, Dublin, 28, 45, 56

Turkey, 148

Turner, Nicholas, chief justice of the common pleas, 125

Ulster, earldom of, 45, 47, 75–6, 92–3, 126–9, 138, 141, 150

province of, 37–8, 40, 69, 71, 74–6, 80, 86, 94, 126, 150, 169, 172, 178–9

Venice, 43

Doge of, 45

de Verdon, John, 73

Theobald, 74

Theobald (II), 74

his daughters: Isabella, Elizabeth, Margery, Joan, 74

de Vere, Edward, 17th earl of Oxford, 65

Vergil, Polydore, historian, 113, 145, 156

Vienna, 125

Wales, 14, 21, 32, 147–8, 150

Walsingham, Francis, secretary of state, 15, 34

Warbeck, Perkin, pretender, 121–3, 125–7, 130

Ware, James, historian, 34, 119–20, 123, 137, 144

Waterford,

city of, 41, 61, 71, 79, 108, 126–7

county of, 54, 69, 71, 77, 92, 98, 128, 170, 177

earl of, see Talbot

Westminster, 125, 128, 142

Wexford, county of, 69–70, 77, 81, 127–8, 163, 168–70

lordship of, 30, 78

Wicklow, castle of, 78
head of, 107
Windsor, 150
Wise, John, chief baron of the exchequer, 41, 130–5
William, sheriff of Waterford, 135, 181–2
Wolsey, Thomas, cardinal and lord chancellor of England, 15, 31, 46, 52, 140, 142, 144–8, 150, 152–5, 183–4
Woodstock, castle of, 78
Wriothesley, Thomas, secretary, 184

Wyatt, Henry, 124, 127
Wyatt, Thomas, royal commissioner, 123

York, 13
York, house of, 13, 53, 93, 113, 117–19, 125, 133, 135, 187
Youghal, 61, 108
Yvers, Walter, chief baron of the exchequer, 127

Zaltieri, Bolognino, printer, 43